# Deleuze and Anarchism

## Deleuze Connections

'It is not the elements or the sets which define the multiplicity. What defines it is the AND, as something which has its place between the elements or between the sets. AND, AND, AND – stammering.'

Gilles Deleuze and Claire Parnet, *Dialogues*

**General Editor**
Ian Buchanan

**Editorial Advisory Board**

Keith Ansell-Pearson
Rosi Braidotti
Claire Colebrook
Tom Conley

Gregg Lambert
Adrian Parr
Paul Patton
Patricia Pisters

Visit the Deleuze Connections website at:
www.edinburghuniversitypress.com/series/delco

# Deleuze and Anarchism

Edited by Chantelle Gray van Heerden
and Aragorn Eloff

EDINBURGH
University Press

Edinburgh University Press is one of the leading university presses in the UK. We publish academic books and journals in our selected subject areas across the humanities and social sciences, combining cutting-edge scholarship with high editorial and production values to produce academic works of lasting importance. For more information visit our website: edinburghuniversitypress.com

Edinburgh University Press Ltd
The Tun – Holyrood Road, 12(2f) Jackson's Entry, Edinburgh EH8 8PJ

First published in hardback by Edinburgh University Press 2019

Typeset in 10.5/13 Adobe Sabon by
Servis Filmsetting Ltd, Stockport, Cheshire

A CIP record for this book is available from the British Library

ISBN 978 1 4744 3907 7 (hardback)
ISBN 978 1 4744 3908 4 (paperback)
ISBN 978 1 4744 3909 1 (webready PDF)
ISBN 978 1 4744 3910 7 (epub)

# Contents

# Acknowledgements

We would like to thank all the anarchists who had the courage to fight systems of oppression, sometimes at great cost to themselves. We thank those who continue to fight for the freedom of all, despite surveillance and systems of control that make it harder than ever before. It is you who help us dream-create a better world. We would like to thank Carol Macdonald at Edinburgh University Press and give a special thanks to Ian Buchanan for encouraging us to take up the project. Finally, we would like to thank all our contributors for their diligence and thoughtful provocations.

# Introduction

## Chantelle Gray van Heerden and Aragorn Eloff

In an interview with Antonio Negri, philosopher Gilles Deleuze memorably states that he and his co-author of many books, Félix Guattari, remained Marxists throughout because of the emphasis Marxism places on capitalist dynamics, an aspect they deem essential to any political philosophy. We see in their individual and collaborative work, then, continued analyses of capitalism, as well as an exploration of mechanisms that can be implemented to prevent the formation of what they term the 'State apparatus' – or hierarchical sociopolitical structures. However, Deleuze and Guattari's insistence on these aspects, as well as the decentralisation of power and the production of the new, have led many anarchists to recognise an anarchist, rather than Marxist, 'sensibility' in their work. There has also, since the publication of Todd May's *The Political Philosophy of Poststructuralist Anarchism* (1994), been observable scholarly interest in this intersection. However, the fact remains that Deleuze and Guattari never identified as anarchists, despite the fact that their oeuvre belies this position through its steady consideration of revolutionary subjectivity and active political experimentation. While this project does not attempt to post hoc label Deleuze and Guattari anarchists, it does look at core anarchist principles in their work, such as non-hierarchical organisation and communalism, and prefigurative politics, action and labour. Prefiguration, which is one aspect of anarchist politics, refers to the enactment and construction of a new political present in the here and now and, as an organisational practice, overlaps in many ways with Deleuze and Guattari's concept of the nomadic war machine. Importantly, a prefigurative politics does not have revolution as its object; instead, it relies on collective experimentation to produce modes of organisation and power relations that are envisioned for future societies by practising them in the present. In the same way, the nomadic war machine does not have war as its object, but a creative line of flight or bifurcation from systems of oppression. This is not to say that either prefigurative politics or the nomadic war machine are not revolutionary but, rather, that there is an 'emphasis on experimentation in contact with the real' (Deleuze and Guattari 1987: 12). Having said this, it is important not to reduce anarchism to prefigurative politics as revolution played a far more significant role historically in the production of new subjectivities.

On that point, it was particularly during the time that Guattari worked at the experimental psychiatric clinic, La Borde, in France, that he began to reconsider the social subject which, according to him and Deleuze, is always produced, created and enacted in relation to individuals, groups, institutions and societies which, in turn, are in relation with other sociopolitical structures. In other words, the social subject is always imbricated in multiple assemblages. One of the important questions they try to answer in their work is how we practically produce different subjectivities within the workings of these complex arrangements. To put it differently, what forms of political organisation and praxes are needed to create new ways of seeing and being in the world? For Deleuze and Guattari it is always a question of desire, of micropolitics, of a revolutionary subjectivity. Anarchists have a long history of thinking about and enacting different ways of being and collectively producing alternatives to the flows and processes that inform subject formation and ensuing subjectivities. As a political philosophy, anarchism includes a critique of both the form and content of hierarchical organisation and the ways in which it creates arbitrary divisions between those with authority and those with less or no authority – the subjugated. Deleuze and Guattari did not identify as anarchists (although Guattari was occasionally, perhaps pejoratively, labelled an anarchist by his friends) and there is little value in attempting to claim them for some or other anarchist 'canon' or tradition. However, as their work has begun to be engaged with in earnest by a significant number of contemporary anarchists, it is perhaps worth considering why.

As a cursory response, we can observe that Deleuze and Guattari share several broad assumptions with anarchism in their work, as we have already hinted at: both traditions (analyses, critique and practices) are anti-State, anti-authoritarian, anti-capitalist and anti-essentialist. More importantly, both traditions imagine and work towards a reality outside of current political and economic configurations and beyond the dogmatic image of thought. Both anarchism, and Deleuze and Guattari, oppose hierarchical relations and simultaneously encourage affirmative praxes that extend to all spheres of life: the social, the economic, the political, the educational, the existential and so on. Moving beyond salient overlaps, this book takes a Deleuzian approach and attempts to operate as a dark precursor that allows these disparate things – *A Thousand Plateaus*, *God and the State*, May '68, Spain '36, Simondon, Bakunin, a people to come, prefiguration, lines of flight, revolution – to resonate together. What does our Deleuze-Guattari-anarchism machine then look like? What are its singular points? Its relations and heterogeneities? The following chapters engage with the tensions and overlaps between anarchism and the philosophy of Deleuze and Guattari in a number of ways and have been divided into three sections.

The first section brings together the series Deleuze *and* Guattari *and* Anarchism, and the introductory chapter by Aragorn Eloff serves to diagram, in broad and suggestive strokes, the Deleuze-Guattari-anarchism machine by following minor threads through the whole of their work, while limning occasionally surprising intersections and resonances with both historical and contemporary anarchist thought and praxis. This is followed by three chapters exploring similar themes, but with more focused approaches and more in-depth discussions. Thus, in Chapter 2, Thomas Nail clarifies what he sees as one of the most important misunderstandings of Deleuze and Guattari's political theory, namely the admixture of their ontological and political anarchisms. He argues that this conflation is unnecessary by demonstrating the difference and articulating their specific relation. He then draws on this to outline the strengths of a strictly political theory of anarchism resulting from Deleuze and Guattari's work, both in its applied and analytic senses. Following on Nail's thorough discussion of absolute and relative deterritorialisation, Andrew Stones, in Chapter 3, accounts for the ways in which these two forms of deterritorialisation are used strategically by indigenous activists and theorists. In particular, he thinks about the relations between struggles 'for' freedom – or *against* the structure of domination – and struggles 'of' freedom – or struggles that take place *within* the structure of domination. Turning to examples of both anarchist and indigenous struggles in India, Africa and Australia, he shows how Deleuze's concepts of 'relative' and 'absolute' deterritorialisation offer concrete strategic resources for resistance to settler colonialism. This is augmented by Paul Raekstad in the final chapter of this section when he looks at Deleuze and Guattari's concepts of the molar and molecular. He argues that while these differ in nature or scale, this does not necessarily mean they differ in size or extension. Based on this argument, Raekstad examines and pinpoints a problem with vanguardist approaches to revolution which, he shows, is not a problem of organisation or unification as such, but of the kinds of organisation and unification that are required to go beyond capitalism and the State.

The second section focuses on theoretical perspectives. Nathan Jun's chapter opens this section by exploring the difference between 'anarchist' and 'anarchistic' thought. Drawing on Michael Freeden's theory of ideology, he thinks about the anarchist tradition in terms of a constellation of diffuse and evolving concepts, rather than a fixed set of principles. Thus, although Deleuze did not identify as an anarchist and was not associated in any meaningful sense with anarchist political movements, Jun argues that he nonetheless displays a strong, if oblique, affinity with anarchism that is particularly evident in his critique of representation. In Chapter 6, Elizabet Vasileva too thinks about representation – one of the many recurring themes in Deleuze's writings. In particular, Deleuze argues against the ontological primacy of identity on which representation is based and proposes instead an ontology of difference – a thread we find in all his work, starting with *Difference and Repetition*. His critique of representation also played a major role in his collaborations with Guattari, right up to their last project, *What Is Philosophy?* Taking 'difference' as the primary ontological category allows for a critique of transcendence, while simultaneously establishing the foundation of a philosophy/practice that does not rely on representation. Vasileva aims at extending and applying this critique of representation to ethics, specifically (post)anarchist ethics. Chapter 7 alloys representation with non-essentialism as Elmo Feiten draws out the overlaps and diversions between the work of Deleuze and Stirner. He shows that both of these theorists developed radical critiques of voluntary servitude and anti-essentialisms and argues, accordingly, that Deleuze's rejection of Stirner is based on a reductive reading of him. The final chapter in this section, by Natascia Tosel, considers Deleuze's critique of voluntary servitude in its fullest iteration by analysing the concept of 'anarchy' in relation to that of 'institution', both conceived of in a Deleuzian way of thinking. The starting point of her argument is the remark that Deleuze makes about Sade in *Coldness and Cruelty* (1967) when he talks about possible strategies to criticise the law. Among these strategies, Deleuze includes a Sadean one that uses irony and leads to a kind of anarchy. Thus, Sade looks for a way out of the law and finds it in perfect institutions, which implies as little intervention from the law as possible. This, Tosel argues, is productive for thinking about how to construct anarchist institutions that establish social relations completely different from those introduced by the law and contracts.

The third and final section of this book establishes relays of a different kind. Thus, in Chapter 9, Jesse Cohn relates his extended encounter with Deleuze, explaining how he went from a fairly sharp mistrust of his philosophy to a place where he finds these problems productive, particularly in terms of thinking about representation, desire, collective forces and even identity politics. The 'drama' has roughly four acts: (1) his initiation into an anarchist thought, laden with humanist, naturalist and rationalist themes; (2) the period when he was taught to read anarchism into the text of deconstruction; (3) his rereading of Deleuze through the anarchist tradition which allowed him to reread anarchism's theoretical commitments through Deleuze; and (4) his current interest in the potentials for Deleuzian anarchist thought to take us past even more false alternatives, including those at the heart of the newer forms of ideology critique (for example, Žižek's), and to help compose new forms of affective intervention. This narrative passage leads to another as we explore, with Alejandro de la Torre Hernández and Gerónimo Barrera de la Torre, an outline of the geography of historical anarchism (from 1871 to 1918) according to three main ideas in which they bring together interdisciplinary contributions from anarchism, geography, history, and Deleuze and Guattari. The first examines the anarchist diaspora and the imaginaries or symbolic geographies that accompanied it through the 'rhizomatic'. This international network, without centre or periphery, and constituted by the flow and mobility of information, capital, people and cultural goods in terms of solidarity and identity, suggests a fluid and ever-changing configuration of nodes and circulation. In the second section, they focus on militant migration and the connections between groups around the world, as analysed through anarchist newspaper records, to highlight the contingency of these networks, but also moments of interruption and eruption. Finally, they draw on the concepts of 'deterritorialisation' and 'becoming' to address the ways in which anarchist thought and praxis were transformed and momentarily fixed through voluntary or compulsory journeys. They argue that anarchist networks can be better understood through a Deleuze–Guattarian framework that acknowledges the continual movement of its members and the contradictory and transformational moments that defined their own of understanding of anarchisms. Chapter 11 moves us into more contemporary anarchist praxis as Christoph Hubatschke thinks about the politics of the face. In the wake of the events of 1968, Guattari, impressed by this extraordinary revolutionary upheaval, wrote a short text entitled *Machine and Structure*. In this text, Guattari introduced the notion of the machine for the first time in order to describe a new form of chaosmotic organising – a form of revolutionary politics without a party, without a specified programme and, most importantly, without representation. Hubatschke sketches a short anarchist theory of the machine and explores what Guattari called 'collectivities of utterance', movements that refuse representation and therefore break with the abstract machines of faciality. In so doing, he focuses on one specific strategy to dismantle the face: the use of masks in current social movements. Political resistance, he argues, must attack the logic of the face to dismantle it and fabulate its own faces. From the ski masks of the Zapatistas to the cartoonish grinning face of Guy Fawkes and the uncompromising 'faceless' black blocs, there are manifold strategies to dismantle the face – but, he asks, what does it mean to become visibly invisible? In Chapter 12, Gregory Kalyniuk addresses the relation of Deleuze's philosophy to anarchism by considering Pierre Clastres's ethnographic research on the stateless peoples of the Amazon basin. Central to Clastres's investigations is his analysis of political power in 'primitive' societies – particularly its regulation through collective levelling mechanisms, which avert social division by means of a systematic dispersal of power. Beginning in *Anti-Oedipus* with the notion of a primitive territorial machine that encodes flows of desire, Deleuze and Guattari propose that its resistance to a primordial Urstaat, or latent form of the State apparatus, would have marked the first stage in a universal history of contingency. With the passage from savage tribes to barbarian empires, however, this primitive mode of resistance would have ultimately come to nought, as the State would become manifest through processes of overcoding, deterritorialisation and stratification. For Clastres, the fundamental condition allowing primitive societies to avoid state capture is war: the threat of war from within, which is warded off by preventing the concentration of power in the chieftainship, and the threat of war from without, which unites the people against enemies and supports the formation of alliances with neighbours. While this may have significantly informed Deleuze and Guattari's concept of the war machine in *A Thousand Plateaus*, they are decidedly more critical in their reception of Clastres this time around and fault him for conceiving the emergence of the State in terms of a sudden and irreversible mutation. Against his apparent falling back into evolutionism, Deleuze and Guattari now present the reality of the war machine and the State apparatus in ahistoricist terms. With this in mind, Kalyniuk asks: What can contemporary anarchism take away from the insight that neither of these two types of social formation enjoys any historical priority over the other? In the final chapter, Chantelle Gray van Heerden argues that plantation logics create a particular appreciative of the spatial coordinates of histories since the carceral, a kind of facialisation of power, is always reliant on binarisation and biunivocalisation. In order, therefore, to bring about any real change in the world, anarchism has to shed this weight, becoming-imperceptible being a necessary step towards the deterritorialisation of stratified micro-powers, the dogmatic image of thought, the sedentary arrangements of enunciation and subjectivisation. The problem, she argues, lies at the surface, when surface equals ground as a condition, because one is then trapped within the circular logic of conditioned/condition. No other condition is possible while the surface grounds itself on the finite synthetic unity of transcendental apperception because this unity is tied to the four aspects that subordinate difference to diversity. This, she contends, leaves us neatly inside the plantation. Deleuze, in *The Logic of Sense*, invites us to reconsider the surface and the ground and this, Gray van Heerden argues, can help us think about how to disrupt the spatial coordinates of the plantation and the racial violence it portends. However, another aspect needs consideration, namely the kinds of subjectivities plantations produce. For her, the problematic lies in the tension between that which is and can be stratified – and therefore regulated – and that which presumably cannot. The intensification of algorithmic regulation and recognition under disciplinary control societies, she argues, means that moving bodies have increasingly come under political governance, which at once owns and disowns them as the figure of the migrant, the moving target par excellence of our time. Migrant frames, as memory devices, signal a problematic related to the temporal dimensions that memory inhabits and catalyses. What Deleuze finds problematic with this is that such a view subordinates time to memory, which remains locked within the extrinsic conditionings of identity and representation. In order to respond meaningfully to the logics of the plantation and the moving target, she contends that anarchism has to desire a politics of time rather than one of memory because, by forgetting, we return to the groundless ground of the surface, leaving behind the conditions that memory ties us to.

In summary, what we explore in this book is a different understanding of what constitutes political thought and action. Deleuze and Guattari, like anarchists, see prefigurative action as a central component of this other politics. In their philosophy, it is presented as a becoming-minoritarian; that is, 'a political affair and necessitates a labour of power (*puissance*), an active micropolitics' (Deleuze and Guattari 1987: 292). Deleuze, and anarchists too, see Nietzschean affirmation and active nihilism as a kind of prefiguration; that is, as opposed to ressentiment.

On practising such a micropolitics or prefigurative labour, Guattari writes the following:

> If there is a micropolitics to be practiced, it consists in ensuring that these molecular levels do not always succumb to systems that coopt them, systems of neutralisation, or processes of implosion or self-destruction. It consists in apprehending how other assemblages of the production of life, the production of art, or the production of whatever you want might find their full expansion, so that the problematics of power find a response. This certainly involves modes of response of a new kind. (Guattari and Rolnik 2007: 339)

All of us, to some extent, live in contradiction with our politics and collude with the State, with capitalism and with other forms of hierarchy and domination. But this does not mean that we have to accept these conditions wholesale. Instead, we can resist the call of nationalists, statists, patriarchs, fascists and capitalists, refusing to belong to the facile, territorialised, homogeneous community of people they invoke, in favour of a people-to-come.

## References

Deleuze, G. and F. Guattari (1987), *A Thousand Plateaus: Capitalism and Schizophrenia*, trans. B. Massumi, Minneapolis: University of Minnesota Press.

Guattari, F. and S. Rolnik (2007), *Molecular Revolution in Brazil*, trans. K. Clapshow and B. Holmes, Los Angeles and New York: Semiotext(e).

May, T. (1994), *The Political Philosophy of Poststructuralist Anarchism*, University Park: Penn State Press.

# PART I

# DELEUZE *AND* GUATTARI *AND* ANARCHISM

# Chapter 1

# Crowned Anarchy-Anarchy-Anarchism – Countereffectuating Deleuze and Guattari's Politics

*Aragorn Eloff*

## Politics Precedes Being

> Nothing more can be said, and no more has ever been said: to become worthy of what happens to us, and thus to will and release the event. (Deleuze 1990a: 149)

> What is an anarchist? One who, choosing, accepts the responsibility of choice. (Le Guin 1974: 32)

In this chapter, I argue that the political philosophy of Deleuze and Guattari is best understood as an anarchist political philosophy. Given the space constraints, I assume some familiarity with their terminology and basic arguments. I also employ their neologisms shamelessly: my intention is not merely elucidation but also, and as importantly, to bring the series *anarchy, Deleuze, Guattari*, and *Deleuze and Guattari* together, in all their heterogeneity, to see what might happen. What resonances are there? What is the dark precursor that creates communication across them? What conjunctive and disjunctive syntheses are produced? To anticipate the argument, I claim that anarchism, as a historical movement, consists of various discrete actualisations of a virtual multiplicity which we can call 'anarchy'. I will draw this anarchy into conversation with the virtual multiplicity 'Deleuze and Guattari'. I will claim that the full practice of anarchism as a series of non-exhaustive selections – various actualisations and counter-actualisations of anarchy – affirms what Deleuze refers to as the crowned anarchy and nomadic distributions of difference in repetition (Deleuze 1994: 47).

What is Deleuze and Guattari's political philosophy? Do they even have one? Badiou observes that Deleuze does not see politics as an autonomous form of thought (Badiou 2006: 68) in his and Guattari's *What Is Philosophy?*, which understands art, science and philosophy as the three planes that cut out sections of the chaosmos. Along with Žižek (2004) and Hallward (2006), Badiou – who has viewed Deleuze as an apolitical elitist since at least the early 1970s – argues that where politics *can* be found in Deleuze and Guattari, it is not a politics that allows for coherent, grounded forms of political organisation and praxis, but one that instead leads to a banal flux of desiring-whatever – what Badiou terms, in a play on the figure of the rhizome, 'the fascism of the potato' (Badiou and Bosteels 2012: 201). How are we to understand this provocative and, I argue, entirely false claim in light of Deleuze and Guattari's statement that 'politics precedes being' (Deleuze and Guattari 1987: 203)? What, exactly, do they mean by this? In delineating this problem, we should take the advice Deleuze gives in his work on Foucault and, instead of picking and choosing from his and Guattari's books as though they were a record, some tracks of which may leave us cold, accept and welcome this work as a whole, following its complex trajectories in order to see what they outline (Deleuze 1997b: 104–5). We should also remember, as Deleuze observes in his work on Nietzsche, that

> the philosophical learning of an author is not assessed by numbers of quotations . . . but by the apologetic or polemical directions of his work itself. We will misunderstand . . . if we do not see 'against whom' its principle [*sic*] concepts are directed. (Deleuze 2006a: 153)

For Deleuze and Guattari, politics names what is in its becoming: the entire actualised plane of force-relations, strata, assemblages and territories, across all scales of organisational complexity, from subindividual to supranational. Politics is the distribution of the actual. This is why Deleuze and Guattari can claim that political practice – what they sometimes term 'schizoanalysis' and refer to as the revolutionary analysis of desire – does not only emerge once the world and its relations have been established, but actively participates in the emergence of the world. 'Before Being, there is politics' (Deleuze and Guattari 1987: 249), a politics that is 'unaware of persons, aggregates, and laws, and of images, structures, and symbols . . . an orphan, just as it is an anarchist and an atheist' (Deleuze and Guattari 1984: 342). Politics, then, is what circulates and communicates beneath things; it is the dynamism of pre-individual singularities and larval selves, without unity or totality, the unfolding of an anarchic multiplicity of differing differences, constantly individuating and dissolving into what there is: a constant process of differentiation.

## Anarcho-Desirants! Spontaneists!

How does this profoundly novel conception allow for anything even close to what we understand as actual, real-world politics? Is Deleuze aristocratic and 'out of this world'? Is Deleuze and Guattari's political maxim really, as Badiou sarcastically claims, 'Unforeseeable, desiring, irrational: follow your drift, my son, and you will make the Revolution' (Badiou 2004: 76)? We can remind ourselves that, for Deleuze, 'thinking's never just a theoretical matter. It ... [is] ... to do with vital problems. To do with life itself' (Deleuze 1997a: 105), but this is not enough to rescue him from the dreaded appellations of 'spontaneist!', 'anarcho-desirant!' Spontaneist. Who has not had this aspersion cast on their politics? For Badiou, Žižek, Hallward and Spivak (1988), Deleuze and Guattari are spontaneist. For Deleuze and Guattari, the anarchists – those anarchist groupuscules that were common in France in the 1960s and 1970s – are the spontaneists. For many anarchists, in turn, it is Deleuze and Guattari themselves who have disowned the class struggle and advocate instead a dangerous spontaneism and becoming-for-the-sake-of-it. For other anarchists, it is anarchism itself that tends towards spontaneism; it must be purged of dreaded lifestylist class enemies and new normativities must be imposed (Bookchin 1995). Travelling further back, is this not the exact same criticism Lenin made of left communism (Lenin 1964: 117–18)? In fact, is this not precisely what Marx and Engels said of Proudhon and Bakunin?

> They are like alchemists of the revolution ... They leap at inventions which are supposed to work revolutionary miracles: incendiary bombs, destructive devices of magic effect, revolts which are expected to be all the more miraculous and astonishing in effect as their basis is less rational. (Marx and Engels 1976: 318)

When engaged in any depth, however, it becomes clear that neither Deleuze and Guattari nor anarchism can really be said to be spontaneist or advocating for the freeing of desire as inherently liberatory, whatever a certain cursory gloss of the sloganeering of *Anti-Oedipus* might suggest. Desire, anyway, always exists as machined (Deleuze and Guattari 2003: 314) and is 'never separable from complex assemblages' (Deleuze and Guattari 1987: 237). It is 'never an undifferentiated instinctual energy' and the 'body without organs' is, in any case, 'opposed not to the organs but to that organisation of the organs called the organism' (Deleuze and Guattari 1987: 175); it has 'its own inner differentiation' (Bell 2006: 159). The 'nomad has a territory; he follows customary paths; he goes from one point to another; he is not ignorant of points' (Deleuze and Guattari 1987: 380). Guattari puts this more directly: 'desire has infinite possibilities of assemblage and creativity, but it can also enter into processes of implosion. I have nothing to do with any liberating mythology of desire for desire's sake' (Guattari and Rolnik 2007: 248). Every desire is also the affair of the people, a molecular affair, as every assemblage is collective. Perhaps the figure of the anarcho-desiring spontaneist is, more than anything, what Max Stirner would call a 'phantasm of the mind' (Stirner 2017: 40) – an abstraction. Indeed, this is how Guattari himself understands it in *Molecular Revolution*, where he observes how

> the Bolshevik phantasy system repressed all suggestions of 'anarchism': barricades, fraternity, generosity, individual liberation, rejection of all hierarchy and constraint, collective exaltation, permanent poetry, daydreaming. All this had seemed dead and buried, just part of a kind of regression or collective infantilism. (Guattari 1984: 211)

## Anarchism and Anarchy in the Work of Deleuze and Guattari

Pointing out their joint dismissal by organisational fetishists is not enough to bring the Deleuze and Guattari and anarchism series together. What, then, do Deleuze and Guattari themselves have to say about anarchism? If we look to their collective biography (Dosse 2011), both were involved in a range of left and communist projects from the 1960s onwards. Both collaborated with Antonio Negri and other autonomist Marxists – a strain of communist thought close to anarchism. Indeed, several of Guattari's friends saw him as, at least in temperament, an anarchist and at one point, in a letter to a friend, he notes that he is writing a manifesto for an 'autonomous-communist-anarchist' movement (Guattari and Rolnik 2007: 87). But no clear picture emerges. Beyond their personal lives, there is no sustained discussion of anarchism anywhere in their work, only a few passing mentions, mostly negative, often figurative, occasionally favourable – for instance, when they discuss the opposition between the socialist and anarchist currents of the nineteenth century on the question of whether to seize or abolish the State and appear to preference the latter, seeing the proletariat, as understood by anarchists, as a form of 'nomadisation power' (Deleuze and Guattari 1987: 558). In short, it does not appear that either Deleuze or Guattari are more than passingly familiar with the history or ideas of anarchism. When Deleuze discusses Proudhon in an early lecture, for instance, it is very clearly Proudhon via the distorting lens of Marx and Engels (Deleuze 2015: 50) and, when Guattari refers to anarchism in *Lines of Flight*, he reiterates Lenin's dubious claim that, like 'social-democratic, economistic, humanist . . . discourse', it is ineffective; what is required is 'the construction of an absolutely new genre of revolutionary machine' (Guattari 2015: 78). Perhaps there is also something like an anxiety around discussing their obvious affinities with anarchism, a distancing from the false and simplistic image of them as elitist anarcho-desirers. Indeed, in some of Guattari's work, most notably that authored with Antonio Negri, anarchism – or at the very least, anarchy as a pejorative term – functions almost as a nervous tic. After critiquing vanguardism in favour of autonomous self-liberation or collective subjectivation, for instance, Guattari is quick to add that 'there is nothing anarchic about this', only to go on to describe a form of revolutionary struggle that almost any anarchist would have affinity with: 'a qualitative autonomy, capable of apprehending the social complexity of movements, and of grasping it as a process of subjective convergence, centered on the quality of life and on the communitarian restructuring of production' (Guattari and Negri 1990: 79).

Elsewhere, anarchism is anachronistic; something subsumed and recuperated, like social democracy, by Leninism. Describing viable political struggle in terms of 'a continuous conquest of (new) arenas of freedom, democracy, and of creativity', Guattari assures us that 'there is nothing anachronistic or retrograde or anarchist in this way of conceiving things' as it understands social transformation on the basis of desire, real needs and productive activity (Guattari and Negri 1990: 36). In some places, strikingly, Guattari even sees anarchism as 'the myth of a return to the pre-technological age, of "back to nature"' and as unable to deal with 'real society' (Guattari 1984: 63). Even more directly, Guattari states that 'it's too late to complain if you've already turned back: Artaud's cry against the Spanish anarchists' (Guattari 2006: 175). Or, most bluntly, 'there is no going back, there is no anarchism' (Guattari and Negri 1990: 92).

In other places still, anarchism is one extreme point of a continuum, on the other extreme of which lies Leninism. This anarchism is a phantasm of defeat, voluntarism and disenchantment, a solitary rebellion and a simple, abstract assertion of singularity. Instead of this, Guattari argues, we need an 'other' movement that is founded on the self-valorisation and self-production of singularities (Guattari and Negri 2010: 77). How sad that Guattari seemingly never read Bakunin, for whom

the very freedom of each individual is no other than the resultant, continually reproduced, of [the] mass of material, intellectual and moral influences exerted on him [*sic*] by all who surround him, by the society in the midst of which he is born, develops, and dies. (Bakunin quoted in Malatesta 1974: 50)

Interestingly, in Deleuze and Guattari, anarchism and anarchy are often mentioned at precisely those points at which they most clearly articulate their political philosophy; at the exact moments that this political philosophy most sounds like anarchism yet simultaneously summarily dismisses the latter. For instance:

1. Like anarchists, they know that the State will never wither away. Anarchists are, however, 'opportunistic spontaneists' (Guattari and Negri 1990: 161).
2. Like anarchists, and like Nietzsche – a common touchstone for both groups – they see destruction as a creative act: 'Destruction is the only way of freeing ourselves from the totality and of becoming free as a segment, as a particularity. A positive social practice can be built on this act of destructive freedom today.' Anarchism, however, is a 'convulsion' (Guattari and Negri 2010: 132).
3. Like anarchists, they argue that we cannot rely on a party or a State apparatus – on better justice – in order to liberate desire; that this liberation must be immanent, must be synthesised by us and must be expressed collectively, functioning by contagion, or an infinite spreading, by plugging into a shared plane of oscillation. But, they continue, 'as long as one alternates between the impotent spontaneity of anarchy and the bureaucratic and hierarchic coding of a party organisation, there is no liberation of desire' (Guattari 2008a: 43). Put otherwise, Deleuze and Guattari want 'to live and to experience a physiology of collective liberation'; they hypothesise another type of power, *puissance*, or what anarchists term 'power to' (rather than power over), as what flows through this physiology, but 'there is no anarchism in this ... because the movement remains none the less collective and challenges individualist implosion' (Guattari and Negri 1990: 91–2).
4. Like anarchists, the desire they wish to liberate consists of 'all forms of the will to live, the will to create, the will to love, the will to invent another society, another perception of the world, and other value systems' (Guattari and Rolnik 2007: 318). Although 'capitalistic subjectivity' may find this conception of desire to be utterly utopian and anarchic, they assuredly do not (318).
5. Like anarchists, they ask how 'human relations [can] be organised without automatically reinforcing hierarchies, segregations, racism,

and the erosion of particularities? How to release an inventive machinic collective passion that would proliferate . . . without crushing people under an infernal discipline' (Guattari 2009: 79)? All the old references are dead, however, including anarchism.

6. Like anarchists, they find value in Pierre Clastres's (1987) work on stateless societies and, like anarchists, they argue that the Urstaat – the abstract machine that is actualised in any given State assemblage – is to be warded off however and wherever possible. The State cannot be wielded against itself (Deleuze and Guattari 1987: 424–73).

Beyond the odd claim that anarchism is anachronistic, as though it cannot and has not differed from itself over the past 170 years, as though it has no becoming or is inherently, diagrammatically constrained (any politics is in some way limited, of course, although anarchism proposes a politics that is itself a diagrammatics), the most salient misconstruals or concerns to be found in this thread of loose, indirect engagement with anarchism appear to be based on a misunderstanding of what kind of organisation anarchists propose, how they understand subjectivity, their ontology, their critiques and their practices. I address this shortly when I bring both series even closer together through an articulation of what a politics might look like that is anarchism-becoming-Deleuze-and-Guattari, Deleuze-and-Guattari-becoming-anarchist. First, I briefly address the various other ways in which they have been understood and deployed.

## Liberals, Marxists, Autonomists, Capitalists?

As we know, the revolutionary problem today is to find some unity in our various struggles without falling back on the despotic and bureaucratic organisation of the party or State apparatus: we want a war machine that would not recreate a State apparatus, a nomadic unity in relation with the Outside, that would not recreate the despotic unity . . . who are today's nomads, who are today's Nietzscheans? (Deleuze 1994: 260)

A brief perusal of the available work on Deleuze and Guattari's political project suggests that there is nowhere near consensus on what their politics either is or does. For some, perhaps most, they are, as they claim, Marxists, albeit each in their own ways (Deleuze 1990b). This Marxism is sometimes compared with autonomism, Zapatismo and Camattian-style communisation theory, but is also occasionally seen, perhaps in the light of, for instance, Guattari's relatively reformist government funded work, as a reasonably mild-mannered socialism. For others, more problematically in my view, the natural implications of Deleuze and Guattari's work are a Rawlsian-style liberal democratic politics (see, for example, Patton 2000 and Tampio 2015), even if this is some sort of aporetic democracy-to-come (Andrew Culp's 2016 *Dark Deleuze* is an excellent corrective here). For the complex systems theorists, whose readings of this aspect of their work are sometimes far from complex, they are theorists of free markets or left market liberalism (DeLanda 1996). And then there is Nick Land's 'mad black Deleuzianism' (2011) which ends up, for all its radical rhetoric and accelerationist zeal, simply conceding, like the 'democratic Deleuzians', entirely to the present in its valorisation of hyper-capitalism. Would it be too surprising to discover that work has been done on a rhizomatic fascism, or a Deleuzo-Guattarian right conservatism?

Although I do not have space to defend this claim here, it seems relatively obvious that when it comes to politics, there is a natural tendency – and the current discussion is by no means immune to this – to preference or isolate particular aspects of Deleuze and Guattari's work in order to defend an existing political affiliation. Just as Manuel DeLanda once claimed that Marx was Deleuze and Guattari's 'little Oedipus' (DeLanda 2003), it appears that when otherwise exceptional scholars arrive at the point at which politics must be discussed, the lens often narrows considerably. Leaving aside the market cyberneticians, I briefly address the argument that Deleuze and Guattari are advocates of Rawlsian-type democracy. As the question of whether or not they are communists of some new but decidedly non-anarchist type is more complex, I shall answer that indirectly when I synthesise/problematise Deleuze–Guattarian libertarian communism. In what follows, a reminder of my original approach is apposite: to welcome the whole of the work and to observe not the frequency of use of any given term but, instead, what the work is directed against; that is, what problems it constructs.

In *What Is Philosophy*, Deleuze and Guattari invoke the term 'becoming democratic' in a register that has subtly Derridean harmonics (Deleuze and Guattari 1996: 113). This encourages some, notably Paul Patton, to elaborate on the importance of jurisprudence in Deleuze's late work and to argue that 'Deleuze's endorsement of rights and jurisprudence clearly commits him to the existence of law and the kind of constitutional state that this implies' (Patton 2010). This is a tenuous claim. In the first case, is not a constitutional State, of any kind, one of the most terrifying things there is for Deleuze and Guattari (1987: 351–423)? Second, jurisprudence implies neither law nor constitution. When Deleuze argues that life unfolds case by case (Deleuze and Parnet 2013: 'G is for Gauche'), it makes far more sense, given his and Guattari's overall political problematic, to understand jurisprudence as an immanent ethics of situated and unique instances functioning via what anarchists and some others refer to as restorative justice. If this, as Deleuze states, gives rise to 'law' and 'life rights' (Deleuze and Parnet 2013: 'G is for Gauche'), then these should be understood descriptively, that is, as a Spinozist law of encounters between forms of life. It is also the case that a straightforward or meaningful endorsement of rights is nowhere to be found in Deleuze, who is more often vehemently critical of rights and rights discourse. Even in the later works, it is unequivocally asserted that 'rights save neither men nor a philosophy that is reterritorialised on the democratic State . . . Human rights say nothing about the immanent modes of existence of people provided with rights' (Deleuze and Guattari 1996: 107). Indeed, Nietzsche, with his hatred of democracy, still lurks in the margins here. For instance, when Deleuze and Guattari discuss the constitution of a new Earth and a new people, they underscore that this is the task of the most aristocratic among us, and that 'this people and earth will not be found in our democracies'. After all, 'democracies are majorities, but a becoming is by its nature that which always eludes the majority' (Deleuze and Guattari 1996: 108).

Lost in the good sense image of Deleuze-and-Guattari-becoming-Rawls, in this incapacity to cross the line, is everything that defines their politics: the critique of normativity, the function of the untimely and the event, the overcodings and axiomatics of a State that is always imbricated with capital, the horrors of the latter, the reification of the actual – of current practices and institutions that are assumed to be neutral forms into which we can inject all our realistic utopian preferences. Is this not precisely what Deleuze criticises as 'equality as an abstract product' (Deleuze 1994: 283)? Does he not see democratic government as a force converter and ordering device far more insidious than any totalitarian regime; a government premised upon the constant modulation of behaviour that 'demands of its bodies . . . a practical acceptance of certain parameters of action, rather than a principled conformity to an absolute ideal' (Massumi 1992: 123)? Or as Stirner, who I claim also subtly haunts Deleuze's work, puts it,

> insurrection leads us no longer to let ourselves be arranged, but to arrange ourselves, and sets no glittering hopes on 'institutions'. It is not a fight against the established, since, if it prospers, the established collapses of itself; it is only a working forth . . . out of the established. (Stirner 2017: 280)

For Deleuze and Guattari, democracy is nothing more than an internalisation of the State-form, a society of legislating subjects who can choose the despotism they most desire so long as it is generalisable, molar, predictable. It is also in some sense a failure to properly practise Deleuze's transcendental empiricism, which Jeffrey Bell succinctly describes as 'the effort to think the conditions for the production of the new that does not reduce the identity of the new to these conditions' (Bell 2009: 6). Perhaps democracy is part of what Deleuze has in mind when he worries about the philosophy of difference appearing as a new version of the beautiful soul: 'the beautiful soul is in effect the one who sees differences everywhere and appeals to them only as respectable, reconcilable or federative differences, while history continues to be made through bloody contradictions' (Deleuze 1994: 64). For Deleuze, remember, it is the name of Marx himself that assuages this concern (1994: 259). If we are to not become beautiful souls and if we are to aim, rightly, I think, for a society that Patton describes as 'characterised by the absence of class or caste privilege and by the implementation of the egalitarian principle of the equal worth of individuals such that no person's life, beliefs, or values are inherently worth more than those of anyone else' (Patton 2010: 164), we should acknowledge that this is irreconcilable with the very principle of state sovereignty; capture is the State's 'interior essence or . . . unity' (Deleuze and Guattari 1987: 427). Let us then look elsewhere.

## Anarchy Becoming Deleuze and Guattari Becoming Anarchy

I am not the first anarchist to claim Deleuze and Guattari as theorists of my specific strain of (anti)political praxis. Anarchists – nomads and smiths that they are – have been constructing war machines and deterritorialising along lines of flight, smashing the Urstaat, finding new weapons and prefiguring the people to come since at least the mid-1980s. Although early work in this field, best exemplified by Hakim Bey's (1985) *CHAOS: The Broadsheets of Ontological Anarchism* and Rolando Perez's (1986) *On (An)archy and Schizoanalysis*, tend towards simplistic misreadings, these have been productive enough to give rise to an entire strain of anarchist thought that sees the political theory and practices set out in the two volumes of *Capitalism and Schizophrenia* as entirely compossible with anarchism, to the extent that contemporary anarchist groups from France to Brazil (the Somaterapia movement, developed by anti-psychiatrist Roberto Freire in the 1970s and now largely the terrain of Brazilian anarchists, is perhaps the most salient example here), including the notorious The Invisible Committee (2008), unproblematically discuss prefiguration and group subjects, molecularity and affinity groups, mutual aid and joyful encounters in the same breath. Like it or not, whether it is in the academic work of postanarchists,[1] whatever the straw men they build out of 'classical anarchism' in order to remedy its Enlightenment humanism with continental theory *du jour*, or in the infiltration of their language into the various anarchist milieus, there is now a deep imbrication of Deleuze and Guattari and anarchism, as evidenced by the bookshelves of almost any anarchist infoshop.[2]

Following this assumption, I now discuss anarchism and Deleuze and Guattari's political philosophy without distinguishing between them. I refer to this coupling of heterogeneous terms simply as 'anarchy' and my approach will be to aim for a maximum density of slogans. Again, my intention is not to speak Deleuzo-Guattarese – or indeed anarchese – for the sake of it, but neither is it to deliver a mere disquisition. While I remain convinced that Deleuze and Guattari's thought can be rendered clear and systematic, it is also more than this. I want to convey a sense of my relation, as an anarchist, to this thought.

What is anarchy? For anarchy, 'politics is active experimentation, since we do not know in advance which way a line is going to turn' (Deleuze and Parnet 2002: 137). Vitally, this experimentation is ground, means and endless end; it is a recognition of crowned anarchy: the fact that what returns is difference (Deleuze 1994: 51). It is an acknowledgement of anarchism: the need to work ourselves out of the present, out of 'the ignominy of the possibilities of life that we are offered' (Deleuze and Guattari 1996: 109–10) towards 'immanent, revolutionary, *libertarian* utopias' (1996: 99, emphasis added). It is the desire for anarchy: a new Earth and new people (99–100) that can affirm the groundless ground. It is ontology, metaphysics, project and Erewhon: utopia-as-process – process because anarchy is, to use a phrase from Deleuze, 'the transcendent object of sociability' (Deleuze 1994: 193). Only in this sense is politics a 'becoming democracy' – in the sense of 'permanent revolution', following an ahistorical line of continuous variation. It is ahistorical because history 'amounts only to the set of preconditions, however recent, that one leaves behind in order to "become", that is, to create something new' (Deleuze 1997b: 171). There is, as Emma Goldman says, no idea whose triumph would eliminate all possible problems from our lives for all time. 'I hold, with Nietzsche,' she argues, 'that we are staggering along with the corpses of dead ages on our backs. Theories do not create life. Life must make its own theories' (Goldman

1909: 9). 'Think about May 1968', says Guattari. 'There was no ideological transmission, but rather the repercussion of events' (Guattari 1995: 37–8).

Our experimentation, our being worthy of the throw of the dice, contains two moments of comprehension and play. First, we must fully determine the conditions of the virtual problem through a specification of adjunct fields; then we must condense singularities, 'which, by dint of ideal events, define the concentration of a "revolutionary situation" and cause the Idea to explode into the actual' (Deleuze 1994: 239) – revolution as plane of immanence, infinite movement and absolute survey (Deleuze and Guattari 1996: 100). Although everything relies on this, nothing should be taken seriously. 'Difference is light, aerial and affirmative. To affirm is not to bear but, on the contrary, to discharge and to lighten' (Deleuze 2004: 54). 'Nietzsche's practical teaching,' Deleuze writes, 'is that difference is happy; that multiplicity, becoming and chance are adequate objects of joy by themselves and that only joy returns' (Deleuze 2006a: 193).

As political practice, anarchy is critical of representation and mediation, of everything that separates us from our capacity to act, from the power we can produce together. For, as Deleuze argues, an image of thought that is premised upon representation and recognition '"rediscovers" the State, rediscovers "the Church" and rediscovers all the current values that it subtly presented in the pure form of an eternally blessed unspecified eternal object' (Deleuze 2004: 136). Instead, we employ diagrammatic thought in mapping, through the contemporary terrain, the virtual multiplicities effectuated within it. This is also a countereffectuation of these multiplicities – a fabulation of new relations, new abstract machines – a cautious smoothing of space that does not seek abolition or de-differentiation but instead to 'attain a life that is the power of the outside' (Deleuze 1988a: 95); not a power of death but, on the contrary, a power of life. Anarchy seeks to counter the microfascisms of everyday life through the coming together in affinity and conflictuality of subject groups working past their myriad subjugations on every level (Deleuze and Guattari 2003: 64). Men [sic] are groups – resultants or collective powers, say Kropotkin (1902) and Proudhon (1861: 128) – not groups consisting of individuals, but arrangements of enunciation, non-denumerable sets consisting of units of desiring subversion, or what Martin Buber, referring to individualist anarchists, called 'concrete singularities' (Buber 2002: 48). The only question is how we can connect our desire with the desires of other groups, with the desires of the masses, producing 'the corresponding creative statements, and establish[ing] the conditions necessary, not for their unification, but for a multiplication favourable to statements capable of producing a rupture' (Deleuze quoted in Lotringer 1977: 104). We are dealing here not with classes but with minorities. The anarcho-syndicalist Victor Griffuelhes underscores this: 'syndicalism, let us repeat, is the movement, the action of the working class; it is not the working class itself' (Griffuelhes 1909: 198).

As social form – or social nature, rather – anarchy is the process of establishing relations that allow for the optimal combinations of bodies. For mutual joy. If we are to maximise our power, our joyful encounters, then we must be able to join together, to evaluate and associate freely; in this sense being is inherently communist – it is 'the composition of a world that is increasingly wide and intense' (Deleuze 1988b: 126). This is our mode of organisation, this ecosophical confederation of monads. It is not chaos but instead a full countenancing of chaos that allows for social arrangements that are not stable, because stability is illusionary, but metastable. This federation of beings implies no higher unity of overcoding. It does not fit together into a whole but is rather a cluster of autonomies, 'a wall of loose, uncemented stones, where every element has a value in itself but also in relation to others' (Deleuze 1997a: 86). This is what Deleuze means when he talks of nature as a tissue of shifting relations:

> nature is inseparable from processes of companionship and conviviality, which are not preexistent givens but are elaborated between heterogeneous living beings in such a way that they create a tissue of shifting relations, in which the melody of one part intervenes as a motif in the melody of another. (Deleuze 1997b: 59)

This is the immanence Bakunin refers to when he says that:

> nature is the sum of actual transformations of things that are and will be ceaselessly produced within its womb ... the universal, natural, necessary, and real, but in no way predetermined, preconceived, or foreknown combination of the infinity of particular actions and reactions which all things having real existence constantly exercise upon one another. (Bakunin quoted in Colson 2001: 60)

The anarchist geographer Élisée Reclus affirms this as 'the intimate link that attaches the succession of human acts to the action of telluric forces' (Reclus 1905: i–ii). This is far from any hylomorphic schema, any transcendence. As Bakunin goes on to say:

> matter is not at all this inert substratum produced by human abstraction ... it is the real ensemble of all that is, of all existing things, including the

> sensations, minds, and wills of animals and human beings. Being which is at the same time a becoming, the movement always and eternally resulting from the infinite sum of all the particular movements down to the infinitely small, the total ensemble of the mutual actions and reactions and the ceaseless transformations of all the things that occur and disappear in turn. (Bakunin quoted in Colson 2001: 185)

Emerging from this is a particular ethos: for Deleuze as for anarchy, ideology – the good sense and common sense of the dogmatic image of thought – is replaced with meta-modelling and resingularisation on all scales. We need assemblages of collective enunciation and creation, not communication. There is no transcendent morality in any of this. If there is a normativity, then it is only in the sense of a meta-norm that preferences conditions for a full unfolding of life (Jun 2012). Furthermore, for anarchy everything is equal, but this equality is said of what is not equal, of being that differs from itself. An equality of unequals, the anarchists call it. As Deleuze argues, equality lies in the ability of beings to go to the limits of their capacities, beyond their limits (Deleuze 1994: 37). Anarchy is also not interested in vanguards – in 'the militant style of a love full of hatred' (Deleuze 2004: 198). In the process of becoming minor we simultaneously 'seed crystals of becoming whose value is to trigger uncontrollable movements and deterritorialisations of the mean or majority' (Deleuze and Guattari 2003: 106) via contagion and propagation. We must always be wary of the tendency to reterritorialise on, or be overcoded by, the party machine. Instead, to propagate transversal becomings, we must, as Simondon says, prime these crystallisations via a pre-revolutionary state of supersaturation (Simondon 1989: 53–4). Anarchy, therefore, is autonomous. 'The nomos came to designate the law, but that was originally because it was distribution, a mode of distribution. It is a very special kind of distribution, one without division into shares, in a space without borders or enclosure' (Deleuze and Guattari 1987: 240).

In summary, as anarchist labour historian and Deleuze scholar Daniel Colson, author of the provocative *Petit lexique philosophique de l'anarchisme: De Proudhon à Deleuze* [Little Lexicon of Anarchism from Proudhon to Deleuze] says,

> the anarchist Idea is neither an ideal, nor a utopia, nor an abstraction; neither a program, nor a catalogue of regulations or prohibitions. It is a force, common to all beings, which expresses the totality of the possibilities that all these beings contain. It is a living force which, in certain circumstances, takes us outside of ourselves. (Colson 2001: 152, own translation)

## Implications

What is the import of all this? For us. Here. Now. In concluding, I can only gesture towards some possibilities.

First, we ought to be done with programmes for political action. Instead, we should be collaborating on producing shared problematics. How do we describe where we find ourselves? How did we get here? What are the intensive flows and processes underlying the world as it is presented to us? What diagrams are we the effectuation of? Can we, via a practice of vice-diction, create new diagrams? We will always get the solutions we deserve as a consequence of how we pose and incarnate these problems.

Organisation is crucial, but let us not forget that for all their differences of instantiation, any group – Marxist-Leninist, Maoist or even anarchist – can lapse into a mode of organisation that repeats the form of the party and hardens into a new dogma defined by unquestioning loyalty, asceticism, and the crushing or recuperation of desire turned against itself. For the former groups, this lapse is perhaps endemic; let us not, however, make the same mistakes with anarchism. Instead, let us heed Guattari's call for 'new micropolitical and microsocial practices, new solidarities, a new gentleness, together with new aesthetic and new analytic practices' (Guattari 2008b: 51). This is not about creating agreement either, because the more we disagree 'the more we create an area, a field of vitality' (Guattari 1998: 196). We should be especially wary of the subjugated groups and their repressed desires, the groupuscules and their channelling of libidinal investments into hierarchies, reform and inertia. What is the viscosity and consistency of our group forms? How do we come together? What flows between us? What are our fluid dynamics?

Attentiveness to the new is crucial: we must overcome stock notions and learn to deal with haecceity. The world now is not the world then and we are not who we were. We must ask what has repeated and how it is different from itself. The new fascism – the Urstaat awakened and given new strength by capitalism – produces a peace more terrifying than war and if we are not careful, then

> all our petty fears will be organised in concert, all our petty anxieties will be harnessed to make micro-fascists of us; we will be called upon to stifle every little thing, every suspicious face, every dissonant voice, in our streets. (Deleuze 2006b: 168)

This does not mean however, that we cannot also, like Nietzsche, act against our time in favour of a time to come.

Engagements on the level of discourse are important but form only part of the picture. Control functions just as much through machinic enslavement of the body – affects, percepts, imaginations, desires, calories, flows of water and electricity – as it does through the social subjection that produces, through the signifying systems that increasingly fill every corner of the world, alienation and ideological hegemony. These new signifying systems also operate in a double movement, whereby they open up the flows of information while simultaneously closing down collective enunciative capacity.[3]

Ressentiment – resentment, revenge and reaction – impedes all revolutionary becoming and will only lead to further oppression, of each other and of ourselves. Do not trust those who spread ressentiment and call for the settling of accounts; they seek only slaves as allies and always reproduce what they aim to destroy. 'To have ressentiment or not to have ressentiment – there is no greater difference, beyond psychology, beyond history, beyond metaphysics. It is the true difference or transcendental typology – the genealogical and hierarchical difference' (Deleuze 2006a: 35).

This is especially true of the cudgel of identity politics. If we remain trapped in a Hegelian spirit of revenge then our victories will always be written into the world as victories as slaves. Identity, even intersectional identity, reifies molar categories in its production of axes of differentiation (race, gender, species, ability). Instead of categories that always repeat the same through false appeals to identity, analogy, resemblance and opposition, we would do better to think of our multiple and always-shifting overlappings as events and encounters, and not as perennial attributes of interpellated subjects. And if we are seeking to hold on to established identities, then what are we resisting? Our own transformation through association with other bodies? Our capacity to expand joy? Is it not precisely the blockage of desiring-production within sedimented identities that has resulted – and continues to result – in relations of hierarchy and domination? And besides, the forces of repression 'always need a Self that can be assigned, they need determinate individuals on which to exercise their power. When we become the least bit fluid, when we slip away from the assignable Self, when there is no longer any person on whom God can exercise his power or by whom He can be replaced' (Deleuze 2004: 138), then perhaps we have a chance. Let us then become liquid; let us fold and unfold and refold in the practice of what Edouard Glissant calls 'Relation identity' (Glissant 1997: 144). This way we can also begin to discover our 'rigid segments', our 'binary and overcoding machines', for 'we are not simply divided up by binary machines of class, sex, or age: there are others which we constantly shift, invent without realizing it' (Deleuze and Parnet 2002: 143) and our true names are not 'pure' but, instead, 'bastard, lower, anarchical, nomadic, and irremediably minor' (Deleuze and Guattari 1996: 109).

At the same time, the struggle on the level of axioms is not unimportant. Sometimes the fight for reforms – for service delivery, for jobs, for a voice – can aid in a minority becoming. We should remember, though, that struggles on this level only facilitate such becomings; they are not, in themselves, these becomings and they are not *always* necessary. These molar politics are, Deleuze and Guattari say, 'the index of another coexistent combat' (Deleuze and Guattari 1987: 520), a micropolitics. At the very least, we must be done with the hegemony of hegemony. Our 'revolutionary organisation must be that of the war machine' (Guattari 2008a: 46). We seek a nomadic revolutionary science, not a royal science of teleologies and base–superstructures and determinations in the last instance. We are multiple, heterogeneous. There are always an infinity of peoples.

We must commit altrucide and suicide. For as long as we remain trapped in the infinite demand of the necessarily othered Other to the self, as long as our focus is on ontological vulnerability, trauma, infinite justice, impossible horizons and melancholia, we are separated from our capacity to act by a reimposed transcendent dialectics of absolute responsibility (Smith 2010: 123–41). There is imbrication in movement, a reciprocal feedback loop; a mutual enfolding of affect and expression, exchange and becoming-other-together (Braidotti 2012: 170–97).

And, of course, let us not deterritorialise too fast. A NO! is just as powerful as a YES! It is all about selection, about learning how to construct a plane of consistency and conflictuality that maximises our connections and our collective capacities.

## Postscript

There is a pause wherein we discover our involuntarism, our freedom; where we hallucinate the whole of history. In this pause we throw the dice and become the quasi-cause of the free and the new. In affirmation of the eternal return of difference; the power of the outside; the constant folding and unfolding and refolding. The dice land and they unsettle the dust of the world. An unhistorical vapour rises around us, invisible. And then, in the rupture, in the cracking of the I, in the endless caesura, there comes the sound of wasps. And orchids. And black flags unfurling. The seed splits open the paving stones. We hold out our hands to the future.

## Notes

1. For an overview of postanarchism and related ideas, see Evren and Rousselle (2011).
2. An infoshop is an autonomous, usually collectively run, radical social centre focused on the distribution of radical literature, the hosting of anarchist events and so forth. See https://en.wikipedia.org/wiki/Infoshop (last accessed 7 August 2018).
3. See Lazzarato (2014) for an extended application of Guattari's thought on social subjection and machinic enslavement in the new millennium.

## References

Badiou, A. (2004), 'The Flux and the Party: In the Margins of Anti-Oedipus, trans. L. Balladur and S. Krysl, *Polygraph*, 15/16: 75–92.
Badiou, A. (2006), *Theoretical Writings*, trans. R. Brassier and A. Toscano, London and New York: Bloomsbury Academic.
Badiou, A. and B. Bosteels (2012), *The Adventure of French Philosophy*, trans. B. Bosteels, London and New York: Verso.
Bakunin, M. (1982), *Œuvres complètes, Vol. VIII*, Paris: Champ Libre.
Bell, J. (2006), *Philosophy at the Edge of Chaos: Gilles Deleuze and the Philosophy of Difference*, Toronto: University of Toronto Press.
Bell, J. (2009), *Deleuze's Hume: Philosophy, Culture and the Scottish Enlightenment*, Edinburgh: Edinburgh University Press.
Bey, H. (1985), *CHAOS: The Broadsheets of Ontological Anarchism and The Temporary Autonomous Zone*, New York: Autonomedia.
Bookchin, M. (1995), *Social Anarchism or Lifestyle Anarchism: An Unbridgeable Chasm*, Oakland: AK Press.
Braidotti, R. (2012), 'Nomadic Ethics', in H. Somers-Hall and D. W. Smith (eds), *Cambridge Companion to Deleuze*, Cambridge: Cambridge University Press, pp. 170–97.
Buber, M. (2002), *Between Man and Man*, New York: Routledge.
Clastres, P. (1987), *Society Against the State: Essays in Political Anthropology*, trans. R. Hurley and A. Stein, New York: Zone Books.
Colson, D. (2001), *Petit lexique philosophique de l'anarchisme: De Proudhon à Deleuze*, Paris: Le Livre de Poche.
Culp, A. (2016), *Dark Deleuze*, Minneapolis: University of Minnesota Press.
DeLanda, M. (1996), 'Markets, Antimarkets and Network Economics', *Manuel DeLanda Annotated Bibliography*, http://www.cddc.vt.edu/host/delanda/pages/markets.htm (last accessed 7 August 2018).
DeLanda, M. (2003), '1000 Years of War: CTHEORY interview with Manuel DeLanda', *CTHEORY.net*, http://www.ctheory.net/articles.aspx?id=383 (last accessed 7 August 2018).
Deleuze, G. (1988a), *Foucault*, trans. S. Hand, Minneapolis: University of Minnesota Press.
Deleuze, G. (1988b), *Spinoza: Practical Philosophy*, trans. R. Hurley, San Francisco: City Lights Books.
Deleuze, G. (1990a), *The Logic of Sense*, trans. C. V. Boundas, London: Athlone Press.
Deleuze, G. (1990b), 'Gilles Deleuze in Conversation with Antonio Negri', *Generation Online*, http://www.generation-online.org/p/fpdeleuze3.htm (last accessed 7 August 2018).

Deleuze, G. (1994), *Difference and Repetition*, trans. P. Patton, New York: Columbia University Press.

Deleuze, G. (1997a), *Negotiations*, trans. M. Joughin, New York: Columbia University Press.

Deleuze, G. (1997b), *Essays Critical and Clinical*, trans. M. Greco and D. Smith, Minneapolis: University of Minnesota Press.

Deleuze, G. (2004), *Desert Islands and Other Texts*, trans. M. Taormina, Los Angeles and New York: Semiotext(e).

Deleuze, G. (2006a), *Nietzsche and Philosophy*, trans. H. Tomlinson, London: Athlone Press.

Deleuze, G. (2006b), *Two Regimes of Madness*, trans. A. Hodges and M. Taormina, Los Angeles and New York: Semiotext(e).

Deleuze, G. (2015), *What Is Grounding?*, trans. A. Kleinherenbrink, Grand Rapids: &&& Publishing.

Deleuze, G. and F. Guattari (2003) [1983], *Anti-Oedipus: Capitalism and Schizophrenia*, trans. R. Hurley, M. Seem and H. R. Lane, Minneapolis: University of Minnesota Press.

Deleuze, G. and F. Guattari (1987), *A Thousand Plateaus. Capitalism and Schizophrenia*, trans. B. Massumi, Minneapolis: University of Minnesota Press.

Deleuze, G and F. Guattari (1996), *What Is Philosophy*, trans. Hugh Tomlinson and Graham Burchell, New York: Columbia University Press.

Deleuze, G. and C. Parnet (2002), *Dialogues II*, trans. H. Tomlinson and B. Habberjam, New York: Columbia University Press.

Deleuze, G. and Parnet C. (2013), *Gilles Deleuze from A to Z*, Los Angeles and New York: Semiotext(e) (DVD).

Dosse, F. (2011), *Gilles Deleuze and Félix Guattari: Intersecting Lives*, New York: Columbia University Press.

Evren, S. and D. Rousselle (2011), *Post-Anarchism: A Reader*, London: Pluto Press.

Glissant, E. (1997), *Poetics of Relation*, Ann Arbor: University of Michigan Press.

Goldman, E. (1909), *San Francisco Bulletin*, 16 January, p. 9.

Griffuelhes, V. (1909), *Le Syndicalisme révolutionnaire*, Quebec: Éditions Espoir.

Guattari, F. (1984), *Molecular Revolution: Psychiatry and Politics,* trans. R. Sheed and D. Cooper. London: Penguin Books.

Guattari, F. (1995), *Chaosophy*, trans. D. Sweet, J. Becker and T. Adkins, Los Angeles and New York: Semiotext(e) Foreign Agents Series.

Guattari, F. (1998), 'Pragmatic/Machinic: Discussion with Félix Guattari (19 March 1985)', in C. J. Stivale (1998), *The Two-Fold Thought of Deleuze and Guattari: Intersections and Animations*, London: Guilford, pp. 191–224.

Guattari, F. (2006), *The Anti-Oedipus Papers*, trans. K. Gotman, Los Angeles and New York: Semiotext(e).

Guattari, F. (2008a), *Chaosophy*, 2nd edn, trans. D. Sweet, J. Becker and T. Adkins, Los Angeles and New York: Semiotext(e) Foreign Agents Series.

Guattari, F. (2008b), *The Three Ecologies*, trans. I. Pindar and P. Sutton, New York: Continuum.

Guattari, F. (2009), *Soft Subversions: Texts and Interviews 1977-1985*, trans. C. Wiener and E. Wittman. New York: Continuum.

Guattari, F. (2015), *Lines of Flight*, trans. A. Goffey, London and New York: Bloomsbury.

Guattari, F. and A. Negri (1990), *Communists Like Us*, trans. M. Ryan, Los Angeles and New York: Semiotext(e).

Guattari, F. and A. Negri (2010), *New Lines of Alliance, New Spaces of Liberty*, trans. M. Ryan, Minor Compositions.

Guattari, F. and S. Rolnik (2007), *Molecular Revolution in Brazil*, trans. K. Clapshow and B. Holmes, Los Angeles and New York: Semiotext(e).
Hallward, P. (2006), *Out of This World: Deleuze and the Philosophy of Creation*, London: Verso.
Jun, N. (2012), *Anarchism and Political Modernity*, New York: Continuum.
Kropotkin, P. (1902), *Mutual Aid: A Factor of Evolution*, London: William Heinemann.
Land, N. (2011), *Fanged Noumena: Collected Writings 1987–2007*, Falmouth: Urbanomic and Sequence Press.
Lazzarato, M. (2014), *Signs and Machines: Capitalism and the Production of Subjectivity*, trans. J. D. Jordan, Los Angeles and New York: Semiotext(e).
Le Guin, U. (1974), 'The Day Before the Revolution', in J. Baen (ed.), *Galaxy Science Fiction*, London: UPD Publishing Corporation, pp. 975–89.
Lenin, V. (1964), 'Left-Wing Communism: An Infantile Disorder', in *Collected Works, Vol 3*, Moscow: Progress Publishers.
Lotringer, S. (1977), *Anti-Oedipus: From Psychoanalysis to Schizopolitics*, Los Angeles and New York: Semiotext(e).
Malatesta, E. (1974), *Anarchy*, trans. V. Richards, London: Freedom Press.
Marx, K. and F. Engels (1976), *Collected Works, Vol. 10: 1849–51*, London: Lawrence & Wishart.
Massumi, B. (1992), *A User's Guide to Capitalism and Schizophrenia: Deviations from Deleuze and Guattari*, Cambridge, MA: MIT Press.
Patton, P. (2000), *Deleuze and the Political*, New York: Routledge.
Patton, P. (2010), *Deleuzian Concepts: Philosophy, Colonization, Politics*, Stanford: Stanford University Press.
Perez, R. (1986), *On An(archy) and Schizoanalysis*, New York: Autonomedia.
Proudhon, P. (1861), *La Guerre et la paix*, self-published.
Reclus, É. (1905), *L'Homme et la terre*, Paris: Librairie Universelle.
Simondon, G. (1989), *Individuation psychique et collective*, Paris: Aubier.
Smith, D. (2010), 'Deleuze and the Question of Desire: Towards an Immanent Theory of Ethics', in N. Jun and D. Smith (eds), *Deleuze and Ethics*, Edinburgh: Edinburgh University Press, pp. 123–41.
Spivak, G. (1988), 'Can the Subaltern Speak?', in C. Nelson and L. Grossberg (eds), *Marxism and the Interpretation of Culture*, Champaign: University of Illinois Press, pp. 271–314.
Stirner, M. (2017) [1907], *The Unique and Its Property*, trans. W. Landstreicher, Berkeley: Little Black Cart.
Tampio, N. (2015), *Deleuze's Political Vision*, Lanham, MD: Rowman & Littlefield.
The Invisible Committee (2008), *The Coming Insurrection*, Los Angeles and New York: Semiotext(e).
Žižek, S. (2004), *Organs Without Bodies: On Deleuze and Consequences*, New York: Routledge.

# Chapter 2

# No Gods! No Masters!: From Ontological to Political Anarchism

*Thomas Nail*

The aim of this chapter is to clarify one the most significant misunderstandings of Deleuze and Guattari's political theory: the conflation of their ontological and political anarchism. My thesis is that the fusing of these two kinds of anarchism undermines both the theory and practice of political anarchism. There is no *necessary* relation between ontological and political anarchism. This chapter thus does three things: it (1) demonstrates the difference between ontological and political anarchism and the dangers of conflating them; (2) shows their specific relation; and (3) shows the practical and analytic strength of a strictly political theory of anarchism derived from Deleuze and Guattari's work.

Deleuze and Guattari describe being as chaotic and lacking origin. This is their ontological anarchism, 'No Gods!' They also say that the aim of revolutionary politics is to create a plane of consistency, in contrast to hierarchical planes of representation. This is their political anarchism, 'No Masters!' But the two are not the same. To reduce political anarchism to ontological anarchism is to say that anarchism is chaos – which it is not. To say that it is, is to repeat the same misunderstanding used by its liberal critics: politics without government is chaos. Furthermore, just because Deleuze and Guattari say being is chaotic and lacking in foundation or origin does not mean that any particular political consequence necessarily follows from this. For example, from Democritus to Alain Badiou, many philosophers have held chaotic ontologies – but this does not mean that they are anarchists or have a political theory of anarchism. 'No Gods!' does not necessarily mean 'No Masters!' (there are atheist capitalists); and 'No Masters!' does not necessarily mean 'No Gods!' (there are Christian anarchists). Therefore, by way of clarification, this chapter proposes to give a clear account of the difference, relation and unique consequences of the ontological and political anarchisms found in Deleuze and Guattari's philosophy.

## Ontological Anarchism

Ontological anarchism is the philosophical position that there is no absolute law, ruler or origin of being – from the Greek word αναρχία, *anarchía*, 'without ruler' or 'without origin'. This is an uncommon but by no means unique ontological position in the history of philosophy. No particular political practice or ideology necessarily follows from this position. This is precisely the point. Anarchic being does not follow any predetermined logical, developmental or evolutionary trajectory. As such, there is no natural, universal or necessary political form of human organisation. Ontological anarchism is therefore a necessary but not sufficient condition for a thoroughly anarchist philosophy.

### *Becoming*

Deleuze's ontological anarchism is distinct in the history of philosophy, however, not merely because being is without God or essence, but because being is *becoming*. Deleuze is the philosopher of process and becoming par excellence. Influenced both by the ontologists of motion (Lucretius, Marx, Bergson) and the great philosophers of vital forces (Duns Scotus, Spinoza, Nietzsche, Leibniz, Whitehead and others), Deleuze was the first to unify these two traditions into a vast synthetic and systematic ontology of becoming. Instead of developing a single ontology limited to a single name for being (space, eternity, force, time, motion and so on), Deleuze developed an inclusive and pluralistic ontology in which all the great names of being are said equally and univocally of the same being – only, however, on the strict condition that this single being be strictly understood as the being of pure becoming or differential process. The ontology of becoming is therefore not a naïve and contradictory affirmation of all other ontologies but, rather, a complete reinterpretation of all ontology itself as process, as becoming. As such, Deleuze develops and applies theories of space, thought, force, time, motion, stasis and others across numerous domains.

This incredible *coup de grâce* at the end of the twentieth century has given birth to a number of derivative efforts extending the application of becoming to new areas. Of particular interest are those Deleuzians like Michael Hardt, Antonio Negri, Manuel DeLanda, Brian Massumi, Erin Manning, Jane Bennett, William Connolly, Rosi Braidotti and others who have made a concerted effort to emphasise in certain ways the becoming of matter and motion in the philosophy of becoming (Hardt and Negri 2007; DeLanda 2016; Massumi 2007; Manning 2012; Bennett

2010; Connolly 2011; Braidotti 2011). Even object oriented ontologists and speculative realists like Levi Bryant (2014), Steven Shaviro (2014) and Didier Debaise (2017) have explicitly drawn on Whitehead and Deleuze to theorise a process philosophy of objects and things. In short, the ontology of becoming has become an extremely fecund starting point for numerous new ontological anarchisms at the end of metaphysics. Deleuze's great contribution to ontological anarchism was therefore to have shown the ontological primacy of becoming over being, the 'and' (*et*) over the 'is' (*est*), and the coherence of this minor historical tradition stretching from Lucretius to Whitehead. But becoming means continuum, matter and motion for Deleuze just as equally as it means difference, thought and stasis. There is a becoming of both – hence the division and ambiguity between what is now called 'new materialism' and 'speculative realism', both drawing on different strands in Deleuze's work. This split, however, attests to the difficulty and perhaps impossibility of affirming both becomings equally without falling back into one or the other, or introducing, as Deleuze ends up doing, a third 'pure becoming' that traverses them all: force. For Deleuze, there is a 'force of thought' (Deleuze 1994: 138) and stasis just as there is a 'force of matter' (Deleuze and Guattari 2014: 95) and motion. Everything becomes because everything is a *force of becoming*.

## Ambivalence

Deleuze's ontological anarchism also confronts a kind of political ambivalence. Where most political theories flow explicitly from their ontologies – for example, Aristotle's naturalised and teleological ontology leads to a *polis* of male, Greek-speaking property owners, or Hegel's nation-state is the end result of spirit's highest self-consciousness in history – Deleuze's ontology does not lead to any particular politics. Being is nothing but pure becoming. 'Affirming Difference in the state of permanent revolution [*affirmer la Différence dans l'état de révolution permanente*]', as Deleuze says in *Difference and Repetition* (75/53), may escape the dangers of vanguardism and the party-state, but it also poses a new danger: that the pure affirmation of Difference will be ultimately ambivalent. Accordingly, ontological anarchism may provide a new, non-representational space of liberty, or it may provide a ruptured 'open' domain for a new discourse of rights and military occupation by the state, or it may merely reproduce a complicity with the processes of capitalism. Slavoj Žižek, in particular, frequently attributes this capitalist ambivalence to Deleuze and Guattari's politics. For example, he imagines a yuppy reading *Anti-Oedipus* and exclaiming: 'Yes, this is how I design my publicities!' (Žižek 2015: 163) But to say, with Alain Badiou, that affirming the ontological potentiality for transformation as such is to affirm a 'purely ideological radicality' that 'inevitably changes over into its opposite: once the mass festivals of democracy and discourse are over, [and] things make place for the modernist restoration of order among workers and bosses', would be to overstate the problem (Badiou and Balmès 1976: 83). Rather, it would be much more appropriate to say, with Paolo Virno, that '[t]he multitude is a form of being that can give birth to one thing but also to the other: ambivalence' (Virno 2003: 131). Accordingly, the affirmation of this ambivalence as a political commitment, and the 'politico-ontological optimism and unapologetic vitalism' it assumes in Hardt, Negri and Deleuze's work, according to Bruno Bosteels, remains an intrinsic danger of ontological anarchism (Bosteels 2004: 95). While the purely creative power of the multitude may be the condition for global liberation from Empire, it is also the productive condition for Empire as well. With no clear political consistency to organise or motivate any particular political transformation, ontological anarchism is politically ambivalent, speculative and spontaneous.

Showing the non-foundational or ungrounded nature of being, and thus of politics, provides no more of a contribution to politics than does the creative potentiality of desire. 'A subject's intervention,' Bosteels suggests, 'cannot consist merely in showing or recognizing the traumatic impossibility, void, or antagonism around which the situation as a whole is structured' (Bosteels 2004: 104). Rather, as Badiou says, a 'political organization is necessary in order for the intervention, as wager, to make a process out of the trajectory that goes from an interruption to a fidelity. In this sense, organisation is nothing but the consistency of politics' (Badiou 1985: 12). And in so far as Deleuze and Guattari, and those inspired by their work, do not offer developed concepts of political consistency and organisation that would bring their affirmation of ontological anarchism into specific political interventions and distributions, they remain, at most, ambivalent towards the practice of anarchist politics (see Nail 2010, 2012, 2013).

## Political Anarchism

The political import of Deleuze's ontological anarchism alone is therefore relatively minimal: it is the nature of being to become, therefore politics is also becoming. But there is no strongly normative imperative to become anything in particular. The most we can extract from such an ontology, as Paul Patton often has, is the quasi- or crypto-normative and Nietzschean interpretation that 'we ought to become different than we are' (Patton 2006: 1–5). But this still leaves our options pretty open and ambivalent, since there are a lot of ways to become different than we are. Thankfully, Deleuze has a robustly descriptive and historical dimension to his work that helps distinguish four political types and how they work. These are not essences, developmental stages or ideologies but, rather, distributions or what they call 'assemblages' or patterns that mix together with one another through history. Through an analysis of these assemblages and their mixtures we can figure out how political situations work and try to make new ones that maximise our pleasure and collective power.

For Deleuze and Guattari, there are four major kinds of assemblages: territorial, state, capitalist and nomadic. Since everything is an assemblage for Deleuze and Guattari, a type of assemblage does not refer to the fact that there are biological, literary, musical and linguistic types of assemblages. Although the content of assemblages is highly heterogeneous, there are four major types or ways of arrangements in which the conditions, elements and agencies of different assemblages are laid out. The analysis of these different types of assemblages is what Deleuze and Guattari call the politics of assemblages. Thus, all assemblages are political in so far as they can be classified according to Deleuze and Guattari's political typology of assemblages. The politics of assemblages is a broader category of analysis than traditional 'political' phenomena, which deals strictly with classical political phenomena: rights, revolutions, governments and so on. In their expanded definition of politics, everything is political. 'Politics,' they say, 'precedes being. Practice does not come after the emplacement of the terms and their relations, but actively participates in the drawing of the lines; it confronts the same dangers and the same variations as the emplacement does' (Deleuze and Guattari 2014: 203). In this sense, everything is political because every assemblage must be practically laid out. It is not just the 'application' of the assemblage that is practical or political, but the very construction of the assemblage – the way it is arranged or laid out. Deleuze and Guattari's political anarchism is defined in the context of this political typology of assemblages. In particular, it is the fourth type that is the more 'revolutionary' and 'anarchist' type of assemblage.

## Territorial Assemblages

The first type of assemblage is the territorial assemblage. Territorial assemblages are arranged in such a way that the concrete elements are coded according to a natural or proper usage. In the case of territorial assemblages, the mutational character of the conditions, elements and personae are arbitrarily delimited according a set of specific limits. For example, Deleuze and Guattari point out that 'the house is segmented according to its rooms' assigned purposes; streets, according to the order of the city; the factory, according to the nature of the work and operations performed in it' (Deleuze and Guattari 2014: 208). Territorial assemblages thus divide the world into coded segments. Each concrete element has a designated place and every persona's life has a plan related to its place in the world:

> As soon as we finish one proceeding we begin another, forever proceduring or procedured, in the family, in school, in the army, on the job. School tells us, 'You're not at home anymore'; the army tells us, 'You're not in school anymore.' (Deleuze and Guattari 2014: 209)

The expansion of these limits is then defined by the progressive expansion of the concrete elements.

Territorial codes define the 'natural' norms of life. They express the pregiven, essential and proper limits and usage of persons and objects in a given assemblage by explaining how the world is related to the past, to an inscription of memory – this is how things are done, how they have always been done. According to *Anti-Oedipus*, these 'qualitatively different chains of mobile and limited code' are formed by three basic actions: (1) 'a selection cut' allowing something to pass through and circulate; (2) 'a detachment cut' that blocks part of that circulation; and (3) a 'redistribution of the remainder' to begin a new chain of code (Deleuze and Guattari 2014: 247).

The first synthesis of territorial coding – the synthesis of connection – attempts to ward off the chaos of ontological anarchy by making a selection cut from fundamentally uncoded flows, allowing some of them to pass through while others are blocked. This primary repression of non-codable flows accomplishes two things: it wards off an absolutely chaotic world by deselecting some of its flows, and it puts into circulation and connection the others to be coded. By marking a separation of some of these non-coded flows, the connective synthesis is able to qualitatively organise them into an identity, or 'coded stock'. The 'entry pole' of selection here initiates a filial line following a genealogical or hereditary descent of hierarchically coded stock: codes of kinship, codes of worship, codes of communication, codes of exchange, codes of location (places of worship, places for eating, places for rubbish and so on). Everything has its proper code: the proper time, the proper place and the proper people to do it. The second synthesis of territorial coding – the disjunctive synthesis or 'detachment cut' – also accomplishes two tasks: it blocks some of these connections from attaching themselves to the assemblage, through code prohibitions, taboos, limits and so on, so that a finite stock of code may circulate within a qualitatively distinct territory, and it detaches a remainder or 'residual energy' in order to begin a new chain of code further along. These are the borders to towns; prohibitions on kinship; and boundaries to racial, ethnic and gender identities. These are the limits produced by the disjunctive synthesis. The third synthesis of territorial coding – the conjunctive synthesis or the 'redistribution of the remainder' – wards off the fusion of all codes into a single qualitative stock by producing a residuum. But it also begins a new line of code by redistributing this surplus through an alliance with new lines of code. There are many different mechanisms for warding off the fusion of codes and redistributing surplus code through alliances with other lines of code: practices of potlatch (giving away wealth in order to gain prestige), practices of struggle (itinerant raids and theft eliminating accumulation), practices of dowry (giving away wealth and establishing alliances with other kinship lines), gifts and countergifts, and so on.

According to Deleuze and Guattari, these coded territories 'form a fabric [*tissu*] of relatively supple segmentarity' (Deleuze and Guattari 2014: 208). The abstract relations change, but only one concrete element at a time as it is selected, detached and redistributed into a new relation. Territorial assemblages thus function like a game of leapfrog. They set up some limits and by doing so create a new limit to cross, and so on itinerantly. Every time a territory is delimited, an outside or surplus is produced through this process of delimitation or 'detachment'. This surplus or credit is then redistributed to another line through an alliance, where it will again produce a surplus and so on in a perpetual disequilibrium, making its very dysfunction an essential element of its ability to function. In the territorial assemblage, the concrete elements become privileged and primary. Change happens progressively, one concrete point at a time.

## State Assemblages

The second type of assemblage is the state assemblage. State assemblages are arranged in such a way that the conditioning relations attempt to unify or totalise all the concrete elements and agencies in the assemblage. Instead of the surplus code generated by territorial assemblages that would normally form an alliance with other concrete elements, a surplus of code may instead begin to form an unchecked accumulation – agricultural, social, scientific, artistic and so on – requiring the maintenance of a specialised body. This special body of accumulation then reacts back on the concrete elements and brings them into resonance around a centralized point of transcendence. According to Deleuze and Guattari, state assemblages

> make points resonate together . . . very diverse points of order, geographic, ethnic, linguistic, moral, economic, technological particularities . . . It operates by stratification; in other words, it forms a vertical, hierarchized aggregate that spans the horizontal lines in a dimension of depth. In retaining given elements, it necessarily cuts off their relations with other elements, which become exterior, it inhibits, slows down, or controls those relations; if the State has a circuit of its own, it is an internal circuit dependent primarily upon resonance, it is a zone of recurrence that isolates itself from the remainder of the network, even if in order to do so it must exert even stricter controls over its relations with that remainder. (Deleuze and Guattari 2014: 433)

In state assemblages, the abstract machine attempts to cut itself off from and rise hierarchically above the concrete relations and personae of the assemblage. What Deleuze and Guattari call 'state overcoding' is thus characterised by centralised accumulation, forced resonance of diverse points of order, 'laying out [*en étendant*] a divisible homogeneous space striated in all directions' (Deleuze and Guattari 2014: 223), and by its vertical and redundant centre (on top), scanning all the radii. Deleuze and Guattari describe three kinds of state arrangements proper to the process of statification: binary, circular and linear. Whereas binary territorial segmentations are defined by multiple binaries that are always determined by a third (an alliance between the two), binary state segmentations are self-sufficient and ensure the prevalence of one segment over the other (hierarchy). Whereas circular territorial segments do not imply the same centre but a multiplicity of centres (round but not quite circular), circular state segments form a resonance of concentric circles around an axis of rotation, converging on a single point of accumulation. Whereas linear territorial segmentation functions by 'segments-in-progress', alignments but no straight line and supple morphological formations, linear state segments function by homogenised segments geometrically organised around a dominant segment through which they pass: a space or *spatio* rather than a place or territory. According to Deleuze and Guattari, there are all manner of state assemblages: statist science (statistics), statist art, statist linguistics (Chomsky) and so on.

## Capitalist Assemblages

The third type of assemblage is the capitalist assemblage. Capitalist assemblages are arranged in such a way that the conditions, elements and agencies of the assemblage are divested of their qualitative relations and codes in order to circulate more widely as abstract quantities. In the capitalist assemblage, it is no longer the concrete elements that drive the process of progressive itinerant change (as in the territorial assemblage), nor the abstract machine that centralises the control over the concrete elements (as in the statist assemblage), but the agent or persona that becomes disengaged from the assemblage and tries to force unqualified concrete elements into strictly quantitative relations. Deleuze and Guattari define the capitalist assemblage by its processes of 'axiomatisation'. An axiom, they say, is precisely this independent or disengaged point that forces unqualified elements into homologous quantitative relations (Deleuze and Guattari 1996: 137–8). Thus, whereas codes determine the qualities of elements (types of places, types of goods, types of activity) and establish indirect relations (of alliance) between these incommensurable, qualified, mobile, limited codes, and statist overcodes capture and recode these elements through extra-economic forces, capitalist axioms establish a strictly economic general equivalence between purely unqualified (decoded) elements. However, Deleuze and Guattari point out that the axiomatic is not the invention of capitalism since it is identical to capitalism itself. Capitalism is the offspring or result, which merely ensures the regulation of the axiomatic; 'it watches over or directs progress toward a saturation of the axiomatic and the corresponding widening of the limits' (Deleuze and Guattari 2003: 252–3). Capitalist axiomatics create denumerable finite representations of assemblages divested of their qualities. Each independent from the others, they are added, subtracted and multiplied to form more-or-less saturated markets for the generation of wealth.

While territorial assemblages arrange qualified pieces of labour corresponding to a particular quantum of abstract labour (activity required to create a given artefact), and state assemblages introduce the general equivalent of currency formally uniting 'partial objects' (goods and services) whose overcoded value is determined by non-capitalist (imperial or juridical) decisions, they neither decode or dequalify exchange to the degree that capitalism does. Capitalism goes further. On one hand, it decodes qualitative relationships through the privatisation of all aspects of social life, free trade, advertising, freeing of labour and capital, and imperialism; on the other, it axiomatises them as 'productions for the market'. This capitalist assemblage thus retains a certain version of immanent relation between the three aspects of the assemblage, but instead of treating them as singularities or qualitative differences, treats them all as globally exchangeable quantities.

## Nomadic Assemblages

The fourth type of assemblage is what they call the 'nomadic' assemblage. This is the most revolutionary and anarchist type of social distribution. Nomadic assemblages are arranged in such a way that the conditions, elements and agencies of the assemblage are able to change and enter into new combinations without arbitrary limit or 'natural' or 'hierarchical' uses and meanings. Deleuze and Guattari call this type of assemblage 'nomadic' because it was invented by historically nomadic peoples without masters whose movement was not directed towards a final end (a static territory or state) but functioned as a kind of 'trajectory'.

For the nomad, Deleuze and Guattari observe,

> every point is a relay and exists only as a relay. A path is always between two points, but the in-between has taken on all the consistency and enjoys both an autonomy and a direction of its own. The life of the nomad is the intermezzo. Even the elements of his dwelling are conceived in terms of the trajectory that is forever mobilizing them. (Deleuze and Guattari 2014: 380)

In contrast to the capitalist assemblage that makes possible unlimited immanent transformation on the condition of global quantification, the nomadic assemblage makes possible a truly unlimited qualitative transformation and expansion of the assemblage. Without the abstraction and dominance of any part of the assemblage, a truly reciprocal change occurs. Thus, the nomadic assemblage does not simply affirm the chaos of heterogeneity or qualitative difference; it constructs a participatory arrangement in which all the elements of the assemblage enter into an open feedback loop in which the condition, elements and agents all participate equally in the process of transformation.

In all kinds of fields – science, art, politics and so on – nomadic assemblages are the ones that create something new or revolutionary for their time. The nomadic assemblage is anarchist in the sense that instead of applying solutions to pregiven problems, such as how to make sure everyone is represented fairly in a presupposed state, or simply affirming that 'other problems are ontologically possible', particular problems are themselves transformed directly by those who effectuate them and who are affected by them. 'When people demand to formulate their problems themselves and to determine at least the particular conditions under which they can receive a more general solution' (Deleuze and Guattari 1987: 470–1), there is a nomadic assemblage: a direct participation without representation or mediation. This kind of participation and self-management thus offers a political alternative absolutely incompatible with territorial hierarchies based on essentialist meanings, state hierarchies based on centralised command and capitalist hierarchies based on globally exchanged generic quantities.

Although Deleuze and Guattari never say 'this assemblage is the best, and the others are bad', it is implicitly or crypto-normatively clear that for them the nomadic assemblage is preferable to the others because it allows for maximal political inclusion, participation and collectively controlled pleasure with the least amount of exclusion, exploitation and hierarchy. Again, these four types of assemblage are never pure; all assemblages are composed of a mixture of these four types to different degrees. In order to understand how a political assemblage works, we need to be able to map out its different tendencies and political types. However, this typology is not yet sufficient for thinking the relationship between ontological and political anarchism, or the task of revolutionary transformation.

## Revolution

What then is the connection between Deleuze's ontological anarchism of becoming and the political anarchism of the nomad? In short, since being is becoming, political being is not necessarily fixed in some universal, developmental or normative pattern, but is open to continual contestation – and ought to change and generate new forms of collective pleasure as much as possible. This is a direct rejection of deterministic interpretations of statism, capitalism, liberalism and Marxism. The affirmation of change, difference and collective pleasure, however, is still a pretty loose category to most people's minds and something that may not always fall into the fourth nomadic or anarchist type of assemblage either. If everything is becoming and changing then any normative imperative to change is redundant and politically ambivalent. Again, Deleuze and Guattari provide a typology of political change or becoming to help describe the kinds of changes we find and direct us towards a fourth kind of 'revolutionary' change that will move us closer to the more nomadic and anarchist type of assemblage. 'In every social system,' Deleuze observes, 'you will always find lines of escape, as well as sticking points to cut off these escapes, or else (which is not the same thing) embryonic apparatuses to recuperate them, to reroute and stop them, in a new system waiting to strike' (Deleuze 2004: 269–70). Every assemblage is always simultaneously criss-crossed with multiple types of processes or change.

The concept they use to describe these four mixed types of change is 'deterritorialisation'. Deterritorialisation is the way in which assemblages continually transform and/or reproduce themselves. If we want to know how an assemblage works, we must ask, 'What types of change are at work?' The four kinds of deterritorialisation or change that define assemblages are: (1) 'relative negative' processes that change an assemblage in order to maintain and reproduce an established assemblage; (2) 'relative positive' processes that do not reproduce an established assemblage, but do not yet contribute to or create a new assemblage – they are ambiguous; (3) 'absolute negative' processes that do not support any assemblage, but undermine them all; and (4) 'absolute positive' processes that do not reproduce an established assemblage, but instead create a new one. Let us look more closely at each of these types of change that define all assemblages.

## Relative Negative Deterritorialisation

Relative negative deterritorialisation is the process that changes an assemblage in order to maintain and reproduce an established assemblage. This is the process by which pre-established assemblages adapt and respond to changes in their relations by incorporating those changes. For example, popular social movements against the policies of governments can often be satisfied through the adaptation of state politics: legal reform, increased political representation and party support. These processes allow the pre-established state assemblage to remain in place precisely through adaptation to popular demands. As Deleuze and Guattari say, 'D[eterritorialization] may be overlaid by a compensatory reterritorialization obstructing the line of flight: D[eterritorialization] is then said to be *negative*' (Deleuze and Guattari 2014: 508). Popular movements against war, poverty, the exclusion of minorities and so on are 'lines of flight' or expressions of political realities different from the established ones. Relative negative deterritorialisation aims to obstruct these lines of flight by offering them an increased incorporation of their desires into the state assemblage. In so doing, these desires become normalised as part of the state itself. Assemblages are thus never total or homogeneous. All assemblages are always undergoing some kind of adaptation or change. The question is, 'What kind of process of trans-formation are they undergoing?' Relative negative deterritorialisations are the processes that simply reproduce an established territorial, statist or capitalist assemblage.

## Relative Positive Deterritorialisation

Relative positive deterritorialisation is the process of change that does not reproduce a pre-established assemblage, but does not yet contribute to or create a new assemblage either (Deleuze and Guattari 2014: 247). These sorts of processes are, in short, ambiguous changes that are not clearly incorporated or incorporable into an established assemblage. Everyone recognises that a new element or agency has escaped the established assemblage, but it is not yet clear whether it will cause a radical transformation of the whole assemblage or whether it will be incorporated into an already established assemblage through a relative negative deterritorialisation. According to Deleuze and Guattari, this type of change is so 'extremely ambiguous' because it is a borderline phenomenon that is split in two. On the one side, it is an 'anomalous' (*anomal*) phenomenon that cannot be represented or incorporated with the current state of affairs; and on the other side, it is like an 'exceptional individual' that expresses the possibility of an entirely new world yet to come (Deleuze and Guattari 2014: 291). It is both the possibility of a new world and the possibility of co-optation.

## Absolute Negative Deterritorialisation

Absolute negative deterritorialisation is the process of change that does not support any political assemblage but undermines them all.[1] These are lines of flight that escape pre-established assemblages but instead of being ambiguously split between the old and the new, they are unam-biguously against the old assemblage *and* any new assemblage that threatens its absolute rejection of all assemblages. However, by reject-ing all forms of organised assemblage, they become fragmented targets easily recaptured by the relative negative deterritorialisations of territorial, statist and capitalist assemblages. 'Staying stratified – organized, signified, subjected – is not the worst that can happen,' Deleuze and Guattari state, 'the worst that can happen is if you throw the strata into demented or suicidal collapse, which brings them back down on us heavier than ever' (Deleuze and Guattari 2014: 161).

## Absolute Positive Deterritorialisation

Absolute positive deterritorialisation is the process of change that does not reproduce a pre-established assemblage, but instead creates a new one. Not only do these sorts of change escape the capture of pre-established assemblages, but they also connect to other such elements that have escaped capture. Their connection is not one that reproduces an alliance, totalisation or commodification; it forms an entirely new form of assemblage. The goal of this type of change is to 'prefigure' a new world; that is, to create a new world in the shell of the old. This absolute positive deterritorialisation does not emerge ex nihilo, but rather simply amplifies the processes of deterritorialisation that are already part of every assemblage and connects them together to form a new assemblage. Deleuze and Guattari describe this type of change as the absolute limit confronted by all other assemblages (Deleuze and Guattari 2014: 161). This process of deterritorialisation is neither transcendent nor oppositional, nor merely potential, but is a creative process that creates something new from the subjects and objects that are continually escaping from all assemblages. Absolute positive deterritorialisation is thus the kind of change that is capable of creating and sustaining a revolutionary movement. It is constructive in so far as it builds an alternative, irreducible to the preconstructed or pre-established assemblages of the past. As such, it is not just a change away from a previous assemblage to a new one but a continual process of stable social mutation. Combined with the nomadic assemblage it offers a way to think about revolution as a continual and immanent process of what we often call 'direct' or 'participatory' democracy in which as many people as possible are included in the process of collective action and enjoyment.

We can now see that the general use of the concepts 'deterritorialisation' and 'becoming' are unhelpful for analysing assemblages without a clear clarification of its four-part typology of change. For Deleuze and Guattari, there are four clearly distinct types of deterritorialisation that we need to make use of in order to understand how an assemblage works. Without such clarification, we risk falling into the valorisation of 'pure change as such', that is, absolute negative deterritorialisation, spontaneism, 'the worst that can happen' (Deleuze and Guattari 2003: 142).

## Conclusion

The thesis of this chapter is simple: ontological anarchism is not the same as political anarchism. There is no necessary relation between one and the other. The affirmation of becoming or 'deterritorialisation' in general is at best politically ambivalent. A robust philosophical anarchism, like Deleuze and Guattari's, requires both the necessary condition of 'No Gods!' and the sufficient condition of 'No Masters!' Furthermore, it requires more than just ontological and political negations. It requires a practical, theoretical and historical description of the political organisation of anarchism (the nomadic assemblage) and a theory of how to get there from here (revolutionary transformation). This chapter is simply an outline of the key ideas needed to connect ontology, politics and revolution together to form a complete theory of anarchism in Deleuze and Guattari's work. The real novelty of Deleuze and Guattari's political anarchism is that there is no longer a static utopia or state at the end of the historical rainbow, only the politics of processes themselves. Therefore, the challenge today is to create a politics equal to our historical conjuncture – a direct and participatory political process uncaptured by gods, masters, territories, states or capitalism. In other words, anarchism.

## Note

1. Absolute deterritorialisation, though, does not simply come after relative deterritorialisation. Rather, 'relative Deterritorialization itself requires an absolute for its operation', and 'conversely, absolute Deterritorialization necessarily proceeds by way of relative Deterritorialization, precisely because it is not transcendent' (Deleuze and Guattari 1987: 636/510).

## References

Badiou, A. (1985), *Peut-on penser la politique?*, Paris: Seuil.
Badiou, A. and F. Balmès (1976), *De l'idéologie*, Paris: F. Maspero.
Bennett, J. (2010), *Vibrant Matter: A Political Ecology of Things*, Durham, NC: Duke University Press.
Bosteels, B. (2004), 'Logics of Antagonism: In the Margins of Alain Badiou's "The Flux and the Party"', *Polygraph: An International Journal of Culture & Politics*, 15/16: 75–92.

Braidotti, R. (2011), *Nomadic Subjects: Embodiment and Sexual Difference in Contemporary Feminist Theory*, New York: Columbia University Press.

Bryant, L. (2014), *Onto-cartography: An Ontology of Machines and Media*, Edinburgh: Edinburgh University Press.

Connolly, W. E. (2011), *A World of Becoming*, Durham, NC: Duke University Press.

Debaise, D. (2017), *Speculative Empiricism: Revisiting Whitehead*, Edinburgh: Edinburgh University Press.

DeLanda M. (2016), *Assemblage Theory*, Edinburgh: Edinburgh University Press.

Deleuze, G. (1994), *Difference and Repetition*, trans. P. Patton, New York: Columbia University Press.

Deleuze, G. (2004), *Desert Islands and Other Texts*, trans. M. Taormina, Los Angeles and New York: Semiotext(e).

Deleuze, G. and F. Guattari (1987), *A Thousand Plateaus: Capitalism and Schizophrenia*, trans. B. Massumi, Minneapolis: University of Minnesota Press.

Deleuze, G. and F. Guattari (1996), *What Is Philosophy?*, trans. H. Tomlinson and G. Burchell, New York: Columbia University Press.

Deleuze, G. and F. Guattari (2003), *Anti-Oedipus. Capitalism and Schizophrenia*, trans. R. Hurley, M. Seem and H. R. Lane, Minneapolis: University of Minnesota Press.

Deleuze, G. and F. Guattari (2014), *A Thousand Plateaus: Capitalism and Schizophrenia*, trans. B. Massumi, Minneapolis: University of Minnesota Press.

Hardt, M. and A. Negri (2007), *Empire*, Cambridge, MA: Harvard University Press.

Manning, E. (2012), *Relationscapes: Movement, Art, Philosophy*, Cambridge, MA: MIT Press.

Massumi, B. (2007), *Parables for the Virtual: Movement, Affect, Sensation*, Durham, NC: Duke University Press.

Nail, T. (2010), 'Constructivism and the Future Anterior of Radical Politics', *Anarchist Developments in Cultural Studies*, 1: 73–94.

Nail, T. (2012), *Returning to Revolution: Deleuze, Guattari, and Zapatismo*, Edinburgh: Edinburgh University Press.

Nail, T. (2013), 'Deleuze, Occupy, and the Actuality of Revolution', *Theory & Event*, 16: 1.

Patton, P. (2006), *Deleuze and the Political*, London: Routledge.

Shaviro, S. (2014), *The Universe of Things: On Whitehead and Speculative Realism*, Minneapolis: University of Minnesota Press.

Virno, P. (2003), *A Grammar of the Multitude: For an Analysis of Contemporary Forms of Life*, Cambridge: Semiotext(e).

Žižek, S. (2015), *Organs Without Bodies: On Deleuze and Consequences: With a New Introduction*, London: Routledge.

# Chapter 3

# Absolutely Deterritorial: Deleuze, Indigeneity and Ethico-Aesthetic Anarchism as Strategy

*Andrew Stones*

'You were the first,' remarked Deleuze to Foucault in 1972, 'in your books and in the practical sphere – to teach us something absolutely fundamental: the indignity of speaking for others' (Foucault 1977: 209). Yet, when it comes to speaking *to* indigenous or subaltern struggles 'for' and 'of' freedom, Deleuze (both separately and alongside Guattari) is often accused of having little to say, if anything at all. Or, worse, when he speaks for those others his vocabulary is not a toolbox for their emancipation, but in various ways mimics the very language of oppression (Spivak 1988; Badiou 1999; Hallward 2006). There is a correlation here between those critiques most frequently ranged against anarchism as a 'strategic political philosophy' (May 1994: 7) and Deleuze's own philosophy of immanence, vitalism and multiplicity when they attempt to speak for those fighting against colonisation, capitalism and the State. If the import of aspects of poststructuralism into contemporary theories of anarchism is now commonplace, our question should not be to what extent Deleuze's philosophy is anarchist but, rather, how must the problem of colonisation be constituted such that a relay, an intensive filiation, can exist between Deleuze and anarchism?

Instead of a dialectical mechanism of oppositions or recognitions, Deleuze posits the idea of a relay or folding between theory and praxis as key to understanding the intellectual and political work of Foucault's Group d'Information sur le Prisons. As a pragmatic and strategic praxis, the lines of filiation, reverberation and disjunction between Deleuze, anarchism and indigeneity must be equally thought such that the political and philosophical problems those identities refer to are transformed and placed into continuous variation. In the examples that follow, I demonstrate how the concept of deterritorialisation performs this work in Deleuze's philosophy in that it helps us think both anarchism and indigeneity as trajectories or becomings rather than states of affairs.

In *A Thousand Plateaus*, Deleuze and Guattari outline two forms of deterritorialisation – relative and absolute – whose interplay characterise the kinds of transformative potential or lines of flight that criss-cross the entire social field. The former refers to deterritorialisations that occur between bodies and social relations in so far as they are constituted as relations between subjects, persons or states of affairs. Where societal transformation (through the representation of previously excluded peoples under the law, or the demand for new rights or institutional change, for example) is articulated, it is presupposed that a body or group of bodies be the 'subject' of those transformations. The latter form of deterritorialisation, therefore, involves the breakdown of those 'spatiotemporal and even existential coordinates' by which subjects and states of affairs can be said to exist (Deleuze and Guattari 2004b: 62). Absolute deterritorialisation follows a trajectory that cuts across the various strata that organise a territory into something like our world. An 'absolute drift', this zigzig line crosses a threshold where bodies, things and their milieus become indeterminate (Deleuze and Guattari 2004b: 62). As a chaotic distribution of elements, this plane underpins the fixed coordinates of the sensible as its absolute limit – not the sensible as it is given to our experience, but that condition 'by which the given is "given" as difference-in-itself' (Deleuze 2004a: 280). The relation between relative and absolute forms of deterritorialisation is not, however, purely one of speed or acceleration:

> What qualifies a deterritorialisation is not its speed (some are very slow) but its nature, whether it constitutes epistrata and parastrata and proceeds by articulated segments or, on the contrary, jumps from one singularity to another following a nondecomposable, nonsegmentary line drawing a metastratum on the plane of consistency. (Deleuze and Guattari 2004b: 63)

Deleuze and Guattari are clear that relative forms of deterritorialisation (the demand for recognition, equality and/or institutional change) are not incompatible with absolute forms of revolutionary change – the kind sought by anarchists, for example – but can in fact precipitate their arrival. Accumulative differences of degree can suddenly become differences in kind. When the problem of colonisation is only conceived as a problem of enunciation (Spivak 1988), this has the effect of collapsing one kind of deterritorialisation (relative) into the other (absolute) so that it appears as if Deleuze and Guattari have no time for the challenges of fostering new forms of political organisation and solidarity between oppressed persons.

Simone Bignall (2010) notes, however, that Deleuze's account of the complex interaction between absolute and relative forms of deterritorialisation already reverberates with the ways in which strategies for achieving social and political change have been used by indigenous activists and theorists themselves. James Tully defines these strategies as struggles 'for and of freedom' (Tully 2001: 36). Struggles 'for' freedom consist of 'struggles against the structure of domination as a whole and for the sake of their freedom as peoples' (2001: 50). Struggles 'of' freedom entail the 'struggle within the structure of domination vis-à-vis techniques of government, by exercising their freedom of thought and action with the aim of modifying the system in the short term and transforming it in the long term' (2001: 50). There is no contradiction between those struggles of freedom, or relative deterritorialisation, and those for freedom, or absolute deterritorialisation, so long as we insist upon the immanence of those revolutionary or absolutist lines within concrete situations of resistance, solidarity and struggle.

As an ethics, struggles for freedom – absolute, open-ended, without recognition – subsist as deterritorialising functions that face towards the plane of consistency or unformed matter, at the same time as they become 'expressed' in the relations between strata (physiochemical, organic, semiotic) within which struggles of freedom – equality, enunciation and subjectification – are articulated. Those struggles, or the relative deterritorialisation of social, political and institutional epistrata, are the *residue* of a politics belonging properly to the plane of consistency itself. This is flush with the anarchist principle that the tools of emancipation are already 'at hand' in everyday life to the extent that our articulation as subjects or persons is political. There is no becoming-political of persons but, rather, a politics of becoming that subsists between our articulation as subjects and our perception of the world as an objective reality. As far as the aesthetic dimension of struggles for freedom is concerned, deterritorialisation is always directed towards 'a new Earth' between or beneath the sensible perception of objects by a subject (Deleuze and Guattari 1994: 99). Anarchism is therefore not only a political practice, but also an aesthetic one in so far as strategies of absolute deterritorialisation express this purely differential potential without identity – the 'being of the sensible' – as it subsists within the institutional, bureaucratic or social apparatuses through which both persons and groups are articulated (Deleuze 2004a: 68). It is not relations of difference between certain social groups that need to be recognised or represented (by a State, for example), but 'difference, potential difference and difference in intensity as the reason behind qualitive diversity' that both Deleuze and anarchism need to account for (Deleuze 2004a: 68). Anarchism takes on an ethical and aesthetic responsibility where its struggles 'for' freedom take on a 'piloting role' (Deleuze and Guattari 2004b: 62) in respect to the politics of the Earth itself – 'a new type of reality' (157) where matter itself becomes expressive and agential (the 'being' of the sensible). Where relative deteritorialisation attempts to rewrite and recode our relation to the land or territory, ethico-aesthetic anarchism is a writing (or painting, or sculpting, or performance or rioting) which 'now functions on the level of the real, and the real materially writes' (156).

How does Deleuze and Guattari's philosophy help us, then, to think 'with' rather than 'for' anarchists and indigenous peoples? If, as Stephen Muecke (2004) attests, 'philosophy is defined by Europe, *the* continent', does the question of an 'indigenous philosophy' become a trap (Muecke 2004: 155)? The contours of a new Earth can only be discerned by 'becoming a nonphilosopher' – by multiplying and diffracting the connections between Deleuze's thought and its non-European, non-philosophical 'outside' in the culture and history of indigenous peoples (Deleuze and Guattari 1994: 109). This would entail nothing less than the transformation of philosophy: creating a relay or circuit-breaker with what is *not* philosophy in order to bring about the permanent decolonisation of thought.[1]

Likewise, anarchism must be seen as both more and less than a politics; that is, not so much a defined set of characteristics as an event or becoming we must 'become worthy of' (Deleuze 2004c: 170). We should not look for an ontology that would determine the coordinates of our praxis. Instead, the separation of art (aesthetics) and life (being) should itself be seen as a normative assumption of a majoritarian culture that seeks, in their separation of these, a means by which to pass judgement on life. As trajectories or paths along a zigzag line, the political philosophies of both Deleuze and Guattari, and anarchism, are an 'ethico-aesthetics' – a ceaseless becoming-other rather than actual states of affairs. This ethico-aesthetics is not an ideology, much less a programme, but a becoming which escapes and dissolves recognition or representation by the subjects who undergo it. If resistance to systems of exploitation and domination is weaker and more perilous than when Deleuze and Guattari published their final collaborative work, this is not for a lack of communication, but more properly a 'lack of resistance to the present' (Deleuze and Guatarri 1994: 108).

What follows is an attempt to map the transverse movements of such an 'ethico-aesthetic anarchism' as it emerges in relation to the struggles of indigenous peoples in different times and places: a cartography of resistances to the present.

## The Papunya Tula Cooperative: Beyond Representation and the State

Since the 1960s, Aboriginal Australian activism has been predominantly conceived from a transnational and rhizomatic perspective influenced by the Black Panthers in America and other black power movements around the globe (Foley 2001). At the same time, the struggles of indigenous people and communities have largely been understood through land rights, such as the 1992 Mabo ruling.[2] Yet the transversal background to these struggles has been less emphasised.[3] If the then Labour government's Native Title Act 1993 established native title claims in Australian common law, this only partially led to the restoration of Aboriginal rights over their traditional lands and reduced the complexity of indigenous activism in the eyes of the State to a demand for recognition (Patton 2001). This, in fact, led to a 'constitutional paradox' whereby the legitimacy of Aboriginal title claims established by landmark rulings, such as the Mabo case, rejected in principle the colonial policy of *terra nullus*, but failed to effect a more thorough or qualitative transformation in the structures of inequality, exclusion and oppression that characterised the relationship between indigenous and non-indigenous peoples in Australia (Patton 2001: 25). This paradox is indicative of what James Tully (2001) refers to as struggles of freedom and Deleuze identifies as processes of relative deterritorialisation. If the Native Title Act partially destratified the legal structures imported from England during the colonial period, this was quickly reterritorialised as a question of reconciliation and recognition of the indigenous 'Other' on behalf of the State – a project that could only succeed in its failure to account for the complexity and multifaceted nature of Aboriginal conceptions of black power, which traversed indigenous, non-indigenous and national boundaries (Foley 2001).

An alternative to this history lies in the creative response to the assimilationist policies of the Australian State in the 1950s by the artists of the Western Australian Desert, most notably at Papunya. The paintings of the Papunya Tula Cooperative since the 1960s embody the capacity for absolute deterritorialisation Deleuze ascribes to aesthetic practice – a becoming-expressive of the landscape of the Western Desert so that it cuts across the paradoxes of Australian responses to the question of Aboriginal land rights.[4]

The 1960 settlement at Papunya agglomerated the Anmatjera, Luritja, Warlpiri and Pintupi communities that, traditionally, had a nomadic relationship to the land. Originally, the indigenous artists who gathered around the teaching of Geoffrey Bardon at Papunya utilised methods of inscription that encompassed carved boards and body decoration as well as ground painting, but by the mid-1980s this was almost entirely transferred to canvas. If, in the first instance, painting at Papunya gave the artists a means of selling their work, by 1971 this was done as a collective with communal meetings held to decide on sales and all earnings being distributed within the group. But this ethical commitment to a group or collective enunciation was combined with an aesthetic praxis which was resolutely non-representational. The inscription of lines and geometric patterns that characterise the paintings of the Papunya Tula Cooperative is a creative deterritorialisation of the ritual practice of 'Dreaming'. Dreaming refers to a supernatural time that is not simply a time antecedent to human history but that subsists alongside the social world as a non-linear temporality. Dreaming exists in an indeterminate state between a verb and an adjective that attaches itself to art-objects, language and practices.

The early paintings of the Papunya Tula Cooperative lack the perspectival conventions of Western art traditions – without an identifiable horizon or separation between land and sky. This non-anthropocentric form of expression, as well as its material 'content' which traverses bodies, the earth and the board or canvas, produces or miraculates the sense of Dreaming as infinity or Aion. In becoming-with the landscape, the Papunya Tula artists enter into an assemblage with the desert that refuses assimilation and recognition by the subject of white Australia: 'In that place the sand was close to all that was said or done; the Aboriginal people made the sand speak as they drew it in their hieroglyphs' (Bardon 1989: 13). For the indigenous communities of central and Western Australia, the desert is already populated by signs; the landscape is a multiplicity of *tjurunga* that mark the disappearance of the supernatural beings of Aboriginal mythology. The painting of the Papunya artists is not set against a void or absence (a blank canvas), but a territory that is itself already expressive.

It is commonly assumed that the Pintupi and other indigenous peoples of Western Australia were some of the last to 'come out of' the desert, but this is not strictly true. In making the landscape of the desert expressive, by rendering the desert as sensation through Dreaming, the Papunya Cooperative brought the desert with them. In the same way that, for Deleuze, the nomad is precisely one who does not travel but rather 'carries' part of their milieu as a deterritorialising refrain, the paintings of the Papunya artists are closer to an aerial cartography or mapping than the forms of landscape painting belonging to the European tradition. Tim Leurah Tjapaltjarri's *Napperby Death Spirit Dreaming* (1980), completed in collaboration with his brother, follows the journey of the Death Spirit rendered as a topography of places and events that link together the artist's life with his tribal history before and after colonisation, as well as the natural formations of the land – the tracks left by animals, smoke, grass and sand – and the windbreaks that mark the inscription of indigenous life in the land itself. Like almost all Western Desert painting, the work lacks any concept of horizon, instead using dotting and smudging to produce a haptic visual effect wherein the terrain is made to 'vibrate' and the figural distinctions between ground and human, animal and territory become indistinct. A chaotic geometry in which the perspectival distance upon which the idea 'landscape' depends disappears so that an *Earth* can emerge.

For the Anmatjera and other indigenous communities in the Northern Territories of Australia:

> Children are born from their ancestor's spirit emerging from the ground, relating a person with their place of birth (and incurring the responsibilities of care for that country) and that, upon their physical, corporeal death, their spirit returns to that place. This is why, upon death, the emphasis is shifted away from the body and towards place as the enduring location of spirit . . . Movement is more important to Aboriginal modes of being than territoriality, and lines (or pathways of movement) more than boundaries. (Muecke 2004: 16)

The European occupation of Australia in part utilised 'spatial technologies, metrical instruments of surveying and measuring' (Muecke 2004: 14) to impose on the indigenous population a capitalist axiomatic which separated body from landscape and nature from culture. It goes without saying that Aboriginal bodies were included in the category of a nature to be dominated and exploited by the settler state. The Dreaming of Tim Leurah Tjapaltjarri and others at Papunya is, by the same token, a deterritorialising praxis (landscape painting led by the hand rather than the eye) through which an idea of place or country emerges at the expense of state-space. The landscape or milieu, rather than an empty container or universal unit of measurement, becomes expressive.[5] The 'becoming expressive' of the country occurs through an indigenous time which,

> while not metrical, was periodised nonetheless and enacted in rituals that brought out Ancesteral power in ever-tightening rhythms, from the

slowest cycle of the ancient dreaming, to the cycle of generations, to the life of one was custodian, to the seasonal ritual cycle to the song cycle itself and its repeated phrasings and stamping of feet into the earth. (Muecke 2004: 17)

The conical or rhythmic movement of indigenous time presupposes the relationships between a people and land as immanent to one another, having no need for the European concept of nature, for all nature is in fact a 'natural-cultural' milieu or becoming. As a place, the desert is populated, but not simply by humans who 'inhabit' or occupy it. Here the Papunya Tula Cooperative can be said to have extended aspects of Deleuze's own preoccupation with the desert as place, country and de/ re-territorialising movement: thinking in things, among things – this is producing a rhizome and not a root, producing the line and not the point, producing population in a desert and not species and genres in a forest, populating without ever specifying (Deleuze and Parnet 2006: 26).

To the white Australian eye, the landscape of the Northern Territories becomes imperceptible at the same time as the desert – an a-signifying, chaotic or haptic sensation – spreads across the canvas. The murals and canvases produced at Papunya were part of a transformation of a ritual form of inscription between bodies and the Earth that allowed the Warlpiri, Anmatjera and other communities to find a form of cultural expression despite the economic, cultural and philosophical violence enacted upon them. But this relative movement of deterritorialisation (the subtraction of elements of ritual from their previous social and religious functions) precisely triggered the kinds of ethical and aesthetic experience unable to be recognised or assimilated by the white gaze. It would be naïve to suggest that the Papunya Tula Cooperative, or the Western Desert Art movement they helped create, constituted an 'anar-chism'. However, in their strategic response to the colonising Australian machine, as well as their evasion of recognition or representation as the horizon of subaltern struggle, their work is instructive for those seeking an alternative to 'this psychotic debate we keeping having with white Australia' (Langton quoted in Muecke 2004: 157). This 'psychotic debate', the ceaseless demand to be recognised, to enunciate as a subject, is in actuality only an apparatus of capture on behalf of the settler. If we think about decolonisation as a question of ethics and aesthetics as well as political organisation, Deleuze and Guattari's philosophy becomes a strategic ally with the theory and praxis of anarchism in the Global South. But these lines of intensive filiation, alliance and escape have only recently begun to be mapped.

## Decolonising Solidarity: The Awareness League

By refusing the representational demands of assimilationist policies, the work of the Papunya Tula Cooperative creates what Deleuze playfully refers to as 'vacuoles of non-communication' that continually short-circuit the means by which the composition of subaltern subjectivity is utilised by the settler State as form of control (Deleuze 1995: 175). This ethical and aesthetic strategy is, moreover, adapted to the situation in which various forms of relative deterritorialisation (such as rights discourses, land titles, political representation and so on) have partially undermined the legal principle of *terra nullus*. But precisely to the extent that Aboriginal bodies are composed *as* subjects (in contrast simply to their 'non-existence' assumed by *terra nullus*), the State can continually defer the process of decolonisation where it relates to the total transformation of the governmental, institutional, legal, cultural and philosophical systems of Australian society by positioning itself as the mediator and ultimate guarantor of any such changes. Ethico-aesthetic anarchism, when it creates vacuoles of non-communication, is in this sense the refusal of minority in favour of becoming-minor. Becoming-minor stands in contrast to the ethics of representation and communication that commonly structure the question of indigeneity in postcolonial discourse. One example of this strategy of creative sabotage – a solidarity between indigenous and non-indigenous activists that does not fall into the trap of speaking for others – is the Awareness League in Nigeria.

From the late 1980s until the end of the 1990s, a loose coalition of activists, academics, students and journalists formed the main opposition to the military rule in Nigeria. The Awareness League grew out of the mostly socialist and Marxist movements that had sprung up in this period, but substantially departed from their intellectual currents in African nationalism to incorporate an anarchist critique of the postcolonial State, capitalism and imperialism. As part of this departure, the Awareness League developed an anthropological critique of anarchism that redistributed its historical and geographical relation to Europe and its relevance to questions of indigeneity and the State in Africa. However, the anarchism they sought was one that did not overcode those social and cultural structures that existed prior to colonialism, nor was it one that would simply offer a different European intellectual tradition:

To a lesser or greater extent, all these traditional African societies manifested 'anarchistic elements' which, upon closer examination, lend credence to the historical truism that governments have not always existed. They are but a recent phenomenon and are, therefore, not inevitable in human society. (Mbah and Igariwey 1997: 27)

At first glance, Sam Mbah and I. E. Igariwey (two of the Awareness League's earliest and most prominent activists in Nigeria) seem to endorse the view that anarchism reflects a 'state of nature' that is reflected in indigenous African cultures, but this is not the case. In fact, Mbah and Igariwey stage a parallel argument to that expressed by Deleuze and Guattari in *A Thousand Plateaus*, where the development of the nation-state is shown to be a contingent and non-linear phenomenon, and the whole discourse of 'development' is undercut by a multiplicity of non-European perspectives. Building on the anthropology of Pierre Clastres, Deleuze and Guattari argue that 'primitive societies' do not lack a politics, but that the manner and orientation of power in those societies is of an entirely different order to the spatial logic of the State:

> Primitive societies do not lack formations of power; they even have many of them. But what prevents the potential central points from crystallizing, from taking on consistency, are precisely those mechanisms that keep the formations of power both from resonating together in a higher point and from becoming polarized at a common point. (Deleuze and Guattari 2004b: 433)

For this reason, Deleuze and Guattari describe the operation of State power as one of capture and resonance between different social structures that those non-State societies are always in the process of warding off.

Instead of an evolutionary movement from non-State or indigenous social structures towards the State, Deleuze and Guattari reveal a mobile and shifting multiplicity of social forces which cannot be made to resonate with State power, and which are absolutely contemporary to Western, capitalist modernity rather than its prehistory. Mbah and Igariwey's analysis of precolonial social structures in Africa likewise transforms their understanding of modernity, the State and the location of an 'indigenous anarchism':

> The manifestations of 'anarchic elements' in African communalism ... were (and to some degree still are) pervasive. These include the palpable absence of hierarchical structures, governmental apparatuses, and the commodification of labour. To put this in positive terms, communal societies were (and are) largely self-managing, equalitarian and republican in nature. (Mbah and Igariwey 1997: 33)

But these 'anarchistic elements' never coalesce into a unity or identity, an 'African anarchism' that was extinguished by colonisation. Instead, these elements are conceived of as trajectories or potentials that striate the formations of power in traditional African societies – a deterritorialising coefficient without an origin or ground to which it gives 'expression'. Communalism was not 'an anarchist utopia', but was in part made possible by relatively low levels of production, the continuation of traditional caste systems and the oppression of women (Mbah and Igariwey 1997: 33). Contrasting both the 'evolutionary' myth of stateless societies and the colonial trope of the 'noble savage' that regard indigenous power dynamics as a state-of-nature, Mbah and Igariwey seek to deterritorialise the meanings of both 'anarchism' as an inherently Western, European political philosophy, while simultaneously refusing the idea of 'indigeneity' as a premodern or primitivist utopia.

Within their schizoid history of indigenous (non)anarchisms in Africa, it is their study of the Igbo peoples of southern Nigeria and the Niger Delta that becomes most productive for this disjunctive synthesis of geography, anthropology and political philosophy. In contrast to the overcoding of the State, Igbo societies functioned by a segmented or serial pattern of organisation:

> against large, centralised political units, Igbo society constructed small units, often referred to as 'village' political units without kings or chiefs ruling over them or administering their affairs . . . Among the Igbo, there is a popular saying, '*Igbo enwegh Eze*', meaning, 'Igbo have no kings'. (Mbah and Igariwey 1997: 35)

As well as the *Umu-ada*, 'a parallel body of women either married into the village or born there [which] played a key role in decision making and implementation processes', they find in Igbo practices of direct democracy and collective decision making a political semiotics able to fold back onto their work and activism in the Awareness League as a whole (Mbah and Igariwey 1997: 36). Here the relay Deleuze identifies in Foucault's work with prisoners is combined with the circuit-breaker as a mode of intellectual sabotage, creatively redistributing the terms 'indigeneity' and 'anarchism' and putting them into variation:

> At the village square, elders outline an issue in detail and the people are expected to air their views as forthrightly as possible, until a consensus is achieved. Neither the elders, the secret societies [such as the *Umu-ada*], nor the age-grades could drag the village into a war or armed conflict without first consulting the general assembly for a decision . . . Igbo social organisation, like that of the Niger-Delta people, Tiv, and Tallensi, manifested a

definite inclination toward leadership as opposed to authority. (Mbah and Igariwey 1997: 36)

These forms of direct democracy, while not fully or formally anarchist, were utilised by the Awareness League in a becoming-indigenous of their overall ethical and political praxis, as well as encouraging those indigenous members of the group to think of their composition as colonised subjects via a series of becomings-anarchist. A transversal line is made to connect indigenous African experience with the political philosophy of anarchism that mutually transforms both, subtracting them from their local spatial and temporal contexts and activating previously impossible relations of solidarity and communication between them.

Since the end of military dictatorship in Nigeria, the Awareness League have ceased to be an active movement. Nonetheless, their methods of creating relays and circuit-breakers between anarchist and indigenous histories can be similarly detected in the newer social movements across the Global South which immediately followed them. The mutual deterritorialisation of the identities of anarchism and indigeneity is key to understanding solidarity between indigenous and non-indigenous activists beyond the problem of enunciation through which indigenous bodies become subjectified. The philosophy of Deleuze and Guattari becomes vital here for thinking the ethico-aesthetic aspects of these movements – in other words, how the demand for relative deterritorialisation of the social body which subjugates indigenous peoples via an apparatus of capture is able to transform into more absolute forms of social, political and environmental deterritorialisation through the invention of a people and an Earth yet to come.

## An Earth, a People Yet to Come: The Shramik Mukti Dal Manifesto

Originally founded in 1980, Shramik Mukti Dal (SMD) (Toilers' Liberation League) quickly became one of the leading activist groups for organising Indian peasant farmers and other indigenous communities around the demand for water rights in the State of Maharashtra. Following the extraction of sand from the Yerala riverbed in the area surrounding the district of Sangli for use in the Indian construction industry, there was growing resistance among indigenous communities to the government-planned irrigation projects designed to replenish the water table. Yet rather than simply demanding relief from drought, centred on the continued economic reliance of indigenous peoples on government work projects, the SMD aimed at 'eradicating drought' entirely (Omvedt 1993: 239). While there has long been a tradition of direct democracy in Maharashtra, the SMD were unique in extending the range of indigenous activism beyond the class-based analysis of Marxism to encompass feminist, anti-caste and ecological concerns.

Against the centralising tendencies of other Indian socialist movements, the SMD 'never built a functioning "democratic centralist" structure' (Omvedt 1993: 239). Instead they expanded horizontally and serially to include several other groups working in solidarity with one another, 'connect[ing] Sangli peasants with a wider political environment' which included anti-caste campaigns, street-theatre performances, demonstrations over drought research at the university in Kolhapur and an autonomous women's activist group (Omvedt 1993: 240). By placing indigenous experience at the forefront of their activities, the SMD's strength lay in creating multiple relays between different areas of indigenous concerns while the question of precisely what those concerns were was left open-ended. This strategy culminated in the four-year struggle to design and build the Bali Raja Memorial Dam in southern Maharashtra against the wishes of the Indian government and, in 1990, a larger irrigation project in Khanapur built and managed by the local Adivasi (indigenous) community.

In contrast to other socialist or Maoist movements in India, the SMD never aimed at taking over or replacing the Indian State, but instead successfully organised to 'ward off' the apparatus of capture by which the State progressively recognises and represents those bodies (both human and non-human) external to it:

> A revolution that creates a new ecologically balanced, prosperous, non-exploitative society is not an 'event' that takes place in one day. It is necessary to start this process of revolutionary transformation from today itself. Briefly, revolution is not a single 'event' but a 'process' that makes change. It is a process of striking one blow after another against the roots of the established capitalist, casteist, patriarchal, social-economic structure, and establishing again and again the roots creating the new society. It is a process of new creation. (Shramik Mukti Dal Manifesto: 1)

What began as an indigenous demand for water rights, the relative redistribution of capitalism's material flows, developed autonomously and in several directions at once into a mutual transformation of the way indigenous and non-indigenous activists related to the land, the State and each other as a collective assemblage of enunciation. Becoming-Adivasi entailed not only relief from the distribution of scarcity imposed by capital, but a process of synthesising entirely new concepts of indigeneity, territory and ecology:

> Now, revolution means . . . the beginning of a struggle to implement a new strategy regarding the relationship between men and women and people of different castes and nationalities. It means alternative ways of organising and managing the production processes, alternative concepts of agriculture/ industry/ecology and alternative health care. (Ramnath 2011: 221)

As with the Awareness League, procedures of deterrritorialisation do not come to rest on the mutual recognition of the Other's right-to-speak, but continually delay the moment of subjectification via which 'thought . . . rediscovers the State, rediscovers all the current values' (Deleuze 2004a: 172). The revolution desired by Shramik Mukti Dal is an immanent decolonisation of everyday life, that is, an entirely 'different logic of anti-colonial struggle' (Ramnath 2011: 21) which 'wards off' the Urstaat wherever it installs itself on social, cultural, political, ecological, psychological or philosophical strata as an abstract machine of colonisation:

> Colonization functioned on multiple levels, through several interlocking modalitites of hard and soft power, from the structural to the psychological . . . Striving for total decolonization would mean working on all these levels in addition to (but not instead of) tackling capitalism and the state, without reducing the struggle to either the material or ideological/discursive plane. (Ramnath 2011: 27)

Instead of staging a moral encounter between Adivasi and non-Adivasi activists, the SMD actively sought out moments of ethical crisis in which the supposed subject of indigeneity became imperceptible to those institutional and governmental apparatuses assumed to speak on their behalf:

> In October 1985 peasants proclaimed their new relationship to the 'world of knowledge' when they demonstrated at the local university at Kolhapur with the demand that either the university do research on drought 'or we'll go into the library and do our own research.' (Omvedt 1993: 240)

Because many Adivasi or indigenous peoples in India reject the term 'tribal' or other universalising terms, the SMD manifesto swerves questions of recognition in favour of a 'collective assemblage of enunciation' that synthesises a zone of solidarity, of becoming, between different subject groups, castes and workers so that it acts as a circuit-breaker to the imposition of the demand for recognition placed on minorities (Deleuze and Guattari 2004b: 89). The goal of the SMD was never to be constituted as a minority, but to 'become minoritarian' as part of an ethical and aesthetic struggle over the structure of everyday life. As Maia Ramnath argues:

> Precolonial reality was dynamic, multifarious, and also horrible for some people. The decolonisation of culture shouldn't mean rewinding to a 'pure' original condition but instead restoring the artificially stunted capacity freely to grow and evolve without forcible outside interference to constrict the space of potential. (2011: 210)

Total decolonisation does not end with the demand for a relative deterritorialisation in capitalism's axiomatic logic of accumulation, but is imminent to those demands as a zone of indeterminacy that dissolves the habitual request for postcolonial bodies to say 'I'. The SMD's manifesto, produced as a collectively written text without an author, does not represent or in other ways signify this 'space of potential', but actively subtracts from it a 'revolutionary process' which operates 'simultaneously in all fields, including the economic, the field of production, social, cultural, literary, art, industrial, agricultural, the production of energy' as an imminent ethics of resistance, and an aesthetic strategy of becoming-minor (Shramik Mukti Dal Manifesto: 3). The relative deterritorialisation of the Indian social body, the demand *of* freedom from 'the unambiguous wrong of dispossession', reaches a threshold where 'those indigenous land claims constitute an argument for a way of relating to place and biosphere that counteracts the ecologically destructive logic of late capitalist consumer society' (Ramnath 2011: 22). In a struggle *for* freedom, the SMD expanded serially and autonomously, combining discursive regimes with both indigenous and non-indigenous institutional networks. By subtracting various lines of deterritorialisation from those economic, social and cultural strata which made them visible to State power, they opened up potential spaces, vacuoles of non-communication, and zones of absolute deterritorialisation out of which a new Earth and a new people might be created.

## Becoming Ungovernable

Dipesh Chakrabarty argues that philosophy is both 'indispensable and inadequate in helping us to think through the life practices that constitute the political and the historical' as postcolonial realities (Chakrabarty 2000: 6). Deleuze does not, therefore, help us uncover an 'Aboriginal philosophy' – whatever that might be – because such a philosophy would entail nothing less than the absolute deterritorialisation of the

European tradition that gave birth to colonialism. Nevertheless, when Marcia Langton speaks about the urgent need to 'forget about this psychotic debate we keep having with white Australia and ... start talking to Asians and people from Eastern Europe and Africa and so on and South America and talk about something else for a change', this is a transversal trajectory in indigenous activism that was there all along and which draws strength precisely from its contingency and heterogeneity (Langton quoted in Muecke 2004: 157).[6]

At a time when global capitalism increasingly demands its own performative opposition via the interminable production of new categories of subjectivity, indigenous and anarchist groups are finding common ground through practices of strategic disappearance. By collapsing the spatial logic of the State (such as at Papunya) or finding a common language that explodes the binary nature–culture (as happens in the Shramik Mukti Dal Manifesto), indigenous activists are finding passages of escape out of 'this world' that are the very condition of an ethics of multiplicity, contingency and autonomy named anarchism. 'The revolutionary problem today', argue Deleuze and Guattari,

> is to find some unity in our various struggles without falling back on the despotic and bureaucratic organisation of the party or State apparatus: we want a war machine that would not recreate a State apparatus, a nomadic unity in relation with the Outside, that would not recreate the despotic unity. (Deleuze 2004b: 260)

The same can be said of reading Deleuze's (and/or Guattari's) philosophy in the twenty-first century, where one is always having to ward off the appearance of a system that would define our (or their) political commitments. We should not look to interpretation, but only to fellow travellers. Here anarchism and indigeneity find conceptual tools in Deleuze, but only by rethinking them creatively so as transform and redistribute both terms of the relation along a line of continuous variation do they become weapons we can use to carve a trajectory from the Outside, to the new Earth.

## Notes

1. The meaning of 'non-philosophy', which I take from Deleuze here, is to be distinguished from Francois Laruelle's related but distinct use of the term.
2. *Mabo* v. *Queensland* (No. 2) 1992.
3. 'Transversality' became a key concept in Guattari's clinical vocabulary during the early 1960s. In contrast to rigidly segmented or hierarchical institutions, transversality aims to maximise the potential for communication flows and affective

encounters between different levels or series, thus producing an immanent rather than transcendent form of organisation without a totalising perspective.

4. The potential for reading the dreaming of Warlpiri painters alongside Deleuze and Guattari's schizoanalysis has notably been explored by Barbara Glowczewski (2016).

5. In Deleuze's philosophy, life is an open whole or becoming. 'Becoming expressive' in this sense is the potential for life to unfold new relations and in new directions on a plane of becoming. Philosophy does not govern life from the outside, developing a structure appropriate to judge life, but must grasp the potential for movement and infinity of expression immanent to life.

6. For more on the history of indigenous activism in Australia and its transversal relation to other radical social movements during the 1960s and 1970s, see www. kooriweb.org

# References

Badiou, A. (1999), *Deleuze: The Clamor of Being*, trans. L. Burchill, Minneapolis: University of Minnesota Press.

Bardon, G. (1989), 'The Gift That Time Gave: Papunya Early and Late 1971–72 and 1980', in J. Ryan and G. Bardon, *Mythscapes: Aboriginal Art of the Desert*, Melbourne: National Gallery of Victoria.

Bignall, S. (2010), *Postcolonial Agency: Critique and Constructivism*, Edinburgh: Edinburgh University Press.

Chakrabarty, D. (2000), *Provincializing Europe: Postcolonial Thought and Historical Difference*. Princeton: Princeton University Press.

Deleuze, G. (1995) [1990], *Negotiations: 1972–1990*, trans. M. Joughin, New York: Columbia University Press.

Deleuze, G. (2004a), *Difference and Repetition*, trans. Paul Patton, London: Continuum.

Deleuze G. (2004b), *Desert Islands and Other Texts*, trans. M. Taormina, New York: Semiotext(e).

Deleuze, G. (2004c), *Logic of Sense*, trans. M. Lester, London: Continuum.

Deleuze, G. and F. Guattari (1994), *What Is Philosophy?*, trans. G. Burchill and Hugh Tomlinson, London: Verso.

Deleuze, G. and F. Guattari (2004a), *Anti-Oedipus: Capitalism and Schizophrenia*, trans. R. Hurley, M. Seem and H. R. Lane, Minneapolis: University of Minnesota Press.

Deleuze, G. and F. Guattari (2004b), *A Thousand Plateaus: Capitalism and Schizophrenia*, trans. B. Massumi, London: Continuum.

Deleuze, G. and C. Parnet (2006), *Dialogues II*, trans. H. Tomlinson and B. Habberjam, London: Continuum.

Foley, G. (2001), 'Black Power in Redfern 1968–1972', *The Koori History Website*, www.kooriweb.org/foley/essays/essay_1.html (last accessed 9 August 2018).

Foucault, M. and G. Deleuze (1977), 'Intellectuals and Power', in M. Foucault, *Language: Counter-Memory, Practice: Selected Essays and Interviews*, trans. D. Bouchard and S. Simon, Ithaca: Cornell University Press.

Glowczewski, B. (2016), *Desert Dreamers*, Minnesota: Univocal.

Guattari, F. (2009), *Soft Subversions: Texts and Interviews*, trans. C. Weiner and E. Wittman, New York: Semiotext(e).

Hallward, P. (2006), *Out of This World: Deleuze and the Philosophy of Creation*, London: Verso.

May, T. (1994), *The Political Philosophy of Poststructuralist Anarchism*, University Park: Pennsylvania State University Press.

Mbah, S. and I. E. Igariwey (1997), *African Anarchism: The History of a Movement*, Tucson: See Sharp Press.

Muecke, S. (1998), 'Cultural Activism, Indigenous Australia, 1972–1994', in K.-H. Chen (ed.), *Trajectories: Inter Asia Cultural Studies*, London: Routledge.

Muecke, S. (2004), *Ancient and Modern: Time, Culture and Indigenous Philosophy*, Sydney: University of New South Wales.

Omvedt, G. (1993), *Reinventing Revolution: New Social Movements and the Socialist Tradition in India*, New York: East Gate Books.

Patton, P. (2001), 'Reconciliation, Aboriginal Rights and Constitutional Paradox in Australia', *Australian Feminist Law Journal*, 15(1): 25–40.

Ramnath, M. (2011), *Decolonizing Anarchism: An Anti-Authoritarian History of India's Liberation Struggle*, Edinburgh: AK Press.

Shramik Mukti Dal, 'Chapter 2', *Shramik Mukti Dal Manifesto*, http://xa.yimg. com/kq/groups/10707696/210021213/name/Shramik+Mukti+Dal+Manifesto. doc (last accessed 9 August 2018).

Spivak, G. C. (1988), 'Can the Subaltern Speak?', in C. Nelson and L. Grossberg (eds), *Marxism and the Interpretation of Culture*, Basingstoke: Macmillan Education, pp. 271–313.

Tully, J. (2001), 'The Struggles of Indigenous Peoples for and of Freedom', in D. Ivison, P. Patton and W. Sanders (eds), *Political Theory and the Rights of Indigenous Peoples*, Cambridge: Cambridge University Press, pp. 36–59.

# Chapter 4

# Micropolitics and Social Change: Deleuze and Guattari for Anarchist Theory and Practice

*Paul Raekstad*

The work of Deleuze and Guattari has much to offer contemporary radical thought. Here I discuss an aspect often mentioned, but rarely explored to the extent I think it deserves, namely the importance of micropolitics for emancipatory social change. To do this, I clarify what the 'micropolitical' is for Deleuze and Guattari and why they think it is important for revolutionary practice. I argue that micropolitics is important for thinking about (1) developing revolutionary subjectivity and (2) developing connections between different organisations and movements that strengthen each other and feed into macropolitical change. I also discuss Deleuze and Guattari's critique of vanguardist approaches to revolutionary organisation and consider some objections to Deleuze and Guattari's emphasis on the micropolitical.

## What Is Micropolitics?

For Deleuze and Guattari, 'everything is political, but every politics is simultaneously a *macropolitics* and a *micropolitics*' (Deleuze and Guattari 2004b: 235). Macropolitics concerns the politics of what they call the level of molar aggregates or assemblages – classes, sexes, nations and so on. The term 'molar' is drawn from the unit of measurement known as the mole, used in chemistry to measure very large amounts of small things, like particles in an ideal gas. This suggests that what Deleuze and Guattari mean by, for example, social class being a molar entity is that social class is a large-scale statistical aggregate composed of large numbers of small units. Viewing politics in such molar terms is common in much Marxist and anarchist theory, for example in thinking about economic oppression. On the other hand, Deleuze and Guattari argue that such molar aggregates always exist alongside molecular entities or assemblages of a different kind. They write:

> If we consider the great binary aggregates, such as the sexes or classes, it is evident that they also cross over into molecular assemblages of a different nature, and that there is a double reciprocal dependency between them . . . [S]ocial classes themselves imply 'masses' that do not have the same kind of movement, distribution, or objectives and do not wage the same kind of struggle. Yet classes are indeed fashioned from masses: they crystallize them. And masses are constantly flowing or leaking from classes. Their reciprocal presupposition, however, does not preclude a difference in viewpoint, nature, scale, and function (understood in this way, the notion of mass has entirely different connotations than Canetti's 'crowd'). (Deleuze and Guattari 2004b: 235)

The differences between the molar and the molecular – 'viewpoint, nature, scale, and function' – need some unpacking. In terms of scale, Deleuze and Guattari write in *Anti-Oedipus* of 'large molar machines' as 'the configurations that the [molecular] desiring-machines *form according to the law of large numbers*' (Deleuze and Guattari 2004a: 316). They go on to write:

> These are the same machines under determinate conditions. By 'determinate conditions' we mean those statistical forms into which the machines enter as so many stable forms, unifying, structuring, and proceeding by means of large heavy aggregates; the selective pressures that group the parts retain some of them and exclude others, organizing the crowds. These are therefore the same machines, but not at all the same *regime*, the same relationships of magnitude, or the same uses of syntheses. (2004a: 316)

The molar and the molecular thus differ in nature or scale in this very specific sense, but this does not mean that they necessarily differ in *size* or *extension*. Although the molecular 'works in detail and operates in small groups, this does not mean that it is any less coextensive with the entire social field than molar organization' (2004b: 237). A molecular phenomenon, such as the worship of a great leader or paranoid xenophobic fear, can be just as widespread as militaristic security politics, and can involve just as many people. Furthermore, the molecular is not solely 'in the realm of the imagination and applied only to the individual and the interindividual' (2004b: 237); each is as social and real as the other.

Here we also see how the molar and the molecular differ in viewpoint. The very same set of people, the very same society, can be considered from the macropolitical point of view (e.g., classes) or from the micropolitical point of view (e.g., particular investments of desire such as fear and hatred, individual and collective fantasies, the reciprocally determining interactions between workers within a workplace or between mothers and daughters, and so on). Distinguishing between micropolitics and macropolitics has important implications for political analysis, since it means that '[p]olitical analysis must therefore always proceed on both levels simultaneously: a society can be defined by its contradictions (as Marxism does) only on the level of macropolitics; on the micropolitical level, a society is defined by its lines of flight' (Holland 2013: 218).

Molar entities can also rightly be said to have certain properties in common; for example, the proletariat can be defined in terms of a determinate position within capitalist relations of production. Based on such common properties, molar entities like classes can also be said to have objective interests; for example, the proletariat as a class can be said to have an objective interest in replacing capitalism with socialism. As a result of this, it is only on a molar level that societies or groups feature material contradictions – for example, in the sense that the expressed interests of the proletariat include the removal of capitalism and the introduction of socialism, whereas the expressed interests of the capitalist class include retaining capitalism and not introducing social-ism. Since a capitalist society necessarily includes, among other things, both a capitalist and a proletarian class, whose objective interests tend to express themselves in and through a process of class struggle, capital-ism is materially contradictory in so far as it generates interests whose expressions logically contradict each other.

Finally, for Deleuze and Guattari it is only on the level of molar phenomena that consciousness and false consciousness come into play, since it is only on the level of molar phenomena that people have objective interests that they can rightly be said to be conscious of. For example, to the extent that people truly and truthfully grasp their interests as members of a class, they can be said to be class conscious. To the extent that they construe their objective interests in a way that falls short of the truth and truthfulness of their situation and is harmful to advancing their interests, they can be said have false consciousness.[1] Although I refer mainly to class here, the same can be said for other molar entities – sexes, races and more. It is not possible to examine all of these here in detail, but it is important to keep them in mind for later discussion as Deleuze and Guattari, like many contemporary radicals, are eager to avoid either ignoring the existence of other sites of social struggle and change or reducing them to class struggle, both of which have troubled certain (but far from all) strands of syndicalism and Marxism.

By contrast, it doesn't make sense to speak about the interests inher-ent in molecular or micropolitical phenomena, at least not in the same sense. For example, it does not make sense to say that the patriarchal father's desire to dominate his spouse is a matter of false consciousness, or likewise the paranoid fear that Southern white Americans felt in the 1950s about, for example, a black boy talking to a white girl. Such fears and desires work on the level of affective structures and processes that are different from, for example, one's beliefs about objective interests in light of one's membership in a particular class, race or sex. As Deleuze and Guattari point out, '[i]nterests can be deceived, unrecognised, or betrayed, but not desire', although it can and does happen that one 'desires against one's interests' (Deleuze and Guattari 2004a: 279). However, the fact that Deleuze and Guattari consider molecular phenomena, as well as affective structures and processes, different from beliefs about objective interests, does not mean that the two are unrelated. The Southern white Americans in question may have believed that segregation was in their objective interests. Their racist beliefs and wider worldview may thus have – and probably did – played an important part in generating and sustaining many of the then circulating affective structures and processes, but this connection should not let the two be conflated.[2] People who are subject to certain kinds of racist fear and misogynist love of domination may well desire something contrary to their objective interests, properly construed, but to explain that they do so in terms of false consciousness – that is, false and harmful beliefs about their interests – is, for Deleuze and Guattari, to make a certain kind of category mistake: it mistakes a molecular phenomenon for a molar one. Finally, it is common to misread Deleuze and Guattari as privileging the micropolitical over the macropolitical, but there is no basis for this in their writings or political practice. This is especially clear in Guattari's writings, as in *Molecular Revolution in Brazil* (Guattari and Rolnik 2007), but Deleuze also points it out in an essay in *Desert Islands* (Deleuze 2004: 193–203). Together, they note:

> The administration of a great organized molar security has as its correlate a whole micromanagement of petty fears, a permanent molecular insecurity, to the point that the motto of domestic policymakers might be: a macropolitics of society by and for a micropolitics of insecurity. (Deleuze and Guattari 2004b: 237)

Micropolitics can be a politics of insecurity and fascism *or* of emancipation, and 'microfascisms are what makes fascism so dangerous' (Deleuze and Guattari 2004b: 237). To take a recent example, the macropolitical fact of Donald Trump's electoral victory and his current policies cannot be properly understood in the absence of the micropolitical fears he marshals or the hopes and wishes he exploits, such as the fear of racialised others and the aspiration to 'make America great again'.

For Deleuze and Guattari, neither macropolitics nor micropolitics is prior to the other; neither is inherently better or worse and they are equally social and real. As Rodrigo Nunes argues, 'there is nothing in Deleuze and Guattari that is *contrary* as such to the scalability, mass mobilisations or forms of organisation that more radical transformations may demand; the front is always both micro- and macropolitical' (Nunes 2010: 123). In fact, they make the point that 'molecular escapes and movements would be nothing if they did not return to the molar organizations to reshuffle their segments, their binary distributions of sexes, classes, and parties' (Deleuze and Guattari 2004b: 239).

However, they do contend that micropolitics is often ignored in favour of macropolitics and argue that this clouds important political phenomena that can help us think about social change and conflict in a satisfactory way. Thus, '[o]nly microfascism provides the answer to the question: Why does desire desire its own repression?' (Deleuze and Guattari 2004b: 236–7). For them, the rise of fascism cannot adequately be understood in terms of ideological deception, passive collective compliance or masochistic tendencies. It is best understood in terms of the many microfascisms that already exist in couples, families, schools and so on, which enable the fascist state to effectively act upon the masses (236–7). On the other hand, some political phenomena can only be understood in micropolitical terms. For Deleuze and Guattari, May '68 in France is one such an example. They diagnose it as 'molecular, making what led up to it all the more imperceptible from the viewpoint of macropolitics', which is why so many party and union leaders 'understood nothing of the event' (238).

Using micropolitics to think about revolutionary politics directs our attention to the affective dimension of political organisation, as well as the micro levels of political processes and interactions. One way to connect this to anarchist theory and practice is in terms of the concept of prefigurative politics and its importance for developing emancipatory revolutionary subjectivity.

## Micropolitics, Revolutionary Subjectivity and Revolutionary Connections

Three main senses of 'prefiguration' can be distinguished. The first is an early Christian concept, according to which prefiguration is a form of 'phenomenal prophecy'; it is 'something real and historical which announces something else that is also real and historical' (Auerbach 1984: 29). The anarchist origin of the concept is entirely different and only started being used in the late 1970s (due to Boggs 1977), although it existed as a practice long before the term did. The anarchist idea that currently goes by the name 'prefigurative politics' differs from the early Christian origin in at least two important ways. First, in the early Christian sense, to prefigure something is not to actually do or try to do it. Thus, Moses can, for example, prefigure Christ without sharing the same goals as Christ or consciously working towards Christ's achievements, simply because he is something real and historical which announces the Christ to come. For anarchists, however, prefigurative politics is all about deliberately bringing about that which they want to enact in the future *by doing it* or *trying to do it* in the now. Second, in the Christian view one can only retrospectively determine whether something prefigures something else; as such it does not guide actions in the present. Anarchists, on the other hand, use a certain vision of a future society to guide organisational structures and practices in the present. Some of the first writings of what we would – but they did not – call prefigurative politics, is found in the Sonvillier Circular of 1871, which states:

> The society of the future should be nothing other than the universalisation of the organisation with which the International will have endowed itself. We must, therefore, care to ensure that that organisation comes as close as we may to our ideal. How can we expect an egalitarian and free society to emerge from an authoritarian organisation? Impossible. The International, as the embryo of the human society of the future, is required in the here and now to faithfully mirror our principles of freedom and federation and shun any principle leaning towards authority and dictatorship. (Quoted in Graham 2005: 97–8)[3]

The same idea is expressed today in anarchist and anarchist-inspired organisations, such as in the Industrial Workers of the World's (IWW) commitment to 'forming the structure of the new society within the shell of the old' (IWW 2014: 4). Similarly, the Solidarity Federation's (SolFed; the British section of the IWA-AIT) commitment to 'building a new society within the shell of the old' within their organisational structures and practices reflects a prefigurative politics (SolFed 2014).

We can distinguish between two slightly different ideas that might be at work here:[4] (1) a narrower conception of prefigurative politics according to which a critical part of emancipatory revolutionary strategy is to develop revolutionary organisations that embody the kinds of structures of deliberation and decision making that a free future society requires;

and (2) a broader conception according to which the organisations of struggle and transition embody 'those forms of social relations, decision-making, culture, and human experience that are [its] ultimate goal' (Boggs 1977: 100). The concept of micropolitics can direct our attention to both of these conceptions, but especially to the latter, broader notion of prefigurative politics. One thing that is sadly missing in Deleuze and Guattari's joint and solo work is an explicit discussion of future and present-day organisational structures of deliberation and decision making, although Guattari did, in a certain sense, prefigure his work at La Borde.[5] As a result, my discussion of the relevance of their thought for prefigurative politics will focus on the latter broader sense, which includes not only forms of deliberation and decision making, but also forms of social relations, culture and human experience.

From a Deleuzian perspective, micropolitics suggests one way of thinking about the importance of prefigurative politics when it comes to generating revolutionary subjectivity. This is important both for revolutionary events that are arguably largely or even wholly micropolitical in character, and for revolutionary events that present themselves in more recognisably macropolitical terms. This is a crucial aspect of their work, since the anarchist notion of prefigurative politics often addresses itself to a macropolitical project, for example how to ensure that the class struggle generates an emancipatory future society. It is also important, as we have seen, for thinking about revolutionary events like May '68 which, even if we reject Deleuze and Guattari's claim that it was entirely micropolitical in character, was overwhelmingly micropolitical in its nature and effects. More than anything else, the events of May '68 were instrumental in generating and promoting a change in values towards greater freedom and equality along with – what might amount to the same thing – a widespread shift in how people relate to and think about one another (Deleuze and Guattari 2004b: 238).

One thing the concept of micropolitics contributes to prefigurative politics is the way it directs our attention to the development of revolutionary subjectivity beyond the more straightforward questions around the formal structures of deliberation and decision making. Like a great deal of early socialist thought – both Marxist and anarchist – Deleuze and Guattari rely heavily on a form of left Spinozism.[6] This view sees subjectivity above all in terms of powers or capacities, and drives or strivings (see especially Deleuze 1988). The concept of drives/strivings is straightforward. Powers can be defined as real possibilities to do and/or to be.[7] For Deleuze, it is vital to understand powers not as itemised properties inhering in stable individual subjects, but rather as relationally and processually constituted in and through an organism's interaction with its natural, social and historical environment. An entity's powers – its real possibilities to do and/or be – include both powers to affect and powers to be affected. This has important implications for thinking about large-scale social change.

According to this view, changing society requires the development of revolutionary subjectivity with the appropriate kinds of powers and drives. On the one hand, it requires the development of revolutionary subjectivity with the real possibilities of organising, interacting and living in new and emancipatory ways. On the other hand, changing society also requires that the real drive or striving towards new modes of social organisation, interaction and life is or becomes stronger than the real forces hindering it, including the drive(s) towards other, non-emancipatory forms like fascism or Stalinism. Micropolitics directs our attention to both these aspects.

On this view, it is important not only that the formal structures of deliberation and decision making mirror those we want to see in a future society, but that we also begin changing the ways in which we interact and relate to one another on a micropolitical level. Only this will develop the powers to organise and live in emancipated ways. As part of such prefigurative organising we need to address a host of micropolitical aspects for both long-term vitality and emancipatory success: (1) how we value different kinds of political work and activity; (2) how we distribute tasks and responsibilities; (3) how we remove and replace toxic patterns of interpersonal interaction; (4) how we collectively address abusive behaviour; (5) how we create political environments conducive to supporting and healing people, and helping them to grow and develop as political agents; and many other aspects. The aim of this, in the words of Raúl Zibechi, writing about Latin American movements, is to create an 'emancipatory climate, which is conducive to the construction of the new world' by 'enhancing the capabilities buried within the people' (Zibechi 2012: 52–3).

In terms of developing real drives or strivings for emancipatory social change, micropolitics directs our attention to the affective aspects of organising. As David Graeber points out, this was a particularly important aspect of Occupy:

> For decades, the anarchist movement had been putting much of our creative energy into developing forms of egalitarian political process that actually work; forms of direct democracy that actually could operate within self-governing communities outside of any state. The whole project was based in a kind of faith that freedom is contagious. We all knew it was practi-

cally impossible to convince the average American that a truly democratic society was possible through rhetoric. But it was possible to show them. The experience of a thousand, or two thousand, people making collective decisions without a leadership structure, motivated only by principle and solidarity, can change one's most fundamental assumptions about what politics, or for that matter, human life, could actually be like. (Graeber 2013: 89)

The basic idea here, central to much of contemporary radical politics, is that people might join a movement or organisation for a variety of reasons: struggling for global justice, improving one's community, fighting against police violence, bettering wages and working conditions and so on (see Holloway 2010; Maeckelbergh 2011; Sitrin 2012; Zibechi 2012). The organisation or movement they join instantiates a certain type of emancipatory political practice that they come to participate in and experience first-hand. As a result of this experience, people often come to change their innermost goals and desires and this, in turn, causes them to change their political activities. Having experienced genuinely more free and equal ways of organising within large groups of people, as well as new ways of interacting and relating to one another, individuals tend to develop a desire to spread these to other areas of their social life and begin striving towards this end.[8] Generating these kinds of experiences is not just about modes of deliberation and decision making – although these do play an important part – but also about the affective dimension. In other words, it is about the feeling of being surrounded by people working to change the world while simultaneously addressing and changing one's own oppressive behaviours; learning new skills and growing as both a political agent and a human being; feeling the joy of acting in concert with one's deepest ethical and political convictions; of overcoming fears with others at one's side; and so forth. These actions and affects can be instantiated – or not – within movements and organisations seeking to advance a variety of different macropolitical goals. They depend not just on formal structures of deliberation and decision making, but also on a host of different micropolitical practices we can and should take seriously as part of prefigurative organising.

Another aspect of successful revolutionary politics is the ability to support struggles of resonance in order to carry out a broader process of social change. As Deleuze and Guattari write:

Flights are everywhere, they are born again each time from the displaced limits of capitalism. And undoubtedly revolutionary flight (the *active* flight . . .) is not the same thing as other kinds of flight, the schizo flight, or the druggie [*toxico*] flight. But this is precisely the problem of marginalities: to make all lines of flight connect on a revolutionary plane. (Quoted in Nunes 2010: 123)

Throughout its history, capitalism has generated different forms of struggle and resistance to the forms of domination, oppression and exploitation it entails. Not all forms of struggle and resistance are equal, and not all can be made to connect to each other as part of a broader process of revolution. Although capitalism 'continually sets and then repels its own limits', it also, in so doing, 'gives rise to numerous flows in all directions that escape its axiomatic' and tend to 'enter into "connections" that delineate a new Land', coming to constitute a machine whose aim is 'revolutionary movement' and which 'opposes both the automation of the capitalist axioms and bureaucratic programming' (Deleuze and Guattari 2004b: 522). One of the major challenges for revolutionary movements has been finding ways to be mutually supportive, thus enabling far-reaching changes in society; that is, a revolution against the forces of both capitalism and bureaucracy (especially the bureaucracy of the State). Responding adequately to these challenges requires, Deleuze and Guattari argue, abandoning the State as the primary vehicle for revolutionary politics – not in opposition to, but in the service of class politics properly understood:

> The power of minority, of particularity, finds its figure or its universal consciousness in the proletariat. But as long as the working class defines itself by an acquired status, or even by a theoretically conquered State, it appears only as 'capital', a part of capital (variable capital), and does not leave the *plan(e) of capital*. At best, the plan(e) becomes bureaucratic. On the other hand, it is by leaving the plan(e) of capital, and never ceasing to leave it, that a mass becomes increasingly revolutionary . . . (2004b: 521)

In other words, anti-capitalist revolution requires leaving capitalist society and its modes of thought and organisation behind and this, in turn, requires not defining revolution or its power in terms of State conquest. This does not mean that Deleuze and Guattari think State power is unimportant, or that they reject taking and using it as a viable part of social change. Rather, their point seems to be that the working class and its struggle (or any other anarchist struggle) should not be defined simply in terms of State power as this will, at best, result in bureaucratism. As they note, seizing the State 'did not prevent the resurrection of a State capitalism' within Russia, nor its gradual erosion (Deleuze and Guattari 2004a: 278).

Importantly, none of this entails a lack of relevance for macropolitical struggles to change the basic components of capitalist society. As Deleuze and Guattari write,

> Once again, this is not to say that the struggle on the level of the axioms [of capitalist society] is without importance; on the contrary, it is determining (at the most diverse levels: women's struggle for the vote, for abortion, for jobs; the struggle of the regions for autonomy; the struggle of the Third World; the struggle of the oppressed masses and minorities in the East or West . . . ) But there is also always a sign to indicate that these struggles are the index of another, coexistent combat. However modest the demand, it always constitutes a point that the axiomatic cannot tolerate: when people demand to formulate their problems themselves, and to determine at least the particular conditions under which they can receive a more general solution (hold to the *Particular* as an innovative form). (Deleuze and Guattari 2004b: 520)

Thus, none of what has been said here, or by Deleuze and Guattari more generally, entails that struggles against the basic components of capitalist society are unimportant. One of the steps that such popular movements have to take, and one of the things that capitalism cannot tolerate of them, is the bold but vital step of formulating their own problems in their own terms, and using that to figure out how, in their particular circumstances, these problems can be solved. This runs completely counter to the bureaucratic structures of capitalism and the state, as well as the top-down bureaucratic structures that these use to co-opt, control, discipline and disarm movements of struggle and resistance.

## Towards a Critique of Vanguardism

If micropolitics can direct our attention to what we want in political movements and organisations, it can also direct our attention to what we should avoid. In a discussion of Guattari's writings, Deleuze writes the following:

> It is certainly true that if the problem of the group's functioning is not posed to begin with, it will be too late afterwards . . . The constancy with which revolutionary groups have betrayed their task is well known. These groups operate through detachment, election, and residual selection: they detach a supposedly expert avant-garde; they elect a disciplined, organized, hierarchized proletariat; they select a residual sub-proletariat to be excluded or reeducated. But this tripartite division reproduces precisely the divisions which the bourgeoisie introduced into the proletariat, and on which it has based its power within the framework of capitalist relations of

production. Attempting to turn these divisions against the bourgeoisie is a lost cause. (Deleuze 2004: 198)

For Deleuze, the strength of Guattari's view 'consists in showing that the problem is not at all about choosing between spontaneity and centralism' (Deleuze 2004: 199). Nor is it an issue of localism versus unification, since 'a revolutionary machine cannot remain satisfied with local and occasional struggles' (199). Instead, the problem concerns how such unification in ongoing organisations is brought about – it 'must function in a transversal way, through multiplicity, and not in a vertical way' (199). In their joint work, Deleuze and Guattari talk about the importance of this in terms of 'revolutionary connections' in opposition to the 'conjugations' of capitalism and the State (Deleuze and Guattari 2004b: 522). Here, connections of social flows and processes refer to the ways in which such flows and processes can interact in ways that increase the power of both, accelerating and augmenting them. On the other hand, conjugations refer to the ways in which one of the flows comes to overcode, interpret and incorporate the others for its own purposes, restricting, blocking and disempowering the others (Patton 2000: 102; Holland 2013: 119).

This pinpoints a problem with vanguardist approaches to revolution. According to Deleuze and Guattari, hierarchical and authoritarian approaches to revolutionary organisation reproduce and strengthen the same kinds of disempowering divisions between potentially revolutionary agents as capitalism does. The problem is not one of organisation or unification as such, but the kind of organisation and unification that is required to go beyond capitalism and the state – the traditional aim of Marxism as well as anarchism. Such organisation and unification must take place in non-authoritarian and non-hierarchical ways, allowing the different social flows and processes that constitute it to connect in ways that empower, augment and accelerate them. By contrast, allowing an elite central committee or would-be revolutionary party to overcode, interpret and incorporate all other social flows and processes, reproducing the disempowering hierarchical divisions of capitalist society within itself, will both weaken any would-be revolutionary movement and render it unable to move beyond capitalism and the state. After all, the structure of vanguard groups prefigures exactly the kind of authoritarian state structures they end up introducing, reproducing forms of division and hierarchy similar to capitalism and easing its restoration (see Lebowitz 2012). As Deleuze and Guattari put it, the 'man of power will always want to stop the lines of flight' (Deleuze and Guattari 2004b: 252).

## Objections and Replies

I will now consider three objections to the view I have been sketch-
ing: (1) that the commitment to the micropolitical entails ignoring or
excluding the macropolitical; (2) that it amounts, or has amounted,
to unproductive navel-gazing; and (3) that it cannot make sense of or
contribute to contemporary political events.

By now it should be clear that the first criticism is erroneous. This
is demonstrated by the argument above that micropolitics expresses
an important aspect of prefigurative politics. If Deleuze and Guattari's
concept of micropolitics contributes something useful to how we think
about prefigurative politics, then it follows that micropolitics is important for at least certain types of macropolitical struggle and change – both
for making sense of them and for contributing to their success. To say
that micropolitics, and attention to micropolitics, entails either ignoring
or excluding macropolitics is then simply false. It is of course possible
for any group or individual to focus only on micropolitics and ignore or
exclude from consideration anything macropolitical, but nothing of the
sort follows inherently either from micropolitics or attention thereon.

As for the second and third points, it should also be clear that a
micropolitics in no way needs to amount to unproductive navel-gazing,
and that micropolitics can in fact help to shed light on contemporary
events, for example the May '68 uprisings and Occupy. Although the
'68 uprisings toppled no governments, conquered no states, established
no autonomous regions and seized no means of production (at least
not in the long term), it is still considered a world revolution (Arrighi
et al. 2012; Graeber 2013). One of the reasons for this is the ethos of
freedom and equality it spread, along with the concomitant demands
and struggles to reorganise social relations on this basis. The state and
capitalism are still with us, true, but a variety of movements for greater
freedom and equality between people of different races, genders, sexual
orientations and so forth have made significant strides since – and arguably buttressed by – the events of May '68.

The recent Occupy movement shows similar characteristics, not only
in terms of an ethos and practice of freedom and equality, but also in
terms of a culture of struggle and, more precisely, a culture of struggle
of a broadly anarchist kind. These forms of struggle are explicitly macropolitical in nature, showing through practice that there is no necessary
contradiction between micropolitics and macropolitics. As in the years
after 1968, which saw an emerging culture of equality and liberation,
the years after Occupy have seen the growth of a culture not just of

resistance, but also of active struggle for positive social change. In the United States, we have seen a new wave of worker militancy, with fast food workers and other low-paid workers, such as those from Whole Foods and Walmart, organising and, for the first time in history, successfully introducing higher minimum wages. Another notable movement is #BlackLivesMatter, although the histories and origins of many of the organisations involved in both of the above-mentioned examples go back many years (see, for example, Taylor 2016).[9]

The effects (and affects) of Occupy are not limited solely to radical movements and organisations, as they have spread to broader and perhaps more popular forms of resistance as well. For one, the years following Occupy saw public discourse shift, even in the USA, to issues of class division, power and struggle – something not achieved by any radical movement or organisation in Europe or the USA in recent history (Wedes 2013; Sitrin 2014). Second, a number of specific campaigns sparked by Occupy have achieved major successes, including disaster relief (for example, in response to hurricanes Sandy and Harvey), struggles to prevent evictions, the Rolling Jubilee's debt cancellations, struggles against the Transatlantic Trade and Investment Partnership and Trans-Pacific Partnership, and the Fight for $15 campaign. Finally, Occupy has contributed to an increasingly critical attitude towards capitalism among ordinary people, which has influenced a new wave of left populism, represented by figures like Jeremy Corbyn and Bernie Sanders. None of this denies the horrors of the current Trump presidency or overlooks the dangers it poses to the world going forward. It does, however, point to some of the more hopeful aspects of ongoing social movements.

Lastly, the tactics and strategies of the more radical movements we are now seeing seem to be profoundly influenced by a number of features that Occupy insisted on. These include a commitment to avoid participating in existing State structures; a serious consideration of how to avoid State and party capture and the resulting deradicalisation and demobilisation; a focus on direct action; and a focus on non-hierarchical and prefigurative modes of social and political organising.[10] This demonstrates the erroneousness of the doctrinaire dismissals of these movements as transient and ineffective. In fact, quite the contrary seems to be true: that we are seeing an emerging culture of active struggle for positive social change of a broadly anarchist kind (for more on this, as well as longer and broader history, see Dixon and Davis 2014; Ness 2014; Sitrin and Azzellini 2014).

Moreover, I think one of the reasons for the continued growth of these movements is their focus on a range of aspects that can rightly be called micropolitical. As Chris Dixon's survey of the 'anti-authoritarian current' of US and English-Canadian social movements shows (Dixon and Davis 2014: 3), a wide variety of radical movements are gaining momentum and developing a social movement orientation, while simultaneously emphasising 'nonhierarchical decision-making structures, efforts to develop more caring ways of relating, and activities aimed at transforming dynamics of privilege and oppression' (2014: 17). Micropolitical concerns are thus important for making sense of these movements and their practices and do not amount to unproductive navel-gazing. Finally, these movements focus not just on micropolitics, but on a range of important macropolitical factors as well, like class-based struggles for better wages and working conditions in the short term, as well as the abolition of capitalism in the long term. It is too early to tell what the effects of these movements will be – whether in micro- or macropolitical terms.

## Conclusion

This chapter has attempted to elaborate Deleuze and Guattari's concept of micropolitics, show how it can be used for thinking about prefigurative political practice, and discuss their related critique of vanguardism. I have not tried to argue that Deleuze and Guattari were anarchists, nor that they thought themselves to be. It is quite clear that they never took themselves to be 'anarchist' thinkers. However, the labelling of thinkers and ideas is always less important and interesting than what they can do for us. If my argument above is at all plausible, then the thought of Deleuze and Guattari is certainly of importance and interest to anarchist theory and practice today.

## Notes

1. This is adapted from István Mészáros's (2011) distinction on p. 193. On the issue of truth and truthfulness, see Williams (2002).
2. I would like to add two caveats here. First, Deleuze and Guattari's insistence on not reducing these micropolitical phenomena to macropolitical ones does not discredit the idea or importance of ideological deception in these cases. Nor does it necessarily deny the ways in which they are connected; think, for example, of the potential importance of white supremacist ideology in mobilising racist fear. If anything, I think the micropolitical analysis here is best construed as a supplement to, rather than a replacement of, theories of ideology (I owe this important point to the comments of a very helpful reviewer). Second, I am not certain about the extent to which I agree with Deleuze and Guattari's views on this point, though I do think that there is some potential use for using this to think about prefigurative politics, which I explore below.

3. For a wealth of information about the *Sonvillier Circular* and its context, see Eckhardt (2016).
4. For further discussion, see Raekstad (forthcoming b).
5. This is not to say, however, that Deleuze and Guattari have no views on organisational issues – far from it. They both explicitly reject 'democratic centralism' and 'spontaneism', and Guattari especially has important insights on reorganising divisions of labour. My point is that they pay relatively little explicit attention to the detailed modes of deliberation and decision making they would like to see.
6. I recognise that this is a highly contentious historical supposition that cannot be properly examined here. I defend parts of it with respect to Marx in Raekstad (2016) and Raekstad (2017).
7. I explore how this can be used as an approach to human development in Raekstad (forthcoming a).
8. For more thoughts on prefigurative politics, see Raekstad (forthcoming b).
9. Importantly, this is not to say that Occupy, as a whole, did an effective job of tackling various forms of racism (see Bray 2013: 94–9).
10. One of the recurring critiques of Occupy (in the USA) is that its aims were not concrete enough. Arguably, this reflects a harmful micropolitical rejection of macropolitics. This critique has two problems. First, in some places, Occupy *did* formulate fairly concrete aims, and it is not clear that this made much difference. Second, it is not clear that this should be blamed on micropolitics, as opposed to, for example, a reliance on strict consensus in mass general assemblies and the highly diverse range of political commitments of its participants. At any rate, micropolitical flows are not necessarily identifiable or conscious. (I would like to thank a very helpful anonymous reviewer for pointing out the need to address this issue.)

# References

Arrighi, G., T. K. Hopkins and I. Wallerstein (2012), *Anti-Systemic Movements*, London: Verso.

Auerbach, E. (1984), *Scenes from the Drama of European Literature*, Minneapolis: University of Minnesota Press.

Boggs, C. (1977), 'Marxism, Prefigurative Communism, and the Problem of Workers' Control', *Radical America*, 11: 99–122.

Bray, M. (2013), *Translating Anarchy: The Anarchism of Occupy Wall Street*, Alresford: Zero Books.

Deleuze, G. (1988), *Spinoza: Practical Philosophy*, trans. R. Hurley, San Francisco: City Lights Books.

Deleuze, G. (2004), *Desert Islands and Other Texts*, trans. M. Taormina, Los Angeles and New York: Semiotext(e).

Deleuze, G. and F. Guattari (2004a), *Anti-Oedipus: Capitalism and Schizophrenia*, trans. R. Hurley, M. Seem and H. R. Lane, London: Continuum.

Deleuze, G. and F. Guattari (2004b), *A Thousand Plateaus: Capitalism and Schizophrenia*, trans. B. Massumi, London: Continuum.

Dixon, C. and A. Davis (2014), *Another Politics: Talking Across Today's Transformative Movements*, Oakland: University of California Press.

Eckhardt, W. (2016), *The First Socialist Schism: Bakunin vs. Marx in the International Working Men's Association*, Oakland: PM Press.

Graeber, D. (2013), *The Democracy Project: A History, A Crisis, A Movement*, London: Allen Lane.

Graham R. (2005), *Anarchism: A Documentary History of Libertarian Ideas, Vol. I: From Anarchy to Anarchism (300CE to 1939)*, New York: Black Rose Books.

Guattari, F. and S. Rolnik (2007), *Molecular Revolution in Brazil*, trans. K. Clapshow and B. Holmes, Los Angeles: Semiotext(e).

Holland, E. (2013), *Deleuze and Guattari's* A Thousand Plateaus: *A Reader's Guide*, London: Bloomsbury.

Holloway, J. (2010), *Crack Capitalism*, New York: Pluto Press.

Industrial Workers of the World (2014), *Preamble, Constitution, & General Bylaws of the Industrial Workers of the World*, available online at http://www.iww.org/PDF/Constitutions/CurrentIWWConstitution.pdf (last accessed 22 August 2018).

Lebowitz, M. (2012), *The Contradictions of Real Socialism: The Conductor and the Conducted*, New York: Monthly Review Press.

Maeckelbergh, M. (2011), 'Doing is Believing: Prefiguration as Strategic Practice in the Alterglobalization Movement', *Social Movement Studies*, 10(1): 1–20.

Mészáros, I. (2011), *Social Structure and Forms of Consciousness, Vol. II: The Dialectic of Structure and History*, New York: Monthly Review Press.

Ness, I. (2014), *New Forms of Worker Organization: The Syndicalist and Autonomist Restoration of Class Struggle Unionism*, Oakland: PM Press.

Nunes, R. (2010), 'Politics in the Middle: For a Political Interpretation of the Dualisms in Deleuze and Guattari', *Deleuze Studies*, 4: 104–26.

Patton, P. (2000), *Deleuze and the Political*, New York: Routledge.

Raekstad, P. (2016), 'Democracy, Socialism, and Human Development: A Realist and Comparative Critique of Capitalism', PhD thesis, University of Cambridge, p. 237.

Raekstad, P. (2017), 'The Democratic Theory of the Early Marx', *Archiv für Geschichte der Philosophie*, 99(4): 443–64.

Raekstad, P. (Forthcoming a), 'Human Development and Alienation in the Thought of Karl Marx', *European Journal of Political Theory*, available with early access: http://ept.sagepub.com/content/early/2015/12/03/1474885115613735.full.pdf+html (last accessed 10 August 2018).

Raekstad, P. (Forthcoming b). 'Revolutionary Practice and Prefigurative Politics: A Clarification and Defense', *Constellations*, available with early access: http://onlinelibrary.wiley.com/doi/10.1111/1467-8675.12319/full (last accessed 10 August 2018).

Sitrin, M. (2012), *Everyday Revolutions: Horizontalism and Autonomy in Argentina*, London: Zed Books.

Sitrin, M. (2014), 'The DNA of Occupy', *Telesur*, 12 September, http://www.telesurtv.net/english/opinion/The-DNA-of-Occupy-20140912-0033.html (last accessed 10 August 2018).

Sitrin, M. and D. Azzellini (2014), *They Can't Represent Us!: Reinventing Democracy from Greece to Occupy*, London: Verso.

Solidarity Federation (2014), *Fighting for Ourselves: Anarcho-Syndicalism and the Class Struggle*, London: Freedom Press.

Taylor, K.-Y. (2016), *From #BlackLivesMatter to Black Liberation*, Chicago: Haymarket Books.

Wedes, J. (2013), 'Occupy Wall Street, Two Years On: We're Still the 99%', *The Guardian*, 17 September, http://www.theguardian.com/commentisfree/2013/sep/17/occupy-wall-street-99-percent (last accessed 10 August 2018).

Williams, B. (2002), *Truth and Truthfulness: An Essay in Genealogy*, Princeton: Princeton University Press.

Zibechi, R. (2012), *Territories in Resistance: A Cartography of Latin American Social Movements*, Oakland: AK Press.

# PART II

# THEORETICAL PERSPECTIVES

Chapter 5

# Deleuze and the Anarchist Tradition

Nathan Jun

The notion that Deleuze is an 'anarchist' thinker – or, at the very least, that his thought may be interpreted in whole or in part as an expression of 'anarchistic' sensibilities – is said to originate with Todd May's formative volume *The Political Philosophy of Poststructuralist Anarchism* (1994).[1] Since that time, May's thesis has become something of a truism among certain students of Deleuze, especially those who identify with the broad and loosely defined movement known as 'postanarchism',[2] and has inspired similar claims regarding Lacan, Derrida, Foucault, Lyotard, Levinas, Rancière and other thinkers (Koch 1993; Jun 2007; Verter 2010; May 2011; Absensour 2013). One of the most often cited criticisms of such claims is that the figures in question were not associated in any meaningful sense with the historical anarchist movement and did not identify themselves as anarchists.[3] The underlying assumption here is that the term 'anarchist' is anchored in a specific tradition characterised by a fixed set of principles, in which case it is incorrectly applied to Deleuze and other thinkers who at best express an affinity with some of these principles or else are interpreted as doing so. For some critics, at least, this further implies that the thinkers in question are completely unrelated to anarchism and, by extension, that it is altogether inappropriate to discuss them in this context.

Drawing on ideas from Michael Freeden's theory of ideology, I contend that the anarchist tradition is better understood as a constellation of diffuse and evolving concepts than as a fixed set of principles. This, in turn, invites a crucial distinction between what I call 'anarchist' thought – that is, thought that emerges within and in response to historical anarchist movements – and 'anarchistic' thought – that is, thought that emerges outside such movements but is conceptually proximate to core anarchist commitments. Inasmuch as the latter has often played a significant role in the historical development of the former, and vice versa, neither can be fully understood apart from the other. As I will argue, this is precisely how we ought to understand Deleuze in relation to the broad anarchist tradition.

## Who Is an Anarchist?

What is required in order for a given individual[4] to qualify as an 'anarchist'? The first and arguably most commonsensical answer is that the individual in question must explicitly identify herself as such. Taken by itself, however, this would seem to imply that *anyone* who self-identifies in this way *just is* an anarchist regardless of her actual political perspective. A better answer, perhaps, is that an individual is properly regarded as an anarchist if she professes distinctively anarchist ideas, beliefs and commitments. This would apply even to individuals who did not – or, indeed, could not – explicitly identify themselves as anarchists, in which case it is possible that anarchists have existed in various cultures throughout human history.[5] The problem, obviously, is that it is by no means clear what qualifies a given belief, idea or commitment as 'distinctively anarchist'. While the prevailing tendency has been to define anarchism as the principled rejection of the State,[6] such an approach 'inevitably creates the impression that anarchism is contradictory as well as unfocused, and renders the theoretical analysis of anarchism a frustrating task at best' (Schmidt and van der Walt 2009: 18). As Michael Schmidt and Lucien van der Walt point out:

> If anarchism can encompass economic liberals, Marxists, radical Christians, Taoism, and more, it is hardly surprising that the standard works on anarchism describe it as 'incoherent'. Such an approach is not useful. Given that there are few intellectual traditions that do not have at least some negative comments about the state and some positive views on the individual, it is not easy to specify an upper limit on the traditions that may be assimilated, in some form, to the anarchist category ... Once ... [the anti-statist] definition is accepted, it is a short step to [Peter] Marshall's work, where the 'anarchist' gallery includes the Buddha, the Marquis de Sade, Herbert Spencer, Gandhi, Che Guevara, and Margaret Thatcher. And if the notion of anarchism can cover so vast a field – and let us not forget that the case can be made to include Marx and his heirs – then the definition is so loose as to be practically meaningless. (Schmidt and van der Walt 2009: 41)

In an effort to avoid this alleged incoherence, Schmidt and van der Walt propose a third answer, namely that anarchism should be strictly identified with the 'core beliefs' of the historical anarchist movement of the nineteenth century. This movement, the origins of which are traced with great specificity to the conflict between Marx and Bakunin in the First International, is explicitly associated with 'class struggle' anarchism (Schmidt and van der Walt 2009: 19). It is characterised first and foremost by its commitment to direct action and the mass organisation of the 'popular classes' in the struggle to replace capitalism, the State and other hierarchical political, social and economic institutions with a 'free [that is, stateless] socialist society based on common ownership, self-management, democratic planning from below, and production for need, not profit' (2009: 6).

Schmidt and van der Walt's proposal has two especially significant ramifications. First, the notion that the historical anarchist movement was necessarily 'a product of the capitalist world and the working class it created' implies that anarchism as such did not – indeed, *could not* – exist in precapitalist contexts (Schmidt and van der Walt 2009: 96). This entails, in turn, that anarchism did not exist as a distinctive political ideology prior to the 1860s, in which case earlier radicals like Godwin and Proudhon cannot be counted among its major proponents. Second, the notion that the historical anarchist movement uniformly espoused a socialistic 'class struggle' orientation implies that individualism and other non-socialist tendencies (for example, post-left anarchy and primitivism) do not qualify as authentic iterations of anarchism, in which case genuine anarchism has been virtually nonexistent in the world since the collapse of that movement following the Second World War.

There are several problems with this approach, a few of which are worth noting in brief detail. In the first place, the notion that the 'broad anarchist tradition' is coextensive with 'class struggle' anarchism assumes that the latter itself can be clearly defined. In lieu of formulating such a definition, however, Schmidt and van der Walt merely enumerate generic beliefs and commitments of the sort cited previously. In so doing, they take for granted that 'class struggle' anarchists share a uniform understanding of concepts like 'direct action', 'common ownership', 'self-management' and the like, thereby overlooking the considerable extent to which different tendencies, orientations and schools of thought within 'class struggle' anarchism itself have disagreed over the meanings of said concepts. On the other hand, virtually all of the individuals Schmidt and van der Walt identify as 'class struggle' anarchists – for example, Kropotkin, Goldman and Malatesta – explicitly deny the notion that anarchism is 'a fixed, comprehensive, self-contained, and internally consistent system of ideas, set of doctrines, or body of theory' (Jun 2012: 49; cf. Rocker 2004: 31) or that it is 'necessarily linked to any [one] philosophical system' (Malatesta

1965: 19). Ironically, this would seem to imply that the rejection of Schmidt and van der Walt's central thesis is itself a core belief or commitment of 'class struggle' anarchism, in which case strictly identifying anarchism as such with a particular form of anarchism is inconsistent if not altogether self-contradictory.

A much more useful approach is provided by Michael Freeden, who defines ideologies in general as complex 'clusters' or 'composites' of decontested political *concepts* 'with a variety of internal combinations' (Freeden 1996: 88). For Freeden, ideologies are not constituted by generic beliefs or commitments but by particular political *concepts* 'characterized by a morphology' (1996: 77) – that is, an inner structure that organises and arranges those concepts and, in so doing, removes them 'from contest by attempting to assign them a clear meaning' (Freeden 2015: 59). The assignment of fixed meanings and degrees of relative significance to concepts is achieved in two ways: first, by identifying, defining and organising their 'micro-components' – that is, the particular referents that specify what they are concepts *of* – and second, by arranging concepts within a hierarchy of 'core', 'adjacent' and 'peripheral' elements, each level of which specifies degrees of relative significance among concepts of the same type and, in this way, determines their overall significance within the ideology itself (Freeden 2013: 124–5). Taken together, these operations allow for 'diverse conceptions of any concept' (124) and an 'infinite variety' of 'conceptual permutations' within 'the ideational boundaries . . . that anchor [them] and secure [their] components' (126, 128, 125). For Freeden, it is precisely conceptual permutations of this sort that account for variation within otherwise stable ideological families as well as their development and evolution 'at variable speeds across time and space' (124).

Deleuze and Guattari's theory of concepts as outlined in *What Is Philosophy?* (1994) displays certain interesting similarities with the foregoing account. Philosophy, they famously maintain, involves the creation of new concepts with a view to analysing 'problems which are thought to be badly understood or badly posed' (Deleuze and Guattari 1994: 16). This is roughly of a piece with conceptual decontestation in Freeden's theory, which seeks to assign fixed meanings to essentially contested concepts and, in so doing, to bring order out of the chaos of ideological dispute. For Deleuze and Guattari, all concepts are essentially contestable in this way precisely because 'the concept has no reference: it is self-referential; it posits itself and its object at the same time it is created' (1994: 22). As in Freeden's account, moreover, the concept is 'defined by . . . its endoconsistency [that is, by its internal 'micro-components'] and exoconsistency [that is, by its relation to other concepts]' (1994: 22).

The notion that anarchism is better understood as a more or less stable cluster of morphologically arranged political concepts than as a fixed set of first-order claims, assertions or propositions strongly belies Schmidt and van der Walt's thesis. Although there is no question that anarchist ideas are 'fluid and constantly evolving' and that their 'central content . . . changes from one generation to another . . . against the background of the movements and culture in and by which they are expressed' (Gordon 2008: 4), different tendencies within anarchism nonetheless 'have largely similar morphologies' (Franks 2012: 63), meaning that they tend to affirm the same set of core concepts even though '[these] are expressed in different ways, depending on context' (Gordon 2008: 4). Were it not the case, it would be difficult to account for the ubiquitous tendency to regard anarchism as a distinct political perspective, let alone the fact that conventional treatments of anarchism consistently highlight particular concepts rather than others. All of this being said, ideologies are not simply abstract conceptual assemblages but

> clusters of ideas, beliefs, opinions, values, and attitudes usually held by identifiable groups that provide directives, even plans, of action for public policy-making in an endeavour to uphold, justify, change or criticize the social and political arrangements of a state or other political community . . . (Freeden 2004: 6)

In other words, ideologies encompass ideational content as well as various forms of concrete political activity. Because this activity, no less than the ideational content it expresses, emerges in response to particular historical circumstances, ideologies cannot be understood apart from the historical contexts within which they arise.

Anarchism, accordingly, is not *just* a collection of ideas but a historically evolving '*movement* composed of dense networks of individuals, affinity groups and collectives which communicate and coordinate intensively, sometimes across the globe, and generate innumerable direct actions and sustained projects' (Gordon 2008: 3, emphasis added). As Gordon notes, the 'major features' of this movement include:

> a shared repertoire of political action based on direct action, building grassroots alternatives, community outreach and confrontation; shared forms of organizing . . . ; broader cultural expression in areas as diverse as art, music, dress and diet . . . ; [and] shared political language that emphasizes resistance to capitalism, the state, patriarchy and more generally to hierarchy and domination. (2008: 3–4)

Although these features are manifestations of an underlying ideational content, that content is itself a product of concrete political activity. Thus, while it is surely a mistake to identify anarchism exclusively with 'a historically-embodied movement or movements (Graham 2015: 2), it is equally mistaken to characterise it as a mere amalgamation of political concepts divorced from historical context.

A distinction must be drawn, therefore, between anarchism as a historically embodied ideological phenomenon, and the range of ideas, beliefs, attitudes, commitments, activities, ways of living and so on that might be termed 'anarchistic' in virtue of their ideological proximity to anarchist movements or to the 'family of shared orientations for doing and talking about politics, and to living everyday life' that are associated with anarchism more generally (Gordon 2008: 4). Although they may lack any explicit connection to anarchism in the former sense, individuals and movements that profess anarchistic beliefs or engage in anarchistic activities have had a profound impact on its historical development and, in many cases, been influenced by it in turn. As I will argue below, this distinction is the key to understanding Deleuze's relationship to the broad anarchist tradition.

While the question of which concepts comprise the ideological core of anarchism – no less than how these concepts have been decontested within the broad anarchist tradition – is very much a matter of dispute, few would deny that anarchism is crucially distinguished by its commitment to *freedom* and corresponding opposition to political, economic and social structures that limit or altogether deny the same. For classical anarchists, at least, the individual's 'consciousness of self, of being different from others' instils a 'craving for liberty and self-expression' (Goldman 1998: 439) and a desire to 'grow to [his or her] full stature . . . [to] learn to think and move, to give the very best of [himself or herself] . . . [to] realize the true force of the social bonds that tie men [*sic*] together, and which are the true foundations of a normal social life' (Goldman 1910: 67). Freedom, accordingly, is associated with the actualisation of 'the material, intellectual, and moral powers that are latent in each person' (Bakunin 1972) and 'the all-around development and full enjoyment of all physical, intellectual, and moral faculties' (Bakunin 1992: 46). Although this 'liberty of actual and active opportunity' is not a '*negative* thing' that involves 'being free *from* something' but rather 'the freedom *to* something . . . the liberty to be, to do' (Goldman 1998: 98), it is only achievable when 'self-thinking individuals' are 'educated to freedom and the management of their own interests' and 'left to act for themselves, to feel responsibility for their own actions in the good or bad that comes from them' (Malatesta 1981: 36). This, in turn, requires the eradication of externally imposed restrictions that 'inhibit or prevent people from participating in determining their actions or the conditions of their actions' (Young 1990: 15).

For the classical anarchists, repression of the latter sort is problematic not only because it prevents human beings from 'bring[ing] to full development the powers, capacities, and talents with which nature has endowed [them]' (Guérin 1998: 57) but also, and more importantly, because it opposes both collective aspirations towards self-determination as well as individual persons' ability to think and act for themselves (Goldman 1998: 98). In this way, it exemplifies what Deleuze calls 'the indignity of speaking for others' (Deleuze and Foucault 1977: 209) – that is, 'the act of representing the other's needs, goals, situation, and in fact, *who they are*, based on [one's] own situated interpretation', thereby 'participating in the construction of their subject-positions rather than simply discovering their true selves' (Alcoff 1996: 100–1). For Deleuze, as for the anarchists, the existence of political, economic and social structures that 'claim to be representative [or] make a profession of speaking for others ... lead[s] to a division of power, to a distribution of this new power' that denies people the ability not only to act autonomously but also to decide who they are and what they (should) want or need (Deleuze and Foucault 1977: 209). If I am right to suggest that the critique of representation is an integral component of anarchism's ideological core, then there is an important sense in which any thinker who significantly emphasises the role that representative practices play in political, social and economic oppression – including Deleuze – may be understood as 'anarchistic' in virtue of operating within close conceptual proximity to anarchism.

## Anarchism and the New Left

Contemporary anarchism is, for the most part, historically discontinuous with the classical anarchist movements of the nineteenth and early twentieth centuries. As Uri Gordon writes:

> the roots of today's anarchist networks can be found in the processes of intersection and fusion among radical social movements since the 1960s, whose paths had never been overtly anarchist. These include the radical, direct action end of ecological, anti-nuclear and anti-war movements, and of movements for women's, black, indigenous, LGBT and animal liberation. (2008: 5)

Although contemporary anarchism 'often draw[s] directly on the anarchist tradition for inspiration and ideas', it is 'in many ways different from the left-libertarian politics of 100, and even 60, years ago' (Gordon 2008: 5). These differences – including the replacement of 'unions and federations' with 'networks of collectives and affinity groups . . . as the organizational norm'; a broadened agenda in which 'ecology, feminism and animal liberation are as prominent as anti-militarism and workers' struggles'; and 'a stronger emphasis . . . [on] prefigurative direct action and cultural experimentation' (2008: 5) – are indicative of the strong influence of New Left, which emerged in the 1960s as an explicit reaction to orthodox Marxism-Leninism and other Old Left ideologies.

Generally speaking, the New Left's critique of such ideologies consists of four basic charges: (1) that they rely on totalising macropolitical discourses which overlook the 'politics of everyday life'; (2) that they reinforce the alienation and reification of individual subjects by subsuming them under abstract, universal categories like 'human nature', 'species-being' and the like; (3) that they deny the creative dimension of power, regarding it instead as a uniformly repressive force that is deployed against otherwise passive, independently constituted subjects; and (4) that they reduce all forms of oppression to a single overarching source (that is, economic oppression). By emphasising 'cultural, psychological, and aesthetic patterns of domination' alongside 'the structural underpinnings of capitalism', New Left movements such as situationism offered a broader conceptualisation of oppression and 'the range of "disciplinary" practices' that serve to maintain it' (Curran 2007: 4). As Richard Gombin notes:

> For the situationists, the bureaucratic system of industrial society [had] considerably increased the sum total of the exploitation and repression of man in comparison with the competitive capitalism and the liberal nineteenth century state. The tremendous development of science and technology . . . led to the individual being completely taken over by the system; the individual is no more than a commodity, a reified object, placed on show, and manipulated by the specialists in cultural repression: artists, psychiatrists, psychologists, psychoanalysts, sociologists and 'experts' of all kinds. (1971: 24)

Commodification and reification of this sort involves *subjectivation*, the process of 'manufacturing images of, or constructing identities for, individuals and groups' and, by extension, divesting them of 'their power to create, transform, and change themselves' (Jun 2012: 127–8). To this extent, the principal mode of oppression in a 'spectacular society' is not so much exploitation, violence or direct physical coercion as it is *representation* – the generic practice of 'giving people images of who they are and what they desire', thereby 'wrest[ing] from them the ability to decide those matters for themselves' (May 1994: 48).

Representation manifests itself not only at the political, social and economic levels of society but at the sexual, psychological and cultural levels as well (Gombin 1971: 24–5). Although 'modes of subjectivation' can be 'foisted upon individuals or groups through direct or indirect . . . coercion', they are typically 'enforced and reinforced more subtly' – for example, through processes of normalisation that encourage individuals and groups 'to identify with the normalized representation, to conform to it, and so to regulate themselves absent any direct coercion' (Jun 2012: 128). For this reason, they are not so much active forces bearing down on already constituted subjects as they are reactive forces that divest subjects of their power and, in so doing, render them docile (Deleuze 1983: 58). Because subjectivation emanates from multiple sites, combating it necessarily requires an 'all-out attack' (Gombin 1971: 24–5) aimed at turning reactive forces against themselves and, by extension, re-empowering the active force of individuals. This, in turn, requires a 'politics of difference' grounded in anti-authoritarianism, personal (and especially sexual) liberation, the celebration of unorthodox 'lifestyles and dress codes' and the deployment of 'Do-It-Yourself direct action' strategies (Curran 2007: 5).

Poststructuralism – the school of thought with which Deleuze is most commonly associated – was both a product of, as well as a major influence on, the French New Left. It comes as no surprise, accordingly, that Deleuze and other 'poststructuralist' thinkers made a common cause of systematically dismantling 'representational barriers between people and who they can become' (May 1994: 131). As Todd May has argued, however, this rejection of representation, no less than other key elements of New Left and poststructuralist critique, is significantly foreshadowed in classical anarchism in so far as the latter denies 'that people have a nature or a natural set of interests that their political liberation will allow them to express or fulfil' and so rejects the practice of 'representing the interests of others as though those interests were either natural or given, even in the unfolding of a historical destiny' (May 1994: 97). In this way, May thinks, classical anarchism is philosophically (if not historically) of a piece with poststructuralism and other New Left-inspired movements, including contemporary anarchism.

In France, the visible culmination of New Left politics was the events of May 1968 – events which, as we will see, had a profound impact on Deleuze's intellectual and political development. Unlike earlier events of this sort, the so-called Paris Spring was 'fomented in mostly spontaneous fashion by a decentralized and non-hierarchical confederation of students and workers' who, despite their otherwise varied political persuasions, tended to share the classical anarchists' rejection of political representation as manifested in 'centralization, hierarchy, and repressive power' (Jun 2012: 165). The most consistently anti-authoritarian among them 'refused to betray their . . . beliefs by taking on leadership roles of any sort [and] repeatedly thwarted attempts by others to consolidate the leadership of the movement, thereby preventing its appropriation by outside political parties' (2012: 166). In place of 'centralized leadership', they organised 'self-managing councils such as the Sorbonne Student Soviet and the Commune of Nantes' (166), transforming the universities into 'cities unto themselves, with virtually everything necessary for normal life' (Decker 1977: 407).

Although there is no doubting 'the existence of anarchist ideas and concepts within the sum total of [their] ideological utterances' nor 'the libertarian character of [their] methods of contestation' (Gombin 1971: 19), the anti-authoritarians of 1968 were mostly unaffiliated with the French Anarchist Federation and other groups associated with the prewar anarchist movement. Indeed, such groups 'supplied very little of the driving force in the events (unlike the FAI and the CNT in the Spanish Civil War)' nor were they 'a direct source of inspiration (as were the Russian anarchists in relation to the Makhnovshchina)' (Gombin 1971: 22). This suggests that the Paris Spring was not so much an anarchist intervention *sensu stricto* as it was a powerful expression of broadly *anarchistic* sensibilities – chief among them the rejection of representation – that significantly challenged the hegemony of orthodox Marxism and opened up a whole new generation of radicals (including Deleuze) to a more straightforwardly anti-authoritarian brand of politics.

## Deleuze and Anarchism

Unlike other figures associated with poststructuralism, Deleuze was largely removed from organised political activity prior to 1968 (Patton 2000: 4). At the time, Francois Dosse writes,

> Deleuze was teaching at the University of Lyon and quickly became quite sympathetic to the student protests. He was one of the rare professors at Lyon, and the only one in the philosophy department, to publicly declare his support for and attend events of the movement. (2011: 177)

Following this initial foray into radical politics, Deleuze 'became involved with a variety of groups and causes, including the *Groupe d'Information sur les Prisons* (GIP) begun by Foucault and others in 1972' (Patton 2000: 4), His work, too, began to follow a much more explicitly political trajectory that reached its apex in the two volumes of *Capitalism and Schizophrenia* (Deleuze and Guattari 1977, 1987).

Poststructuralism, as noted previously, may be understood as radically extending the anarchistic critique of representation beyond the narrow boundaries of the political. Yet whereas Derrida and Foucault conceived of this project in largely epistemological and sociolinguistic terms, Deleuze's own account draws on a complex ontological framework that had already been developed in *Difference and Repetition* and other earlier works. At the centre of this framework is the notion that Being itself is an expression of difference or multiplicity rather than identity (Deleuze 1994: 36–40). For Deleuze, reality does not consist of stable, transcendent entities that exist external to and independent of the forces that act upon them; rather, it emerges from the material actualisation of 'relationship[s] of forces', where force itself (which Deleuze refers to as 'desire') is a virtual capacity for the expression of such relationships (Deleuze 1983: 40). This actualisation or expression, Deleuze writes, is 'on the one hand an explication, an unfolding of what expresses itself, the One [that is, force as such] manifesting itself in the Many [that is, particular relationships of force]' (Deleuze 1990: 16). On the other hand, because 'the One remains involved in whatever expresses it, imprinted in what unfolds it, immanent in whatever manifests it' (Deleuze 1983: 40), its expression as multiplicity is always already an expression of unity. In this way, Being is wholly immanent; it is neither constituted nor determined by fixed identities but by multiplicities – that is, variable processes, operations and relations of force.

As Deleuze writes, 'every force is related to others . . . [that] it either obeys or commands' (Deleuze 1983: 40). Whereas those of the latter sort (active forces) are capable of transforming themselves by affecting weaker forces, to 'go to the limit of what [they] can do', those of the former sort (reactive forces) are capable of being transformed by stronger forces but strive to prevent this by 'separat[ing] active force from what it can do' by taking away 'a part or almost all of its power' (58). In so far as desire (that is, force as such) is immanent to all particular relations of force and, in this way, constitutes the ultimate source of their affective qualities, it 'must itself have qualities, particularly fluent ones, even more subtle than those of force . . . the immediate qualities of becoming itself' (53–4). These qualities of desire (affirmation versus negation), which Deleuze elsewhere describes as qualities of power or life (Deleuze 1983: 85; cf. Deleuze 1990: 102, 218), are 'immanent to every force, every expression of or relation among forces' and, as such, 'actual force is not only determined by its own quality (its sense) but by the quality of the virtual desire . . . immanent to it (its value)' (Jun 2012: 171). Thus, every force – whether active or passive – has the capacity to either affirm or deny life (Deleuze 1983: 67).

Because epistemological representation – which Deleuze refers to as 'the dogmatic image of thought' – is founded on identity rather than fluid and variable relations of force, it 'fails to capture the affirmed world of difference' (Deleuze 1994: 55–6). The same is true of political representation which, as a species of the dogmatic image of thought, relies on already-constituted individuals with uniform, rationally appreciable interests. In rejecting the concept of identity in general, Deleuze also rejects the concepts of universalisable human subjectivity (Deleuze 1992: 162) and universal 'reason' (Deleuze 1995: 145–6), redefining them as, or replacing them with, 'variable processes of rationalization . . . [and] subjectivation' (Smith 2003: 307). In *Capitalism and Schizophrenia* Deleuze and Guattari refer to such processes as 'machinic'. Unlike the universalisable subject of traditional political theory, a machine is 'fluid, mobile, and dynamic . . . capable of changing, of connecting and reconnecting with other machines . . . immanent to the connections they make, and vice versa' (Jun 2012: 171). It is not a 'bounded whole with an identity and an end'; on the contrary, it is 'nothing more than its connections; it is not made by anything, and has no closed identity' (Colebrook 2002: 56; cf. Deleuze and Guattari 1972: 1).

The quality of machines is a function of the quality of whatever forces are dominant within the relations that comprise said machines (Deleuze and Guattari 1972: 135). Thus, a machine that 'dams up, channels, and regulates' (1977: 33) flows of desire is dominated by reactive forces, whereas a machine that expands or proliferates these flows is dominated by active forces. The same is true of social or political assemblages, which are themselves constituted by relations among machines. Assemblages that are dominated by machines of the former sort 'overcode' flows of desire in the form of people, money, labour and commodities through processes of domination and control ('molar lines'). These processes, which seek to 'territorialise' subversive machinic processes ('molecular lines' or 'lines of flight') and so prevent them from decoding flows of desire (1977: 223–4; cf. Deleuze and Parnet 1987: 130), are representational in nature; they suppress difference by constructing fixed identities that serve to identify, order and discipline individuals.

When Deleuze and Guattari claim that the state 'makes points *resonate* together, points that are not necessarily already town-poles but very diverse points of order, geographic, ethnic, linguistic, moral, economic, technological particularities' (Deleuze and Guattari 1987: 433), they mean that it organises various kinds of machines into an interdependent relationship with itself and with each other and, in so doing, uses these machines to overcode flows of desire and to territorialise lines of flight. Capitalism, in contrast, does not seek to control so much as to *commodify*; it does this by implementing a generic ('axiomatic') framework within which flows of desire are decoded, reterritorialised as exchange value and, finally, enclosed within the axiom of circulation and trade (Deleuze and Guattari 1977: 224). That said, both rely on capturing flows of desire, suppressing difference and representing others to themselves; to this extent, they are clearly expressions of reactive force. At the same time, every social and political assemblage is defined by 'the variable lines and singular *processes* that constitute it as a multiplicity: their connections and disjunctions, their circuits and short-circuits and, above all, their possible transformations' (Smith 2003: 307). In other words, their nature is determined not only by what they do but also by the conditions of possibility for their doing otherwise – that is, their 'lines of flight' (Deleuze and Guattari 1987: 216; cf. Deleuze and Parnet 1987: 125). This means that resisting reactive or oppressive assemblages is ultimately a matter of escaping along 'lines of flight' by decoding and deterritorialising flows of desire.

Deleuze's philosophy provides a sophisticated descriptive analysis of oppressive political, social and economic systems – one that highlights the role that representation plays in their operation as well as in resistance to them (Deleuze and Foucault 1977: 206–7; Deleuze 1988: 23; Deleuze and Guattari 1994: 47; Deleuze 1995: 85). To this extent, at least, there is no question that it bears an affinity to classical anarchism. For anarchists of all stripes, however, oppression is not (or not just) an empirical phenomenon that needs to be studied and understood; oppression is a wrong that needs to be condemned, combated and, ultimately, defeated. Traditional normative judgements of this sort, predicated as they are on transcendent values, are seemingly absent in Deleuze's work. Although he directly impugns the practice of 'speaking for others' and often seems to ascribe positive value to active, life-affirming modes of existence, he nonetheless fails to provide an explicit 'moral' critique grounded in what I have elsewhere termed '*nomological* (that is, law-, principle-, or rule-based) normative principles' (Jun 2011: 99). As Todd May writes:

> For Deleuze, as for Nietzsche, the project of measuring life against external standards constitutes a betrayal rather than an affirmation of life.

> Alternatively, an ethics of the kind Spinoza has offered . . . seeks out the possibilities life offers rather than denigrating life by appeal to 'transcendent values'. Casting the matter in more purely Nietzschean terms, the project of evaluating a life by reference to external standards is one of allowing reactive forces to dominate active ones, where reactive forces are those which 'separate active force from what it can do'. (1994: 127)

There is no question that Deleuze rejects the 'abstraction, universality, and exteriority to life' that are hallmarks of traditional ethical thinking (Jun 2011: 99). Such thinking, after all, 'generates norms that do not and cannot take account of their own deterritorialization or lines of flight . . . [because] they cannot provide self-reflexive criteria by which to question themselves, critique themselves, or otherwise act upon themselves' (2011: 101). Far from rejecting any and all ethical thinking, however, Deleuze instead identifies deterritorialisation itself as an 'overriding norm' (Patton 2000: 9) which, rather than generating extensive normative criteria, provides the means 'to critique and transform [such criteria], that is, to create something new' (Smith 2003: 308). In this way, deterritorialisation functions as an *intensive* normative criterion that is 'categorical, insofar as it applies to every possible norm as such, but . . . not transcendent . . . immanent to whatever norms (and, by extension, assemblages) constitute it' (Jun 2011: 101).

As it turns out, all of this is remarkably similar to the core anarchist concept of *prefiguration* which demands that the means and methods employed in achieving a desired end must reflect or 'prefigure' that end (or, more specifically, the values that are promoted by achieving it) (Bakunin 1984: 7; Avrich 1987: 7–8, 29; Goldman 2003: 261). In the absence of prefiguration there are no grounds upon which to critique the extensive norms that motivate and justify political action, which, by extension, invites the betrayal of those same norms by reproducing the very objects to which they are applied in the first place. Prefiguration is analogous to deterritorialisation, accordingly, because it serves as an intensive criterion by which to judge extensive criteria, where this, in turn, is a matter of determining whether said criteria themselves inhibit the creation of new normative criteria and, in so doing, give rise to the 'micro-fascism' of the avant-garde (Deleuze and Guattari 1977: 214–15).

## Conclusion

The foregoing has highlighted two important senses in which Deleuze may be understood as an 'anarchistic' thinker – that is, a thinker who stands in a significant relation of proximity to the conceptual core of anarchism. In the first place, as we have seen, Deleuze recognises that existing political, social and economic assemblages are inexorably wedded to representational practices that separate active force from what it can do and, in so doing, inhibit or deny the realisation of latent possibilities for creativity and development. In this way, such assemblages are shown to be inherently at odds with freedom as anarchists understand it. Deleuze goes even further, however, by highlighting the extent to which oppressive assemblages actually *determine* individuals' identities and desires, which denies people the ability not only to act for themselves but also to decide for themselves who they are or what they can become. Freedom, accordingly, can only be achieved by thinking, doing and *becoming* otherwise. This requires more than the abolition of oppressive assemblages; it requires actively creating and experimenting with new possibilities at both the individual and the social levels, which in turn requires a rigorous interrogation of the conditions of possibility for what is as well as what could be.

Like the classical anarchists before him, Deleuze interrogates not only the conditions of possibility for thinking, doing and becoming otherwise but also, and more importantly, the normative framework within which these conditions can be met. Both are interested in explaining how and why ostensibly liberatory political movements end up transforming into the very monsters they seek to combat, no less than what must be done to prevent this transformation from occurring. In the end, both contend that axiomatised values or norms inhibit or altogether eliminate the capacity for self-critique that is necessary for political actors to secure and maintain the ends to which they aspire. Put another way, both insist on prefiguration (or, in Deleuze's parlance, 'absolute deterritorialisation') as a minimal requirement for a genuinely liberatory politics that avoids the self-destructive impulse towards microfascism.

## Notes

1. The basic themes of *The Political Philosophy of Poststructuralist Anarchism* were first articulated in May's 1989 article 'Is Post-Structuralist Theory Anarchist?'.
2. Representative postanarchist texts include Newman (2001, 2010, 2015), Call (2002), Day (2005) and Rousselle and Evren (2011).
3. Indeed, some explicitly repudiated the label. See, for example, Derrida (2002: 22).
4. The analysis to follow takes for granted that this question also applies to texts, as well as political organisations, movements, practices and the like.
5. This is precisely the position favoured by Kropotkin, Nettlau, Rocker and other notable anarchist thinkers, to say nothing of more recent writers such as George

Woodcock, Peter Marshall and Robert Graham. See, for example, Kropotkin (1970: 287), Woodcock (1975: 13, 15, 19), Nettlau (1996: 277–8), Rocker (2004: 9–33), Graham (2005: xi–xii) and Marshall (2010: 4).
6. Arguably the most significant source of this tendency is Paul Eltzbacher's *Anarchism: Exponents of the Anarchist Philosophy* (1960, originally published 1900). See especially pp. 189, 194, 201.

# References

Abensour, M. (2013), 'An-archy Between Metapolitics and Politics', in J. Blumenfeld, C. Bottici and S. Critchley (eds), *The Anarchist Turn*, London: Pluto, pp. 80–98.

Alcoff, L. (1996), 'The Problem of Speaking for Others', in J. Roof and R. Wiegman (eds), *Who Can Speak? Authority and Critical Identity*, Chicago: University of Illinois Press, pp. 97–119.

Avrich, P. (1987), *Bakunin and Nechayev*, London: Freedom Press.

Bakunin, M. (1972), *Bakunin on Anarchy: Selected Works by the Activist-Founder of World*, New York: Knopf.

Bakunin, M. (1984), *Marx, Freedom, and the State*, London: Freedom Press.

Bakunin, M. (1992), *The Basic Bakunin*, Buffalo: Prometheus.

Call, L. (2002), *Postmodern Anarchism*, Lanham, MD: Lexington Books.

Colebrook, C. (2002), *Gilles Deleuze*, New York: Routledge.

Curran, G. (2007), *Twenty-First Century Dissent: Anarchism, Anti-Globalization and Environmentalism*, Basingstoke: Palgrave Macmillan.

Day, R. (2005), *Gramsci Is Dead: Anarchist Currents in the Newest Social Movements*, London: Pluto.

Decker, J. (1977), 'Direct Democracy and Revolutionary Organization in the 1968 French Student–Worker Revolt', *Proceedings of the Annual Meeting of the Western Society for French History*, 5: 406–14.

Deleuze, G. (1983), *Nietzsche and Philosophy*, trans. H. Tomlinson, New York: Columbia University Press.

Deleuze, G. (1988), *Spinoza: Practical Philosophy*, trans. R. Hurley, San Francisco: City Lights Books.

Deleuze, G. (1990), *Expressionism in Philosophy: Spinoza*, trans. M. Joughin, New York: Zone Books.

Deleuze, G. (1992), 'What Is a "Dispositif"?', in *Michel Foucault: Philosopher*, trans. T. Armstrong, New York: Routledge, pp. 158–66.

Deleuze, G. (1994), *Difference and Repetition*, trans. P. Patton, New York: Columbia University Press.

Deleuze, G. (1995), *Negotiations*, trans. M. Joughin, New York: Columbia University Press.

Deleuze, G. and M. Foucault (1977), 'Intellectuals and Power', in D. Bouchard (ed.), *Language, Counter-Memory, Practice*, trans. D. Bouchard and S. Simon, Ithaca: Cornell University Press, pp. 205–17.

Deleuze, G. and F. Guattari (1972), 'Deleuze et Guattari s'expliquent . . . ', *La Quinzaine Littéraire*, 143 (16–30 June): 15–9.

Deleuze, G. and F. Guattari (1977), *Anti-Oedipus: Capitalism and Schizophrenia*, trans. R. Hurley, M. Seem and H. R. Lame, New York: Viking Press.

Deleuze, G. and F. Guattari (1987), *A Thousand Plateaus*, trans. B. Massumi, Minneapolis: University of Minnesota Press.

Deleuze, G. and F. Guattari. (1994), *What Is Philosophy?*, trans. H. Tomlinson and G. Burchell, New York: Columbia University Press.

Deleuze, G. and C. Parnet (1987), *Dialogues II*, trans. H. Tomlinson and B. Haberjam, New York: Columbia University Press.

Derrida, J. (2002), *Negotiations: Interventions and Interviews, 1977–2001*, trans. E. Rottenberg, Stanford: Stanford University Press.

Dosse, F. (2011), *Gilles Deleuze and Félix Guattari: Intersecting Lives*, New York: Columbia University Press.

Eltzbacher, P. (1960) [1900], *Anarchism: Exponents of the Anarchist Philosophy*, London: Freedom Press.

Feenberg, A. and J. Freedman (2001), *When Poetry Ruled the Streets: The French May Events of 1968*. Albany: SUNY Press.

Franks, B. (2012), 'Anarchism and Analytic Philosophy', in R. Kinna (ed.), *The Bloomsbury Companion to Anarchism*, New York: Bloomsbury, pp. 50–71.

Freeden, M. (1996), *Ideologies and Political Theory: A Conceptual Approach*, Oxford: Clarendon Press.

Freeden, M. (2004), 'Ideology, Political Theory and Political Philosophy', in G. Gaus and C. Kukathas (eds), *Handbook of Political Theory*, London: SAGE, pp. 3–17.

Freeden, M. (2013), 'The Morphological Analysis of Ideology', in M. Freeden, L. Tower Sargent and M. Stears (eds), *The Oxford Handbook of Political Ideologies*, Oxford: Oxford University Press, pp. 115–37.

Freeden, M. (2015), *Liberalism: A Very Short Introduction*, Oxford: Oxford University Press.

Goldman, E. (1910), *Anarchism and Other Essays*, New York: Mother Earth Publishing Association.

Goldman, E. (1998), *Red Emma Speaks*, New York: Humanity Books.

Goldman, E. (2003), *My Disillusionment in Russia*, Mineola, NY: Dover.

Gombin, R. (1971), 'The Ideology and Practice of Contestation Seen Through Recent Events in France', in D. Apter and J. Joll (eds), *Anarchism Today*, New York: Doubleday, pp. 17–40.

Gordon, U. (2008), *Anarchy Alive! Anti-Authoritarian Politics from Practice to Theory*, London: Pluto Press.

Graham, R. (2005), *Anarchism: A Documentary History of Libertarian Ideas, Vol. I: From Anarchy to Anarchism (300CE to 1939)*, Montreal: Black Rose Books.

Graham, R. (2015), *We Do Not Fear Anarchy – We Invoke It: The First International and the Origins of the Anarchist Movement*, Oakland: AK Press.

Guérin, D. (1998), *No Gods, No Masters*, Oakland: AK Press.

Jun, N. (2007), 'Deleuze, Derrida, and Anarchism', *Anarchist Studies*, 15(2): 132–56.

Jun, N. (2011), 'Deleuze, Values, and Normativity', in D. Smith and N. Jun (eds), *Deleuze and Ethics*, Edinburgh: Edinburgh University Press, pp. 89–103.

Jun, N. (2012), *Anarchism and Political Modernity*, London: Bloomsbury.

Koch, A. (1993), 'Poststructuralism and the Epistemological Basis of Anarchism', *Philosophy of the Social Sciences*, 23(3): 327–51.

Kropotkin, P. (1970), *Kropotkin's Revolutionary Pamphlets: A Collection of Writings by Peter Kropotkin*, New York: Dover.

Malatesta, E. (1965), *Malatesta: Life and Ideas*, London: Freedom Press.

Malatesta, E. (1981), *Fra Contadini: A Dialogue on Anarchy*, trans. J. Weir, London: Bratach Dubh Editions.

Marshall, P. (2010), *Demanding the Impossible: A History of Anarchism*, Oakland: PM Press.

May, T. (1989), 'Is Post-Structuralist Theory Anarchist?', *Philosophy and Social Criticism*, 15(2): 167–82.

May, T. (1994), *The Political Philosophy of Poststructuralist Anarchism*, University Park: Pennsylvania State University Press.

May, T. (2011), 'Kant via Rancière: From Ethics to Anarchism', in J. Casas Clausen and J. Martel (eds), *How Not to Be Governed: Readings and Interpretations from a Critical Anarchist Left*, Lanham, MD: Lexington Books, pp. 65–82.

Nettlau, M. (1996), *A Short History of Anarchism*, London: Freedom Press.

Newman, S. (2001), *From Bakunin to Lacan: Antiauthoritarianism and the Dislocation of Power*, Lanham, MD: Lexington Books.

Newman, S. (2010), *The Politics of Postanarchism*, Edinburgh: Edinburgh University Press.

Newman, S. (2015), *Postanarchism*, London: Wiley.

Patton, P. (2000), *Deleuze and the Political*, New York: Routledge.

Rocker, R. (2004), *Anarcho-Syndicalism: Theory and Practice*, Oakland: AK Press.

Rousselle, D. and S. Evren (2011), *The Postanarchist Reader*, London: Pluto Press.

Schmidt, M. and L. van der Walt (2009), *Black Flame: The Revolutionary Class Politics of Anarchism and Syndicalism*, Oakland: AK Press.

Smith, D. (2003), 'Deleuze and the Liberal Tradition: Normativity, Freedom, and Judgment', *Economy and Society*, 32(2): 299–324.

Verter, M. (2010), 'The Anarchism of the Other Person', in N. Jun and S. Wahl (eds), *New Perspectives on Anarchism*, Lanham, MD: Lexington Books, pp. 67–84.

Woodcock, G. (1975), *Anarchism: A History of Libertarian Ideas and Movements*, London: Penguin Books.

Young, I. M. (1990), *Justice and the Politics of Difference*, Princeton: Princeton University Press.

# Chapter 6

# Immanent Ethics and Forms of Representation

*Elizabet Vasileva*

The aim of this chapter is to address the anti-representational principle in (post)anarchist ethics. Most commonly referred to in relation to representative politics, this principle is also taken to be at the core of anarchist ethical conduct, reflected in the anarchist practices of not speaking for others (as in representative democracy), using direct action rather than turning to authorities for solutions, applying a DIY ethos and so forth. Here I critically examine the anti-representational principle and discuss its ontological dimensions. Using Deleuze's critique of representation, I argue that the (post)anarchist move towards anti-representation needs to be further developed along two simultaneous paths: first, as an affirmative acceptance of a certain type of representation in metaphysics and subsequent politics and, second, as a move towards performativity.[1] Following Deleuze, I claim that we cannot simply get rid of representation and formulate anti-representation as an ethical principle. Rather, I argue that this problem refers not to representation per se, but to a specific type of representation derived from transcendent metaphysics and Platonic idealism. The standpoint from which I work is informed by a Deleuzian arrangement of theory-practice where the two arise from and affect each other (rather than being binary). This stands in contrast with the notion that theory is representative of practices, or that the two are separate processes.

It has been roughly thirty years since postanarchism appeared as a theoretical field.[2] Its origins are difficult to determine; some authors attribute the coining of the phrase to Andrew Koch, some to Hakim Bey, some to Lewis Call.[3] Regardless, it is interesting to note that anarchist theory and practice in the late 1980s in the United States revolved around a debate between the anarcho-primitivism of John Zerzan and the social eco-anarchism of Murray Bookchin. Bey pointed to this argument as an exemplar of the stagnation within the anarchist movement, indicating the need for an urgent update. The primary authors associated with postanarchism attempt to interrupt this situation by grounding themselves in poststructuralism – in some cases trying to theorise the political implications of poststructuralism and arriving at a different version of anarchism (Todd May), in others claiming to more accurately describe contemporary anti-authoritarian thinking (Saul Newman). Whether or not they have been 'successful' in their endeavours,[4] it would seem that postanarchism is here to stay.

One of the most important contributions of postanarchist theory is its problematisation of ethics, which many anarchists have placed at the forefront of radical political thought. Newman, for example, claims that anarchism is first and foremost an ethical position (Newman 2001: 166); Simon Critchley paraphrases Kant (1959 [1785]), saying that 'ethics without politics is blind' (Critchley 2007: 120); and numerous postanarchist writings have engaged in ethical debates.[5] Anarchism, many have claimed, is a political position derived from a commitment to ethical values like freedom, equality and personal autonomy. However, the entry point of postanarchists is a critique of the foundation of these values, namely the essentialist and universalising tendencies they have discovered in 'classical' anarchist ethics. Utilising (most commonly) Foucault, Derrida and/or Deleuze, they question the assumptions about a benevolent human nature that certain anarchist ontologies rely upon, as well as universal truths about freedom, equality and a 'good' life. Closely bound to questions of essentialism and universal truths, we find a fundamental tenet of the postanarchist critique of 'classical' anarchism – representation. Starting with the infamous split between Marx and Bakunin, the key to understanding anarchism, May argues, is acknowledging its central theme – the rejection of representation (May 1994: 29).

May identifies several primary postanarchist ethical principles, the first of which is anti-representation (May 1994: 72). Foucault, Deleuze and Lyotard, he claims, all strive to affirm difference and 'the indignity of speaking for others' (Kay 2006), which is translated into the ethical position that representing others ought to be avoided.[6] May identifies the principle as follows: 'People ought not, other things being equal, to engage in practices whose effect, among others, is the representation or commendation of certain intentional lives as either intrinsically superior or intrinsically inferior to others' (May 1995: 48). Later on, in *The Political Philosophy of Poststructuralist Anarchism*, May bases his argument against representation in radical politics on two main points. First, he argues, representing people is oppressive in itself because it limits the possibilities of what or who they can become; for example, if we take a Barbie doll to be a representation of women, we create certain limits around what kinds of body shapes and appearances can constitute a 'woman'. Second, it helps reinforce existent oppressive social relationships; for example, we are less inclined to accept fat, black, or Asian women as 'women' (May 1994: 72). May supports this claim with Foucault's critique of practices of normalisation:

> One might argue here that what poststructuralism resists is not representation per se, but only a specific kind of representation: 'normalization'. Normalization is, as its name implies, a practice of defining what is normal in a group and attempting to hold people to that norm . . . [The power of the sovereign] is a representation designed to discourage deviance and to ensure obedience; and it is presented by Foucault with no more sympathy than modern practices of normalization. (1994: 73)

In summary, when talking about anti-representation, May refers to only two particular types of *political* representation that are unacceptable in poststructuralist anarchism as opposed to more general *ontological* types of representation. Representation is condemned in so far as it 'presents', again and again, certain lives as better, more normal, more acceptable or intrinsically superior to others. Thus, anti-representation is presented as an ethical principle that underpins poststructuralism and is directly derived from a commitment to difference and diversity. The principle of actively promoting difference and diversity, May argues, can be found in Deleuze and Guattari's *What Is Philosophy?* and in Foucault's final writings on alternative practices of being (May 1994: 75).

Like May, Saul Newman draws his critique of representation from Deleuze and Guattari's *Anti-Oedipus* and the work of Foucault. Acknowledging the different ways in which these thinkers conceptualise desire, Newman nevertheless finds a uniting thread – the rejection of the tendency to speak for others: '[Deleuze and Guattari's] critique of representation in psychoanalysis is similar to Foucault's attack on various discourses – political, medical, psychiatric, etc. – which attempt to speak for the individual' (Newman 2001: 101). Indeed, Newman acknowledges his indebtedness to May by referring to anarchism as a critique of political representation in the form of government representatives – always 'a relationship of domination' (2001: 102). As such, anarchism can never accept vanguardism (either of the party or the proletariat in general) since a vanguard is representative of the people. Newman goes on to claim that 'representative thinking is a domination of thought, in the same way that anarchists argue that representative politics is a domination of the individual' (105). He supports this statement by referencing Deleuze and Guattari's critique of psychoanalysis, which shows that representing the subconscious is a way of suppressing rather than liberating desire. Moreover, by attacking certain norms of truth and rationality, Newman is able to simultaneously expand anarchism and critique its reliance on such representative thinking. Representation, he argues, is based on essentialist thinking – the idea that there is an authentic object, truth or place (or even an objective subject in some instances) that thinking refers to and which is often constructed dialectically (2001).

It would seem that for many postanarchists political anti-representationalism is of primary importance as a value; liberation can occur only in so far as people are able to retain their power and agency rather than surrendering it to a 'representative'. The notion that representational thought is oppressive is not new in anarchism,[7] yet it would appear that it needs further unpacking. In the next section, I examine the meaning of anti-representation as an ethical principle and the implications of a political ontology that rejects the primacy of representation.

## Representation and Transcendence

We talk about representation, both politically and philosophically, in many ways. Some stem from, or were developed by, poststructuralist theorists. As Claire Colebrook remarks, there are two main tendencies in poststructuralist engagement with representation (Colebrook 2000: 1). On one hand, it is argued that there is nothing outside representation and that the world is textual and readable. On the other hand, representation is posited as a problem that needs to be overcome; in other words, all entities are defined as re-presentations, copies or images of something 'outside'. This outside is the unquestioned transcendent which serves to ground thought in most Western philosophy.

In relation to postanarchism, representation is broadly identified as epistemological – a symptom of 'classical' anarchist thought. Newman, for example, claims that in classical anarchism notions such as human essence or universal truths hold metaphysical authority over their 'representations' in the physical world, thus creating a relationship of domination that is unethical in itself (Newman 2001: 161). Similarly, Colebrook observes that there is a clear link between epistemological representation and political representation. After all, 'it is only because we can think of an "empty" human subject that representative democracy can work: democracy is not just the collection of self-seeking interests and the expressed desires of competing individuals' (Colebrook 2000: 15). Representation, in this sense, is tightly bound to, and reliant upon, an ontology of transcendence.

Representation, be it political, social and/or linguistic, is about resemblance – a copy in another form. The closer the copy is to the original, the better the representation is. This involves transferring something from one medium to another. For example, if we take two copies of the same book, we do not usually think of one of them as a representation of the other. But if we take one book and one photograph of that book, we typically understand the photograph to be a representation of the 'real existing' book. This type of representation is what many linguistic theories consider speech to be – words representing or describing life. Thus, both in linguistics and in sociopolitical thought, we have the material world on one side and the symbolic, representational world on the other.[8] This totalising view of representation is reliant upon a specific type of thinking that Deleuze, in the chapter of the same name in *Difference and Repetition* (2004), calls the dogmatic Image of Thought. The chapter reveals the implicit forms of representational thinking found in most Western philosophy and demonstrates how they produce an exclusionary and contrived approach to metaphysics, providing justification for Deleuze's engagement with difference as a primary ontological category.

Thought, Deleuze claims, always relies on implicit presuppositions, and the search for the 'purest' place to begin philosophy has (mis)guided many thinkers (Deleuze 2004: 164). Philosophy, according to Deleuze, can begin from either objective or subjective presuppositions. Objective presuppositions could be defined as those that explicitly require other concepts for support; for example, by saying that 'anarchists are violent' we rely upon presuppositions about the sense of both 'anarchists' and 'violence'. Subjective presuppositions, on the other hand, are more implicit – the Cartesian 'I think therefore I am', for instance, where it is expected that every 'I' knows, independently of definitions or discourse, what it is to think and to be. In philosophy, this is taken to be a pure beginning, as it refers all presuppositions back to the empirical self (2004). Examples of this include Hegel's pure being and Heidegger's pre-ontological Being. Deleuze, however, argues that this creates an Image of Thought that is circular, always repeating itself, attempting to identify that which does not rely on other concepts for its existence. These subjective presuppositions, he claims, take the form of an 'everybody knows' – that which no one can argue against (Deleuze 2004: 165). By taking this form of what Deleuze refers to as *common sense* as its starting position, the Image of

Thought becomes a form of representational thinking – it re-presents what is known to be universally acknowledged. In other words, the Image of Thought is based on a particular *form* of thinking that is oriented towards finding the Truth; different philosophers only change the *content*, which takes the shape of their starting premises or postulates. This is what Deleuze calls the dogmatic or moral (in Nietzsche's terms) Image of Thought – most Western philosophy that calls itself 'rationalist' or 'empiricist' is based on this (2004: 167). To operate outside of representational thinking, Deleuze says, we need 'a radical critique of this Image and the "postulates" it implies' (167).

The critique of the dogmatic Image of Thought, as well as Deleuze and Guattari's work on the role of philosophy more generally, imply that the totalising tendencies of representation in politics are derived from a transcendent ontology. In other words, the form of representation that postanarchists have identified and argued against is in fact a symptom of a deeper problem – representational thinking that always refers to something 'outside'. Deleuze's response to the dogmatic Image of Thought is to argue that the world simply *is* – there is nothing transcendent in which we can ground ethics, politics or reality. Moreover, the idea of a 'subject' in whose mind the world is represented is a *result* of practices of knowledge rather than the foundation for them. Thus, non-representation is, for Deleuze, not a stance against *all* representation, but a rejection of an anthropocentric conception of the subject whose point of view determines the physical world through representation. As Colebrook observes,

> [a]s soon as thought regards itself as other than such an affirmation [of existence] – if it regards itself as the representation of some outside – then it becomes the very opposite of affirmatory; it becomes slavish, reactive and in denial of its own possibility. (2000: 58)

Similarly, the danger in creating an ethical principle from anti-representational practices lies in the fact that it sustains the dogmatic Image of Thought. In other words, we change the content, but not the form of ethics. Replacing one transcendent value with another does not radically question the framework in which ethics takes place, a charge we might also lay against May. To move fully beyond political representation, as postanarchists convincingly argue we need to do, it is essential that we reject transcendence in favour of an immanent approach to ethics. In the next section, I begin to reconstruct a theory of immanence-in-itself as it might apply to anarchist politics; immanence that is not subsumed under a transcendent category. This move allows us, following Deleuze, to start constructing a metaphysics of difference. This is important in the consideration of an anarchist ethics as it is linked to the 'liberation' from the notion of representation and from the trap of transcendence. In other words, whereas morality, duty and obligation are based on a representational image of thought, immanent ethics are built on affirmation and active forces (the will to power).

## Immanence and Representation

What is the role of representation, then, for immanent metaphysics? It is clear that we cannot deny representation's role as a common cognitive tool. Neither is it possible to structure our lives politically if we reject all forms of representation.[9] So far, we have identified one form of representation – an epistemological one that describes the relationship between transcendent ideals, forms, essences and the physical world or subject. Levi Bryant has appropriately named this 'the problem of hegemony of epistemology', problematising the view of subjects as 'fixed and stable', to be contrasted with 'events and processes' (Bryant 2011: 13–14). The question of the representation of an object through the subject thus becomes of utmost importance for the way in which we understand the object itself; in other words, is this representation independent of the object, independent of our own mind, or entirely within it? Epistemological realists are concerned with making a representation as true (accurate) to reality as possible. This is, in a way, the goal of the Enlightenment project – the discovery of the true nature of the world in a manner that is objective and not biased by culture, society, religion and so on. Anti-realists, on the other hand, argue that representation falls entirely within the domain of the subject and that there are no criteria by which we can determine whether representation is accurate, or merely a product of our imagination. This constructivist position also leads to an understanding of truth as subjective – a shared representation rather than a direct correspondence between representation and reality (2011: 14–16). The result of these two approaches, Bryant argues, is that the question of objects, of what they are (ontologically) becomes a question of how we know objects (epistemologically). Representation, in this sense, is the 'mediation' between things that makes possible the comparison between the Idea and the copy. Does the copy represent the pure form well? Is it a 'good' copy? Representation, in the form of resemblance, is the mechanism at the heart of the Neoplatonic triad.[10] The claim is validated only on the basis of its resemblance to the original, and not just any resemblance, but an internal noetic resemblance to the

Idea of the object. Of course, this naturally leads to the question of essence in Plato – the goal of Platonism is to detach each object from what it is immanent to and evaluate it in relation to a transcendent Idea of its pure essence. For example, a table is not taken as that which it is in relation to this immanent moment (the table for our picnic was the grass), but in relation to what the Idea of a table is in the abstract (the grass is not a table). This is the error Deleuze observes in Plato – difference is again subsumed under Identity and resemblance.

Thus far, I have discussed two types of representation: linguistic, where language is taken to 'represent' reality, and Platonic, where objects in reality are re-presented in the realm of Ideas. However, there is another type of relationship between subject and object; following Deleuze again, we call this 'repetition'. At the heart of Deleuze's metaphysics lies the concept of difference-in-itself that comes to be through repetition. Repetition, as Deleuze makes clear from the very first page of *Difference and Repetition*, should not be thought of in terms of representation or some form of identity: '[r]epetition is not generality' (Deleuze 2004: 1). For instance, while looking at two objects that share the same characteristics, a relationship of resemblance would identify both objects as chairs if they were referenced according to the general concept of 'chair'. This is how repetition differs from resemblance – resemblance is what would allow us to generalise. Deleuze instead claims that 'to repeat is to behave in a certain manner, but in relation to something unique or singular which has no equal or equivalent' (2004: 1), a 'repetition-in-itself'. In this sense, repetition is never purely the repetition of the same since the object of repetition is never the same in a concrete sense for each instance. Therefore, repetition and difference always exist together – one's existence relies upon the other. The significant difference between representation within a framework of transcendence and repetition within an immanent framework is production or creation. Repetition creates something; changing the assemblage produces something new. Indeed, non-representational theory emphasises that representation, liberated from the need to resemble Ideas, is creative:

> First, to repeat is to differ and defer. The same that returns ineluctably returns otherwise. Representation is inevitably transformation and differentiation, even when it is a transposition of the semblance of one medium into that of another. By necessity, it brings forth more than the same. (Doel 2010: 132)

To illustrate this productive aspect of 'representation', I briefly turn to Deleuze and Guattari's discussion on linguistics in *A Thousand Plateaus*

(Deleuze and Guattari 2013: 87). Deleuze and Guattari identify two expressions of assemblage, which are neither ontologically distinct nor binary. 'Machinic assemblages' vaguely correspond to the physical world, bodies, their structures and processes, while 'collective assemblages of enunciation' relate to the domain of language, signs and the symbolic, but also the practices that create them. Their primary argument is that collective assemblages of enunciation are more than just a 'representation' of the world and that their main purpose is not to describe or convey information but, instead, to create. In support of this, Deleuze and Guattari invoke J. L. Austin's theory of speech acts and the notion of performativity. Their interest lies in Austin's critique of logical positivism – the view that the role of language is to represent the world – as unable to provide an accurate description of feelings, objects, humans and the rest of reality. Drawing on Austin and Searle, Deleuze and Guattari point out three aspects of language: locutionary, or what is said; illocutionary, or what the intention is; and perlocutionary, the result of the action (of speech) (2013: 90). The illocutionary is particularly important as this is where the idea of language as performative arises, in the sense that it not only describes or represents, but also *does* what it says; that is, the act occurs through the speech itself. By saying 'I swear', one performs the act of swearing itself; 'I promise' is the act of promising, but so too could the statement 'I love you' be, depending on the context. These 'incorporeal transformations' are a function of language that is not representative or descriptive but, instead, changes the symbolic attachments that come with a particular body. When a judge proclaims a 'guilty' verdict, a body is transformed from a 'bank manager' to a 'convict'. Moreover, these transformations are highly contextual and immanent – they require an analysis of all the complex processes involved in the transformation rather than the simple equation of signifier = signified.

Our account of postanarchist ethics needs to take into consideration the two main points I have outlined so far. First, a rejection of representation within a transcendent ontology and its transformation into repetition within an immanent one; and second, an affirmation of the productive role of repetition. Following Deleuze, we have 'liberated' the concept of representation from referring to a transcendent entity (essence, Platonic forms, rationality) that it re-presents again and again in the physical world and instead chosen to view it as immanent – as a form of repetition that is performative. Following from this, we see that a radical concept of 'representation' inevitably includes difference – there is no obligation to produce any resemblance between 'reality' and 'representation'. A painter can draw the face in cubic forms or use one black line to represent the feeling of pain. Representation, then, is productive or, rather, it is not a slave to resemblance but an affirmation of difference. Moreover, as Jeffrey Popke has suggested, non-representational thinking has created a different kind of ethics, one that

> takes the form of an ethos rather than a morality or a set of principles grounded in universal norms or juridical constructs. Such an ethos works toward encounters that open us to a generous sensibility, one that might be capable of re-enlivening our affective engagements with others and fostering a heightened sense for what might be possible. (2006: 84)

In the final section, I outline the kinds of problem these ethics might solve in anarchist organisation.

## Immanent Anarchist Ethics

In both 'classical' and 'post' anarchism there seems to be a struggle to reconcile means and ends – to overcome the separation and hierarchy between the two. If seen as a political ideology with demands for internal consistency and a need to reconcile its values with its methods, anarchism inevitably creates tension between practices that are closer to this anarchist ideal and those that are not. This leads to either moral universalism, which postanarchists claim is the case for classical anarchism, or moral relativism which, for Newman, is exemplified by Stirner. Attempts to create anarchist ethics that avoid swinging between the two (or that dispense with the question entirely) need to start by questioning the existence of a standard – the ideal as the standard and reality as 'lower', as that which needs to be brought to the level of the standard. One example here is the overly discussed pacifism versus 'radicalism' debate, which the Invisible Committee outline in *To Our Friends* (Invisible Committee 2015: 135). Both pacifists and radicals, they claim, strive for purity – either of violent action or of non-violent action – reaching even the point of handing each other over to the common enemy, the police:

> Since the catastrophic defeat of the 1970s, the *moral* question of radicality has gradually replaced the *strategic* question of revolution. That is, revolution has suffered the same fate as everything else in those decades: it has been privatised. It has become an opportunity for personal validation, with radicality as the standard of evaluation ... What happens instead is that a *form* is extracted from each [revolutionary act]. (Invisible Committee 2015: 142)

Thus, a transcendent measure by which revolutionary acts are rated as 'radical' emerges and people come to aspire to a level of radicality rather than to real world change. There seems to be a similar intrusion of moral radicality in queer and intersectional organising, particularly in recent debates around 'Oppression Olympics'. Abbie Volcano provides a hypothetical situation that many activists might find familiar:

> 'As a working class person, I have to say . . . ' (a few nods of agreement)
> 'As a poor woman, it seems to me . . . ' (even more nods)
> 'As a poor lesbian of color, I think . . . ' (even more furious nodding, making sure everyone registers each other's frenetic agreement). (Volcano 2013: 34)

In the same way that there is a quest here for the most 'authentic' voice or the most oppressed person, the quest for radicality can become yet another search for the 'ideal' anarchist, who has the moral high ground and whose opinion therefore matters most. Volcano continues: '[o]ften this tactic of agreeing with "the most marginalised in the room" will be used as a substitute for developing critical analyses around race, gender, sexuality, etc.' (Volcano 2013: 34). Without wishing to take up a position on these particular debates, it seems to me that there are many more examples with a similar structural framework.

Essential to this transcendent framework is a particular type of epistemology that prioritises fixed and stable identities that are representations of a universal standard. In the example above, this is reflected in the construction of 'queer' as an identity with its own implications and limitations. To be perceived as the bearer of a queer identity, one needs to act in certain ways – going to queer events, engaging in non-heteronormative sexual practices, dressing in certain ways and so on. Moreover, what follows from this is the view that the rest of the world is also composed of stable and fixed identities – humans, nature, animals and cultures are all seen as capable of being defined and separated from each other, relating only through the medium of a standard ideal. Finally, this ideal needs to be more or less permanent (or at least presented as such), universally accepted and unchanging so that other people can aspire to achieve it. The product of such transcendent frameworks is not necessarily that they result in an essentialist understanding of identities (although they often do), but that they result in new types of norms where the existence of these assumptions and limitations cannot be easily challenged.

The problems this presents for anarchist ethics are twofold. On one hand, it is possible to claim that an ontological hierarchy between means and ends – and the subjugation of our reality to a higher standard – is in opposition to the anarchist value of non-hierarchy, as is the case with certain types of ontological anarchism discussed by Newman (Newman 2010: 53). This claim is already an ethical stance that presupposes an anarchist ideology against hierarchy on all levels, including the onto-logical. On the other hand, we could say that measuring life against a transcendent ideal requires us to evaluate our embodied knowledge of the world according to an imposed standard (even if it is one created by ourselves; even if it is an anarchist one). For example, we know that not all women are gentle, kind and helpful, but we may nevertheless expect all women to behave according to this ideal. This refers particularly to situations where various socially accepted practices are presented as historically unchangeable and universal – a problem Foucault exposes in his critique of the treatment of sexual practices. If we were to accept that most (or even some) practices, structures and identities are socially constructed, then positioning our actions as ahistorical truths based on ideals is simply incorrect. Without repeating Foucault's entire argu-ment, it is possible to draw on his conclusion that most human societies revolve around historically contingent 'truths' that have nevertheless been presented as universal and normalised.[11] If – and here we might refer to Benjamin Franks's idea of prefigurative ethics based on various telē – we are aware of these 'truths' and accept them as valid only within our own immanent reality, then the possibility of even having a telos to compare them to is exposed as another contingent concept that cannot be evaluated as 'good' or 'bad' without appealing to a transcendent framework.[12]

Finally, I extend one further practical critique of deontological, teleological or even postanarchist ethical frameworks that are not based on a foundation of pure immanence, to be found in the 'poverty'[13] or weakness of applied ethics that most ethics teachers will immedi-ately recognise. Sitting in a classroom and applying a set of rules to a given problem is a common methodology in these classes. Similarly, in anarchist meetings or discussions, there are often people establishing a number of 'anarchist' rules and defending their position in relation to them. However, the problem often arises that one can defend virtually *any* position with these rules. In practice, it is possible to perform mental and linguistic gymnastics with ethical rules in order to reach a desired outcome. For instance, when engaging with the topic of abortion we can use Kantian deontology, which would require us to ascertain whether the action is universalisable. If we encounter no contradictions and the action is still possible, then it is an ethical action, and this holds for both sides of the common debate. We are required to look at the action as detached from its context and probable outcome, purely in relation to its universalisability. Similarly, we can use utilitarian ethics to discuss the right to abortion and arrive at completely different conclusions. But none of these frameworks gives us a reason why we should commit to that particular framework or what the moral action should actually be. Franks attempts to answer that question with a prior commitment to anarchist values, with contextual rules stemming from them, but it is still possible to employ the aforementioned mental gymnastics within a value-based prefigurative framework. Of course, Spinoza already suggested this critique: 'we do not endeavour, will, seek after or desire because we judge a thing to be good. On the contrary, we judge a thing to be good because we endeavour, will, seek after and desire it'.[14] The only 'redeeming feature' of such mental gymnastics is to stipulate a transcendent ideal or duty that never changes. But such an epistemology of transcendence relies on sameness as the fundamental ontological category and difference as its derivative. To match people to a standard or fit them into categories implies that they are in some way comparable to each other, that they are similar on some level. Difference is constructed as the negation of the same and thus as inferior to it, in turn automatically creating the categories of One and Other.

On the contrary, immanent ethics allows for the unfolding of complex phenomena in ways that allow us to better understand and approach them. Non-representational thinking and performativity play a crucial role in such an ethics. They *enable* us, creating the conditions in which we can respond to reality. They increase our capacity to be 'ethical' by demanding recognition of all the relations involved in an ethical event and increase our accountability as ethical agents. In this context, performativity also relates to the active and reactive forces in Nietzsche. *Ressentiment*, or reactive force, renders us unable to act; we can only be acted on. Active force, on the other hand, brings us closer to our capacity to act. Moreover, performativity precludes the possibility of mental gymnastics as it removes the need to 'justify' or 'evaluate' an action and instead posits relations as values. Rosi Braidotti, for example, has long suggested similar practices of location, embodiment and accountability, as have numerous anarchists and activist zine authors.[15] I illustrate this through a brief engagement with some recent debates on the concept of ally-ship in anarchist organisation.

The principle of anti-representation in anarchism has fed into the idea of allies and ally-ship. Ally-ship puts responsibility in the centre – an immanent responsibility of those who are privileged[16] to support those who are not. It recognises that everyone's experiences are different and that nobody can 'speak for' anybody else. Allies are often encouraged to take a step back and let oppressed people lead the struggle while providing what protection or mobilisation they can through their privileged position afforded to them from within hierarchical structures. In fact, '[i]t is a well-worn activist formula to point out that oppressed groups must be placed front and centre in struggles against racism, sexism, and homophobia' (Tipu's Tiger 2015: 51). However, as many anarchists have discovered, the problem is more complex than choosing to not 'represent' oppressed groups. For example, white allies of indigenous groups can generate problems such as when self-appointed indigenous leaders claim authority based upon the legitimacy afforded them by white people. At other times, allies may become passive due to being overcome with guilt. This imposition of (ethical) rules on the basis of the transcendent ideals of ally-ship or 'non-representation' inhibits action, with consequences like burnout, rejection and an inability to work together. In response to this, groups like Indigenous Action Media have started referring instead to 'accomplices', suggesting a new form of organisation based on performativity and relationships:

> Accomplices are realised through mutual consent and build trust. They don't just have our backs; they are at our side, or their own spaces confronting and unsettling colonialism. *As accomplices, we are compelled to become accountable and responsible for each other; that is the nature of trust.* (Indigenous Action Media 2015: 96)

For an immanent ethics, politics is enacted, embodied and performed rather than prejudged or evaluated. An ethical response does not rely upon justifying our actions on the basis of certain (transcendent) values, but instead emerges from engagement with a complex situation.

## Conclusion

I have argued that the anti-representation principle in (post)anarchism needs to be further developed in order to successfully found itself upon solid ontological ground. Utilising Deleuze's metaphysics of difference and extending his critique of transcendence to anarchist ethics has revealed that anarchism need not be against representation per se, despite defining itself as anti-representational. I have shown that it is not necessary to reject representation in an immanent ontology when it takes the form of productive repetition. Moreover, political or ontological representation that relies upon a transcendent framework perpetuates relations of domination and leads to dogmatic thinking in both philosophy and anarchism. Siding with Levi Bryant, I would like to claim that the rejection of representation, essentialism and transcendence is not a primary factor of Deleuze's ontology but a *consequence* of it (Bryant 2008: 4). This is a very important distinction in so far is it encourages us to avoid starting from an ethical position opposing these things and, instead, allows us to critique them and understand their genesis in a way that allows for new configurations to emerge. Finally, I suggested a new type of relationship – performative – where the need to 're-present' is bypassed, making us more accountable for the complexities and changes that anarchists encounter.

## Notes

1. The choice of this term comes from J. L. Austin's speech act theory, rather than the work of Judith Butler. Though her use popularised the term, this chapter develops a different meaning which will be expanded upon later.
2. I use this term as it has been most commonly adopted. I include the poststructuralist anarchism of Todd May here. For more on this rupture, see Kuhn (2009) and Antliff (2011).
3. For the origins of postanarchism see Adams (2003).
4. Postanarchist theorists have been criticised for their reductive and oversimplified presentation of 'classical' anarchism. This is not treated here but is well covered in Franks (2007), Kinna, (2007) and Cohn and Wilbur (2003).
5. See, for example, Day (2005), Rousselle and Evren (2001) and Cohn (2006).
6. It has been noted that the normative theory May proposes is not congruent with the poststructuralist epistemological theories he draws it from. For a more extensive outline of this critique, see Jun (2012).
7. See, for example, Cohn (2006).
8. The classic Cartesian divide of immaterial mind and material body.
9. Would that include rejecting language? Art? Fighting for animal rights?
10. The triad of the unparticipated, the participated and participant is what produces a hierarchy on the basis of proximity with the 'original'.
11. For a summary of this argument, see Foucault (1976).
12. For discussion of this, see Swann (2010).
13. For an excellent critical discussion, see Houle (2014).
14. Spinoza (1996), Ethics, III, P9 Schol.
15. See, for example, Tipu's Tiger (2015), Gorrion and Celeste (2012), Williams (2014) and CrimethInc. (n.d.).
16. Due to space constraints, I am unable to present a full treatment of this term as an analytic concept. For relevant debates, see Gelderloos (2010), Escalating Identity (2012), sasha k (2009) and CrimethInc. (2014).

## References

Adams, J. (2003), 'Postanarchism in a Nutshell', *The Anarchist Library*, https://theanarchistlibrary.org/library/jason-adams-postanarchism-in-a-nutshell   (last accessed 13 August 2018).

Amster, R., DeLeon, A., Fernandez, L., Nocella, A. J., and Shannon, D. (eds) (2009), *Contemporary Anarchist Studies: An Introductory Anthology of Anarchy in the Academy*, London and New York: Routledge.

Antliff, A. (2011), 'Anarchy, Power and Post-structuralism', in D. Rousselle and S. Evren (eds), *Post-Anarchism: A Reader*, London and New York: Pluto Press.

Bryant, L. (2008), *Difference and Givenness: Deleuze's Transcendental Empiricism and Ontology of Difference*, Evanston: Northwestern University Press.

Bryant, L. (2011), *The Democracy of Objects*, Michigan: Open Humanities Press.

Cohn, J. (2006), *Anarchism and the Crisis of Representation: Hermeneutics, Aesthetics, Politics*, Selinsgrove: Susquehanna University Press.

Cohn, J. and S. Wilbur (2003), 'What's Wrong with Postanarchism?', *Institute for Anarchist Studies* 31, https://theanarchistlibrary.org/library/jesse-cohn-and-shawn-wilbur-what-s-wrong-with-postanarchism (last accessed 13 August 2018).

Colebrook, C. (2000), 'Questioning Representation', *Substance*, 2(92): 47–67.

CrimethInc. (n.d.), 'Accounting for Ourselves', *CrimethInc.*, https://theanarchistlibrary.org/library/crimethinc-pfm-accounting-for-ourselves (last accessed 13 August 2018).

CrimethInc. (2014), 'Ain't No PC Gonna Fix it Baby', *CrimethInc.*, https://theanarchistlibrary.org/library/crimethinc-anonymous-ain-t-no-pc-gonna-fix-it-baby (last accessed13 August 2018).

Critchley, S. (2007), *Infinitely Demanding: Ethics of Commitment, Politics of Resistance*, London: Verso.

Day, R. (2005), *Gramsci Is Dead: Anarchist Currents in the Newest Social Movements*, London and New York: Pluto Press.

Deleuze, G. (2004), *Difference and Repetition*, trans. P. Patton, New York: Continuum International.

Deleuze, G. and F. Guattari (2013), *A Thousand Plateaus: Capitalism and Schizophrenia*, trans. B. Massumi, London: Bloomsbury.

Doel, M. (2010), 'Representation and Difference', in B. Anderson (ed.), *Taking Place: Non-Representational Theories and Geography*, Farnham: Ashgate, pp. 117–30.

Escalating Identity (2012), 'Who is Oakland', *The Anarchist Library*, https://theanarchistlibrary.org/library/escalating-identity-who-is-oakland (last accessed 13 August 2018).

Foucault, M. (1976), 'The Political Function of the Intellectual', *Radical Philosophy*, 16, https://www.radicalphilosophy.com/article/the-political-function-of-the-intellectual (last accessed 13 August 2018).

Franks, B. (2007), 'Postanarchism: A Critical Assessment', *Journal of Political Ideologies*, 2(12): 127–45.

Gelderloos, P. (2010), 'Lines in Sand', *The Anarchist Library*, https://theanarchistlibrary.org/library/peter-gelderloos-lines-in-sand (last accessed 13 August 2018).

Gorrion, A. and A. Celeste (2012), 'The Broken Teapot', *The Anarchist Library*, https://theanarchistlibrary.org/library/anonymous-the-broken-teapot (last accessed 13 August 2018).

Houle, K. (2014), *Responsibility, Complexity, and Abortion*, Lanham, MD: Lexington Books.

Indigenous Action Media (2015), 'Dangerous Allies', in C. Millstein (ed.), *Taking Sides*, Edinburgh: AK Press, pp. 85–96.

Invisible Committee (2015), *To Our Friends*, London: MIT Press.

Jun, N. (2012), *Anarchism and Political Modernity*, London: Continuum.

Kant, I. (1959) [1785], *Foundations of the Metaphysics of Morals*, Indianapolis: Bobbs-Merrill.

Kay, J. (2006), 'Intellectuals and Power: A Conversation between Michel Foucault and Gilles Deleuze', *Libcom*, http://libcom.org/library/intellectuals-power-a-conversation-between-michel-foucault-and-gilles-deleuze (last accessed 13 August 2018).

Kinna, R. (2007), 'Fields of Vision: Kropotkin and Revolutionary Change', *Substance*, 2(36): 67–86.

Kuhn, G. (2009), 'Anarchism, Postmodernity, and Poststructuralism', in R. Amster, A. DeLeon, L. A. Fernandez, A. J. Nocella II and D. Shannon (eds), *Contemporary Anarchist Studies: An Introductory Anthology of Anarchy in the Academy*, London and New York: Routledge, pp. 18–25.

May, T. (1994), *The Political Philosophy of Poststructuralist Anarchism*, University Park: Pennsylvania State University Press.

May, T. (1995), *The Moral Theory of Poststructuralism*, University Park: Pennsylvania State University Press.

Newman, S. (2001), *From Bakunin to Lacan: Antiauthoritarianism and the Dislocation of Power*, Lanham, MD: Lexington Books.

Newman, S. (2010), *Politics of Postanarchism*, Edinburgh: Edinburgh University Press.

Popke, E. J. (2006), 'Geography and Ethics: Everyday Mediations through Care and Consumption', *Progress in Human Geography*, 4(30): 504–12.

Rousselle, D. and S. Evren (2001), *Post-Anarchism: A Reader*, London and New York: Pluto Press.

sasha k (2009), '"Activism" and "Anarcho-Purism"', *The Anarchist Library*, https://theanarchistlibrary.org/library/sasha-k-activism-and-anarcho-purism (last accessed 13 August 2018).

Spinoza, B. (1996) [1677], *Ethics*, London: Penguin Books.

Swann, T. (2010), 'Can Franks' Practical Anarchism Avoid Moral Relativism?', *The Anarchist Library*, https://theanarchistlibrary.org/library/thomas-swann-can-franks-practical-anarchism-avoid-moral-relativism (last accessed 13 August 2018).

Tipu's Tiger (2015), 'Dangerous Allies', in C. Millstein (ed.), *Taking Sides*, Edinburgh: AK Press, pp. 48–63.

Volcano, A. (2013), 'Police at the Borders', in C. B. Daring (ed.), *Queering Anarchism*, Edinburgh: AK Press, pp. 33–43.

Williams, K. (2014), 'The Politics of Denunciation', *The Anarchist Library*, https://theanarchistlibrary.org/library/kristian-williams-the-politics-of-denunciation (last accessed 13 August 2018).

# Chapter 7

# Deleuze and Stirner: Ties, Tensions and Rifts

## Elmo Feiten

### An Encounter That Never Happened: Stirner and Deleuze

When investigating the relationship between Deleuze and anarchism, the thought of Max Stirner has special relevance. More so perhaps than any other anarchist critique of the State, Stirner's extreme radicalism critiques the way that State power is embedded in our subjectivity. He shows how the elevation of symbolic language from a tool to an ideal makes us internalise our own oppression so that it systematically takes hold of our desires. Stirner's thought resonates strongly with Deleuze and Guattari's *Anti-Oedipus*, the book which perhaps best encapsulates the spirit of May '68, the fierce and joyous uprising that marked a decisive break not just with Marxist accounts of revolution centred on the party, but also with a whole way of thinking and living that was complicit in oppression (Buchanan 2008: 1–19). May '68 is also a primary reference point for histories of postanarchism, an umbrella term for those strains in twentieth-century anarchist thought strongly influenced by predominantly French postmodern and poststructuralist theory (Evren 2011: 5–7). It is the anti-essentialism of these anarchist positions and their broadened understanding of how domination works in different social contexts that underpins both their affinity for the thought of Gilles Deleuze and the potential of a renewed reception of Stirner's thought in this contemporary context.

The reception of Stirner's thought has been fraught with strong emotional reactions and persistent misreadings. Stirner is considered anathema in some intellectual contexts and many thinkers have only admitted partially, or in private, the extent to which Stirner's thought has influenced them (Laska 1996: 7–9). The question of whether Stirner can be considered an anarchist produces a wide range of positions, from those who see him as a founding figure of anarchism to those who firmly reject his admission to even a broad anarchist tradition (Feiten 2013: 117–20). Whether or not he has influenced poststructuralist thought is equally contentious. While the general scholarly view seems to be that poststructuralists have only a very cursory knowledge of Stirner, Wolfgang Essbach claims that Henri Arvon – who pointed out Stirner's significant role in the genesis of historical materialism – is also responsible for Stirner's influence on poststructuralism: 'The reading of Stirner inspired by Arvon clearly left its mark on Foucault, Deleuze and Derrida. Arvon contributed substantially to the anti-totalitarian profile of these thinkers' (Essbach 2012, own translation). This is a curious statement because it makes an extraordinary claim in an offhand fashion and provides no further source or argument. In keeping with this tradition of disagreement and confusion, Stirner has also been used in vastly different ways in the debates around postanarchism. For instance, Stirner has been read as an anarchist in order to argue against the idea that poststructuralism has significant affinities with anarchism, with Simon Choat pointing out that Deleuze rejects Stirner as a dialectician and a nihilist (Choat 2010: 60–1). In one of the first postanarchist texts, published in 1993, Andrew Koch proceeds in the opposite direction, treating Stirner as both an anarchist and a precursor to poststructuralism. Koch contrasts the ontological perspective of nineteenth-century anarchists with an epistemological defense of anarchism that he bases on the theories of Stirner, Nietzsche and poststructuralism. His depiction of Stirner correctly identifies key aspects of this thought but also introduces certain inaccuracies and ambiguities that prevent an accurate assessment of Stirner's relation to poststructuralism:

> Stirner argued that the concept of self represents a link between culture and institutionalized power. If the self cannot validate its understanding through the belief in transcendent truth, and if social discourse consists of metaphors, traces of reified metaphysics, and power, then the self has only the self through which to validate being. As a result, Stirner embraced the concept of the ego. (Koch 2011: 38)

In Koch's account, the breakdown of symbolic power is presented as a loss in that the self cannot continue as the subject into which it has been made and is left with itself only. This stands in contrast to Stirner's fundamentally joyous and affirmative act of self-empowerment against the rule of symbolic thought, when he describes how 'a jubilant whoop throws off year-long burdens' (Stirner 1995: 133). We will encounter this misjudgement of temperament again in Deleuze's reading of Stirner. The more important mistake in Koch's reading is when he identifies 'the concept of the ego' as central to Stirner's thought. Stirner's term 'ego' (or the better translation of the German *der Einzige*, 'unique one') is not merely unrelated to the Freudian concept of the ego, but is not a concept in the way we usually understand concepts to operate. Rather, the ego is a purely referential phrase used to point at the material existence of individual human beings, devoid of any descriptive content. According to Koch, Stirner's thought is ultimately incompatible with poststructuralism's denial 'that any concept of self can be independent of language' (Koch 2011: 39). Koch misses the entire point of Stirner's term, which lies in the fact that it is not a concept. Stirner's thought is thus introduced into postanarchism with a misunderstanding.

Many postanarchist works do not mention Stirner at all, even if the political philosophy they describe is highly reminiscent of Stirner's thought. One example is Gabriel Kuhn's excellent exposition of a strongly Deleuzian postanarchism in *Tier-Werden, Schwarz-Werden, Frau-Werden* [Becoming-Animal, Becoming-Black, Becoming-Woman] (2005). Although Kuhn himself is critical of the label 'postanarchism', he sees strong potential for the strengthening of anarchist struggles through poststructuralist theory. One aspect of this potential is what he identifies as a 'critique of the subject that liberates us from the need to conform to fixed identities and opens a never-ending playground to create and permanently recreate subjectivities in self-determined processes' (Kuhn 2009). Even though this is a perfect summary of Stirner's critique of humanism and other forms of essentialism, Kuhn does not reference Stirner in his combination of anarchist and poststructuralist theory. By following up on this unexplored similarity, we might gain a new understanding of the history of radical anti-essentialism and its relevance for anarchist thought and practice.

Perhaps the most influential voice on Stirner within postanarchism is that of Saul Newman. Newman's work deserves much credit for the popularisation of postanarchism in general and for developing original contextual readings of Stirner, whom he variably interprets as either a precursor to poststructuralism or an anarchist (Newman 2001a, 2001b, 2001c, 2011). His reading of the relationship between Deleuze and Stirner is of specific relevance (Newman 2001c).

Newman's text is an example of what could provocatively be called the founding myth of postanarchism: the idea that classical nineteenth-century anarchism works with a fixed idea of human nature that is overcome by the anti-essentialism of poststructuralist thought. According to Newman, 'Stirner's work is a rejection of the idea of an essential human subjectivity, a human essence that is untainted by power', whereby it constitutes, together with Deleuze's thought, 'a new theoretical terrain beyond classical anarchism' (Newman 2001c). Newman correctly points out many parallels between the two thinkers in their views on power, desire, revolution and the State. Despite his stated aim 'not to ignore the differences between them, but on the contrary, to show how these differences resonate together', Newman ends up focusing on the similarities. This is quite understandable since he writes on a completely new topic and highlighting the parallels serves to justify the validity of the whole venture. However, merely pointing out those points where Deleuze and Stirner agree does not give us any new theoretical tools. Only if we find the points at which the comparison produces problems, forcing us to make decisions and develop new ideas, can we actually gain new insights and tools for radical thought. This is one of the primary motivations for the present analysis, but it can only be successful if it is based on a nuanced understanding of Stirner's thought.

Stirner wrote only one book, *The Ego and Its Own* (1995), as well as a series of essays. The most important of these is *Stirner's Critics* (2012), in which he deals with the criticism levelled at his book by his contemporaries. While Stirner's presentation of his thought in *The Ego and Its Own* is an attempt to free himself from the Hegelian tradition, his clarifications in *Stirner's Critics* are far clearer. The first enunciation of Stirner's egoism seems to oscillate between an ironic deconstruction of his contemporaries' theories and the exposition of his own position, which uses terms like 'egoism' and 'property' with drastically altered meanings and employs purely referential terms to point at that which exists prior to language. This has led to a continuous stream of misreadings, from the time of publication of *The Ego and Its Own* to the present day. In contrast, Stirner's reply to his earliest adversaries in *Stirner's Critics* is more direct and uses clear language to explain the misreadings of his book by Szeliga, Hess and Feuerbach. Many lingering misunderstandings about Stirner could be rectified by reading *Stirner's Critics*. By taking its significance into account, we are able to progress beyond the current state of research on the relationship between Deleuze and Stirner.

## Deleuze's (Mis)Reading of Stirner in *Nietzsche and Philosophy*

While Deleuze recognises Stirner's work in *Nietzsche and Philosophy* (1983), he ultimately rejects Stirner's position. It appears that Deleuze actively caulks his reading of Nietzsche against Stirner's impetus by identifying Stirner as a Hegelian dialectician and a nihilist. Deleuze's assessment of Stirner goes hand in hand with his emphasis on the anti-Hegelian character of Nietzsche's thought. He argues that it is likely that Nietzsche 'had a profound knowledge of the Hegelian movement, from Hegel to Stirner himself' and that we can only understand the core concepts of Nietzsche if we understand against whom they are directed (Deleuze 1983: 162). These opponents of Nietzsche he identifies as Hegel, Feuerbach and Stirner (162). Deleuze sees Stirner as the thinker who completes the Hegelian dialectic, as the end point of Hegelian philosophy:

> It is clear that Stirner plays the revelatory role in all this. It is he who pushes the dialectic to its final consequences, showing what its motor and end result are. But precisely because Stirner still thinks like a dialectician, because he does not extricate himself from the categories of property, alienation and its suppression, he throws himself into the nothingness which he hollows out beneath the steps of the dialectic. (1983: 163)

The reading of Stirner as the final Hegelian has been advanced by Lawrence Stepelevich (1985) and attacked by Andrew Koch (1997). Interestingly, Koch's argument rests solely on *The Ego and Its Own* and does not refer to *Stirner's Critics* at all. When we take into account Stirner's own clarifications, the anti-Hegelian impetus of his work is quite clear both theoretically and rhetorically. One of his most well-known terms, the 'spook', is after all a mockery of Hegel's spirit. Spooks, according to Stirner, are concepts that we mistakenly believe to have authority over us and to which we subjugate our desires and our pursuit of happiness, internalizing our own oppression (see Stirner 1995: 40–1). In a critique of religious, humanist and liberal ideologies, Stirner describes how spooks haunt us and identifies Feuerbach's move from Christianity to anthropology not as a liberation, but as a refinement of symbolic domination: 'The most oppressive spook is man' (1995: 69). The anti-Hegelian make-up of Stirner's thought becomes even more obvious in his explanation of the ego or unique one, one of the very central elements of his work:

> The unique, however, has no content; it is indeterminacy in itself; only *through you* does it acquire content and determination. There is no conceptual development of the unique, one cannot build a philosophical system with it as a 'principle', the way one can with being, with thought, with the I. Rather it puts an end to *all conceptual development*. Anyone who considers it a principle, thinks that he can treat it philosophically or theoretically and inevitably takes useless potshots against it. Being, thought, the I, are only

*undetermined* concepts, which receive their determinateness only through other concepts, i.e., through conceptual development.

The unique, on the other hand, is a concept *that lacks determination* and cannot be made determinate by other concepts or receive a 'nearer content'; it is not the 'principle of a series of concepts', but a word or concept that, as word or concept, is not capable of any development. (Stirner 2012: 56)

Stirner's central term is not developed via the Hegelian method but is in fact an empty phrase, empty of conceptual content so as to preserve the full referential function. It is not derived from other concepts through the Hegelian method and no other concepts can, as a result, be derived from it. As a term, 'the unique' not only functions apart from the specifically dialectical logic of Hegelian philosophy, but in fact breaks with the entire idea that a word can represent its meaning, with representational thought as such: 'What Stirner *says* is a word, a thought, a concept; what he *means* is neither a word, nor a thought, nor a concept. What he says is not the meaning, and what he means cannot be said' (Stirner 2012: 55).

While Deleuze reads Stirner as the final Hegelian dialectician, his reading of Nietzsche is often quite close to Stirner's thought. This makes his claim that '[n]either ego nor man is unique' (Deleuze 1983: 163) quite puzzling. Although this almost seems like a pun on the different translations of Stirner's *Einziger* as 'ego' and 'unique', the context suggests that it is not. Thus, when Deleuze highlights how Nietzsche's Overman differs from Feuerbach's species being and Stirner's ego, he explains that '[t]ransvaluing is opposed to current values but also to dialectical pseudo-transformation' (1983: 163). The same is true of Stirner's position – the insurrection of the unique one against the logic of representation. This is not to suggest that there are no differences between Nietzsche and Stirner, but the way in which they are presented by Deleuze is misleading.

Deleuze seems to be intent on showing that Stirner had no influence on Nietzsche and that the latter rejected the former's thought. The question of a possible influence of Stirner on Nietzsche has in fact been discussed at length, if not necessarily in detail, since the 1890s (Laska 2002). Most commentators who deny Stirner's influence on Nietzsche seem to either argue that Nietzsche did not know Stirner's work or suggest that he did not find it worth commenting on. Deleuze follows a different route; after arguing that Nietzsche (who never mentioned Stirner in writing) was probably aware of his work, he clarifies: 'The philosophical learning of an author is not assessed by numbers of quotations, nor by the always fanciful and conjectural check lists of libraries, but by the apologetic or polemical directions of his work itself' (Deleuze 1983: 162). Deleuze's reading is that Stirner played a significant role in Nietzsche's thought, but only as an adversary against whom Nietzsche's concepts were developed. If this holds true, an analysis of how exactly Nietzsche's thought counters Stirner's would be very insightful. Since Deleuze includes Stirner in his account of how Nietzsche overcomes various kinds of nihilism, we should read this account carefully and critically.

The problem with a word such as 'nihilist' is, of course, that it is attached to any number of different conceptions, with meanings that sometimes overlap or are complementary and sometimes disjunctive or even contradictory. This is not a problem in *Nietzsche and Philosophy*. In the chapter 'The Overman: Against the Dialectic', Deleuze provides us with a systematic account of consecutive modes of nihilism that Nietzsche overcomes (Deleuze 1983: 147). In accordance with his account of Stirner as the final dialectician, we would expect this development of nihilism to culminate in the 'extreme nihilism' of Stirner (1983: 162). However, the picture we get is quite different: 'negative nihilism is replaced by reactive nihilism, reactive nihilism ends in passive nihilism' (151). In negative nihilism life is 'depreciated from the height of higher values', 'God, essence, the good, truth' (148, 147). Reactive nihilism results in a 'pessimism of weakness' because it 'denies God, the good and even truth', leaving behind 'a depreciated life which now continues in a world without values, stripped of meaning and purpose' (148). And where reactive nihilism is led by a 'will to nothingness', in passive nihilism the reactive forces break with will completely, 'fading away passively rather than being led from outside' (148–9). This is Deleuze's account of Nietzsche's analysis of nihilism, which he links to a historical sequence of different systems of thought: 'Negative, reactive and passive nihilism: for Nietzsche one and the same history is marked out by Judaism, Christianity, the reformation, free thought, democratic and socialist ideology' (152). Two things are immediately obvious: first, the historical progression of thought is practically identical to that which Stirner attacks at length in *The Ego and Its Own*, the second section of which is structured into the ancients, the moderns and the free, who in turn are differentiated into political, social and humane liberalism (Stirner 1995: vii); second, the 'extreme nihilism' that is attributed to Stirner and allegedly overcome by Nietzsche does not figure in this account at all (Deleuze 1983: 162).

Ronald Hinner has pointed out several ways in which Stirner's perspective anticipates Deleuze's account of Nietzsche's thought (Hinner

2013: 17–23). One of these is the central role of enjoyment and affirmation. For instance, Deleuze describes the difference between Nietzsche's method and dialectics: 'For the speculative element of negation, opposition or contradiction, Nietzsche substitutes the practical element of difference, the object of affirmation and enjoyment. It is in this sense that there is a Nietzschean empiricism' (Deleuze 1983: 9), and Hinner (2013: 17) sees this mirrored in Stirner's statement that 'uncouth jubilation still has the potential, if necessary, to become critical jubilation, an egoistic critique' (Stirner 2012: 72). According to Hinner, we find in Stirner's egoism the radical elaboration of '[i]rresponsibility – Nietzsche's most noble and beautiful secret' (Deleuze 1983: 21). This assessment seems quite accurate considering how much energy Stirner devotes to attacking what Deleuze describes as the two elements of responsibility, as well as central elements of 'our way of thinking and interpreting existence in general'; that is, 'ressentiment (it's your fault) and bad conscience (it's my fault)' (21). Two examples of this are Stirner's critique of resentment in the category of the inhuman and his attack on self-renunciation and the suppression of one's libido in the passage on the young girl whose 'habit of renunciation cools the heat of [her] desire' (Stirner 1995: 59). Deleuze himself begins his systematic treatment of nihilism thus:

> In the word nihilism nihil does not signify non-being but primarily a value of nil. Life takes on a value of nil insofar as it is denied and depreciated. Depreciation always presupposes a fiction: it is by means of fiction that one falsifies and depreciates, it is by means of fiction that something is opposed to life. (1983: 147)

To anyone who has read Stirner it is clear that he does not depreciate life but, on the contrary, radically affirms it. It is equally clear that he does not achieve this by means of fiction and falsification but, conversely, by destroying the fiction of the higher value of spooks. Unlike Nietzsche, Stirner does not require the metaphysics of the eternal return in order to overcome nihilism. According to this description, Stirner's thought cannot qualify as nihilism. On the contrary, Stirner fights against idealism, and the ideologies that succeed it, on the grounds that they are fictions which denigrate the lives of those who cannot see them as such.

Deleuze sees Stirner as a Hegelian who shows that the inevitable result of the dialectic is 'the ego which is nothing' (Deleuze 1983: 162). Against this, Stirner asserts: 'I am not nothing in the sense of emptiness, but I am the creative nothing' (Stirner 1995: 7). What this creative nothing is may become clearer when we compare Stirner's thought to Deleuze and Guattari's *Anti-Oedipus*.

## The Unique One and the Anti-Oedipus

We have seen that Deleuze rejects Stirner's thought by including it in the successive forms of nihilism overcome by Nietzsche. And yet Stirner does not seem to quite fit into this account of nihilism. By comparing several aspects of Deleuze and Guattari's *Anti-Oedipus* to Stirner's work, I attempt to show that these two critiques of voluntary servitude share some of their relevance for anarchist thought, but also highlight potential limits to a combination of their perspectives. The analysis focuses on the use of Nietzsche and Marx as sources in *Anti-Oedipus*, on the identification of domination in different social contexts, as well as on the concepts of 'desiring-production' and 'schizoanalysis'.

We have seen that Deleuze's rejection of Stirner is based on a misreading. Just as many of the points Deleuze takes up from Nietzsche in his monograph were originally made by Stirner, this reference to Nietzsche in *Anti-Oedipus* echoes one of Stirner's core points:

> God dead or not dead, the father dead or not dead, it amounts to the same thing, since the same psychic repression (*refoulement*) and the same social repression (repression) continue unabated, here in the name of God or a living father, there in the name of man or the dead father. (Deleuze and Guattari 1983: 106)

Diagnosing a continuity of repression between religion and humanism, between God and man, is a central aspect of Stirner's book. In his criticism of Feuerbach's movement from Christianity to anthropology, he asks: 'Who is his God? Man with a capital M! What is the divine? The human!' (Stirner 1995: 55). Stirner identifies this transition as a 'change of masters' and humanism as 'nothing more or less than a new – religion' (55). However, he also sees a difference between the successive subjugation to God and to man in that the relation of domination is internalized by the subject: 'To expel God from his heaven and to rob him of his "transcendence" cannot yet support a claim of complete victory, if therein he is only chased into the human breast and gifted with indelible immanence' (1995: 47). It is this criticism of Feuerbach's humanism as a continuation of repression that prompted Marx to break with Feuerbach as well and develop historical materialism.

The debate among the Young Hegelians escalated in the 1840s, with mutual critiques becoming more aggressive and acidic, until reaching a point where any further communication became impossible once the issue of sexuality was broached (Essbach 1982). Stirner refuses to accept sexuality as the truth of the subject and Feuerbach, Marx and Engels use precisely this refusal to be subjected to the 'Oedipal triangle, father-mother-me' (Deleuze and Guattari 1983: 351) to critique him. Stirner's position on desire and sexuality is radically emancipatory, attacking the societal injunctions against masturbation, incest and the compulsion of heterosexual monogamy in the form of the institution of marriage. Against this, Marx and Engels take a classical position of sexual repression and heteronormativity. They ridicule Stirner for his lack of focus on genital intercourse and reproduction (Essbach 1982: 342). When they link the unique one's squandering of his sexual energy on non-procreative joy to the extinction of the human race, they use the issue of biological reproduction to reproduce across generations the normative relation in which living beings are made subservient to the abstraction of the species being. This resonates to some degree with the position of the psychoanalysts criticized in this passage of *Anti-Oedipus*:

> But psychoanalysts are bent on producing man abstractly, that is to say ideologically, for culture. It is Oedipus who produces man in this fashion, and who gives a structure to the false movement of infinite progression and regression: your father, and your father's father, a snowball gathering speed. (Deleuze and Guattari 1983: 105)

While Stirner pioneered some aspects of the critique which Deleuze and Guattari take from Nietzsche, the situation with Marx is in some sense reversed. Marx and Engels champion a conservative perspective against Stirner's attempt to free the expression of desire from socially established norms and ideological prescriptions.

Newman points out the similarities between the notion of desire in *Anti-Oedipus* and Stirner's concept of insurrection (Newman 2001c). Indeed, when Deleuze and Guattari write that 'desire is revolutionary in its essence . . . and no society can tolerate a position of real desire without its structures of exploitation, servitude, and hierarchy being compromised', the Stirnerian translation would be to say that desire is insurrectionary. Thus, we find a parallel here with Stirner who derives his enmity towards the State from the fact that the expression of his desire is incompatible with morality, whereas the State 'cannot last without morality, and must insist on morality' (Deleuze and Guattari 1983: 120; Stirner 1995: 161). Their analyses of the failure of past revolutions are also fundamentally similar:

> That is why, when subjects, individuals, or groups act manifestly counter to their class interests – when they rally to the interests and ideals of a class that their own objective situation should lead them to combat – it is not enough to say: they were fooled, the masses have been fooled. It is not an

ideological problem, a problem of failing to recognize, or of being subject to, an illusion. It is a problem of desire, and desire is part of the infrastructure. (Deleuze and Guattari 1983: 118)

Or in Stirner's words, '[a] revolution certainly does not bring on the end if an insurrection is not consummated first' (Stirner 1995: 281). Not only are the critiques of classical notions of revolution in *Anti-Oedipus* and Stirner very similar, but even the strategy of attack is the same: aim not for the structure, but for its foundation. 'Oedipus disintegrates because its very conditions have disintegrated' and the insurrection 'is not a fight against the established, since, if it prospers, the established collapses of itself' (Deleuze and Guattari 1983: 105; Stirner 1995: 280).

Stirner sees the domination of a nominally secularised morality at work not just through State power, but throughout social institutions like marriage, schools and hospitals, which Mark Seem in the introduction to *Anti-Oedipus* calls 'oedipalized territorialities' (Seem 1983: xvii). Stirner describes how the State marks everyone who does not attempt to conform to the normative ideal of humanity as inhuman, and 'it locks him up, or transforms him from an inhabitant of the state into an inhabitant of the prison (inhabitant of the lunatic asylum or hospital, according to communism)' (Stirner 1995: 159). He also sees a connection between the State, the family and the institution of marriage: 'Family concerns are altogether state concerns' and individuals 'are members of a family in the full sense only when they make the persistence of the family their task' (1995: 200, 195). The family and the State form a social structure which recruits individuals for its reproduction by making them conform to its ideals, and Stirner criticises Feuerbach for defending the basic logic of this mechanism in his assertion that '[m]arriage is sacred' (quoted in Stirner 1995: 55). The principle of essentialism produces subjects according to normative ideals that are perpetually at odds with their own desires and diverts their energy towards the maintenance of this symbolic authority. Another key institution in this process, according to Stirner, is the school: 'the court has the object of forcing people to justice, the school that of forcing them to mental culture' (1995: 200). The young are 'driven through school to learn the old song' and 'stuffed with imparted feelings' until 'they twitter like the old' (62). According to Stirner, the way in which institutions exert power over individuals based on their ability to administrate the dominant ideological truths is also the mode in which the violence of authoritarian revolutionary forces is meted out: 'Because the revolutionary priests or schoolmasters served *man*, they cut off the heads of *men*' (74). This resonates with Foucault, who lists as one of the key adversaries of *Anti-Oedipus* the '[b]ureau-crats of the revolution and civil servants of Truth' (Foucault 1983: xii).

When comparing Stirner, who focuses so much on self-empowerment, with Deleuze and Guattari, we should at least consider the claim from *A Thousand Plateaus* that 'the self is only a threshold, a door, a becoming between two multiplicities' (Deleuze and Guattari 1987: 249). On one hand, we can point out Stirner's clarification that he is not talking about an abstract, fixed subjectivity but 'only the self-dissolving ego, the never-being ego, the – finite ego is really I' (Stirner 1995: 163). Stirner's ego is very close to Deleuze and Guattari's idea of becoming. On the other hand, this points at a tension in our understanding of the term desiring-production that needs to be addressed: in some passages of *Anti-Oedipus* desiring-production seems to be a process in the subsymbolic, presubjective regions of the psyche that is hampered by fixed identities and representations, which seek to reroute its energies and flows. This notion of desiring-production is fully compatible with Stirner's account of the creative nothingness (which is a nothingness only at the symbolic level, the level of philosophical abstraction on which Stirner is articulating his theory of what lies below – desiring-production). In other passages, desiring-production seems to be closer to something like a basic life force that suffuses everything (freely travelling between individual psyches). This latter reading is supported by Marc Roberts, who reminds us that Deleuze explicitly identifies desire with Nietzsche's will to power in *Dialogues II* (Roberts 2007: 116). It is hard to see how Stirner's notion of creative nothingness could be reconciled with a '"fundamental principle" of ontology ... which "underlies" the world itself and all of existence, and which operates "through" us as human beings' (Nietzsche quoted in Roberts 2007: 116). This is not necessarily because it is incorrect (although the suspicion does arise when we note how the will to power version of desiring-production seems to fulfil a similar ontological function as Reich's 'orgone'), but because any a priori description we make of our desires (and this is what desiring-production as a fundamental principle seems to result in) clouds our own access to them. One might say that a notion of desiring-production that is modelled on Nietzsche's intentional invention of a 'new ideal' is in danger of overcoding the psyche (Deleuze 1983: 21). On the one hand, such a fundamental principle seems to counter the radical openness which Stirner explores after getting rid of idealist notions of essence. On the other, this ontological aspect of desiring-production seems to describe a process in the world from which the individual perspectives of private selves and their experiences arise as secondary effects, whereas Stirner treats the privileged access of a self to the particular experiential world that it inhabits as primary. 'Does Feuerbach live in a world other than *his own*? Does he perhaps live in Hess's world, in Szeliga's world, in Stirner's world?' (Stirner 2012: 63). According to Stirner, 'like Feuerbach, no one lives in any other world than his own' (63). This points towards thorny issues at the interface of ontology and epistemology, and addressing them in detail might furnish anarchist thought with new ways of conceptualising how we live in the world.

While the notion of desiring-production does not have a direct equivalent in Stirner's work, whose terms at any rate do not translate easily into Deleuzian concepts, the practices that result from the two approaches are very much alike. Marc Roberts's summary of schizo-analysis illustrates this:

> schizoanalysis can be understood as a practice that seeks to 'destroy' all forms of representation in order to liberate and affirm the process of desiring-production. Thus, its 'negative' or 'destructive' task demands the undoing of 'the representative territorialities and reterritorializations through which a subject passes in his individual history. For there are several layers, several planes of resistance that come from within or are imposed from without' ... Against this, schizoanalysis engages in the on-going 'destruction' of all territorialities, undoing any notion of a fixed identity, essential characteristics, and fundamental or authentic being in order to affirm and 'work with' the productive process of becoming. (2007: 124)

In some ways, the process of schizoanalysis is remarkably similar to the way Stirner describes the self-empowerment of the conscious egoists. Other aspects, such as the central role of the body in this process of shedding fixed identities, are specific to Stirner: 'a stretching of the limbs shakes off the torment of thoughts' (Stirner 1995: 133). Either through intellectual analysis or sheer somatic health and strength, the egoists throw off all notions of identity or essence that constrain the free expression of their desire. Instead of developing a notion of authentic self or being, Stirner writes: 'I do not presuppose myself, because I am every moment just positing or creating myself' (1995: 135). It is this free and fluid play of creative selfhood that fosters an ability to react spontaneously to situations and enables the egoist's move towards the fulfillment of their needs and desires in the context of the present.

Stirner's thought offers an opportunity for critiquing the often pathological relationship we have to ourselves, as well as others – human and non-human. Without a doubt, there are no ready-made solutions to be found in Stirner's work, but many promising avenues for critique and self-empowerment. In many ways, his attacks on voluntary servitude resonate with the work of Deleuze and Guattari, but in other ways their perspectives appear to be at odds. Yet perhaps it is precisely this tension between the similarities and differences that might drive us towards the creation of new ways of living and thinking. Hopefully, further work on the relationship between these two modes of thought on the margins of anarchism can bring us closer to a joyous, spontaneous and flowing contact with our surroundings. Maybe it is possible to live and think unencumbered by symbolic representations that predetermine the meaning of any situation and force us to perform a script with a meagre selection of choices.

## Conclusion

The relation between Deleuze and Stirner is anything but obvious. It is deeply intertwined with the troubled history of the reception of Stirner's work as well as with Deleuze's readings of Nietzsche and Marx, both of whom have their own highly controversial relationship to Stirner's thought (Bernd Laska has written extensively and with extraordinary erudition on this topic). My analysis of *Nietzsche and Philosophy* shows that Deleuze's reading of Stirner as a dialectician and a nihilist fails to account for the radicality of his thought. The discussion of *Anti-Oedipus* demonstrates the very close ties between the two thinkers, as well as the tensions and rifts between Deleuze and Stirner, and demonstrates, furthermore, that our understanding of this relationship is only just beginning to unfold.

Anarchism is sometimes reduced to a fixation of resistance against State power in the narrow sense by its detractors. In contrast to this, the history of anarchist struggles shows a broad movement against domination in all social spheres. It is by analysing how State power operates through the subject in all these spheres, and by developing ways of resisting the symbolic order, that Deleuze and Stirner provide useful tools for these struggles. Beyond debates about the boundaries of anarchism and postanarchism, it is this possibility of developing more effective tools for resistance that makes further research on the relationship between Deleuze and Stirner a promising endeavour.

## References

Buchanan, I. (2008), *Deleuze and Guattari's Anti-Oedipus: A Reader's Guide*, London and New York: Continuum.
Choat, S. (2010), 'Postanarchism from a Marxist Perspective', *Anarchist Developments in Cultural Studies*, 1: 51–71.

Deleuze, G. (1983), *Nietzsche and Philosophy*, trans. H. Tomlinson, New York: Columbia University Press.

Deleuze, G. and F. Guattari (1983), *Anti-Oedipus: Capitalism and Schizophrenia*, trans. R. Hurley, M. Seem and H. R. Lame, Minneapolis: University of Minnesota Press.

Deleuze, G. and F. Guattari (1987), *A Thousand Plateaus: Capitalism and Schizophrenia*, trans. B. Massumi, Minneapolis: University of Minnesota Press.

Essbach, W. (1982), 'Sexualität und Gesellschaftstheorie', in W. Essbach, *Gegenzüge*, Frankfurt am Main: Materialis Verlag, pp. 322–36.

Essbach, W. (2012), 'Späte Gerechtigkeit für Sankt Max', *Frankfurter Allgemeine Zeitung*, 29 February 2012, p. 3.

Evren, S. (2011), 'Introduction: How New Anarchism Changed the World (of Opposition) after Seattle and Gave Birth to Post-Anarchism', in S. Evren and D. Rousselle (eds), *Post-Anarchism: A Reader*, London and New York: Pluto Press, pp. 1–19.

Feiten, T. E. (2013), 'Would the Real Max Stirner Please Stand Up?', *Anarchist Developments in Cultural Studies*, 1: 117–37.

Foucault, M. (1983), 'Preface', in G. Deleuze and F. Guattari, *Anti-Oedipus: Capitalism and Schizophrenia*, trans. R. Hurley, M. Seem and H. R. Lame, Minneapolis: University of Minnesota Press, pp. xi–xiv.

Hinner, R, (2013), 'Deleuze und der Nihilismus: Zur Sekundärverdrängung von Max Stirner', *Academia.edu*, https://www.academia.edu/3152489/Deleuze_und_der_Nihilismus._Zur_Sekund%C3%A4rverdr%C3%A4ngung_von_Max_Stirner (last accessed 13 August 2018).

Koch, A. M. (1997), 'Max Stirner: The Last Hegelian or the First Poststructuralist', *Anarchist Studies*, 5: 95–107.

Koch, A. M. (2011), 'Post-Structuralism and the Epistemological Basis of Anarchism', in S. Evren and D. Rousselle (eds), *Post-Anarchism: A Reader*, London and New York: Pluto Press, pp. 23–40.

Kuhn, G. (2005), *Tier-Werden, Schwarz-Werden, Frau-Werden: Eine Einführung in die Politische Philosophie des Poststrukturalismus*, Münster: Unrast Verlag.

Kuhn, G. (2009), 'Anarchism, Postmodernity, and Poststructuralism', in R. Amster, A. DeLeon, L. A. Fernandez, A. J. Nocella II and D. Shannon (eds), *Contemporary Anarchist Studies: An Introductory Anthology of Anarchy in the Academy*, London and New York: Routledge, pp. 18–25.

Laska, B. (1996), *Ein dauerhafter Dissident*, Nuremberg: LSR-Verlag.

Laska, B. (2002), 'Nietzsche's Initial Crisis', *LSR*, http://www.lsr-projekt.de/poly/ennietzsche.html (last accessed 13 August 2018).

Newman, S. (2001a), 'Spectres of Stirner: A Contemporary Critique of Ideology', *Journal of Political Ideologies*, 6(3): 309–30.

Newman, S. (2001b), *From Bakunin to Lacan: Anti-Authoritarianism and the Dislocation of Power*, Lanham, MD: Lexington Books.

Newman, S. (2001c), 'War on the State: Deleuze and Stirner's Anarchism', *The Anarchist Library*, https://theanarchistlibrary.org/library/saul-newman-war-on-the-state-stirner-and-deleuze-s-anarchism (last accessed 13 August 2018).

Newman, S. (2011), *The Politics of Postanarchism*, Edinburgh: Edinburgh University Press.

Roberts, M. (2007), 'Capitalism, Psychiatry, and Schizophrenia: A Critical Introduction to Deleuze and Guattari's *Anti-Oedipus*', *Nursing Philosophy*, 8(2): 114–27.

Seem, M. (1983), 'Introduction', in G. Deleuze and F. Guattari, *Anti-Oedipus: Capitalism and Schizophrenia*, trans. R. Hurley, M. Seem and H. R. Lame, Minneapolis: University of Minnesota Press, pp. xv–xiv.

Stepelevich, L. (1985), 'Max Stirner as Hegelian', *Journal of the History of Ideas*, 46(4): 597–614.

Stirner, M. (1995), *The Ego and Its Own*, Cambridge: Cambridge University Press.

Stirner, M. (2012), *Stirner's Critics*, trans. W. Landstreicher, Berkeley: LBC Press.

# Chapter 8

# Anarchy and Institution: A New Sadean Possibility

*Natascia Tosel*

> Sade often stresses the fact that the law can only be transcended toward an institutional model of anarchy. The fact that anarchy can only exist in the interval between two regimes based on law, abolishing the old to give birth to the new, does not prevent the divine interval, this vanishing instant, from testifying to its fundamental difference from all forms of the law. (Deleuze 1991a: 87)

In 1967 Gilles Deleuze wrote an important book, titled *Masochism: Coldness and Cruelty*. Most critics do not give the text much consideration, except for acknowledging the originality of Deleuze's reading of Sacher-Masoch. However, there is another important figure in this book, namely the Marquis de Sade, who 'is far from absent in the text: *Coldness and Cruelty* is bookended by detailed interpretations of Sade's novels' (Harris and Lauwaert 2015: 192). The principal aim of the book is to establish the incompatibility between the sadistic system of thought and the masochistic one. It is thus an attempt to critique the psychiatric (Krafft-Ebing 1939) and the psychoanalytic (Freud 1975) interpretations of sadomasochism. For Deleuze, it is impossible to unify Sade and Masoch, because he considers their 'pathologies', writing styles and theories very different from each other. However, the Deleuzian reading does not concern only the psychological and artistic elements of the two authors; on the contrary, it deals with an analysis of two different philosophies and, moreover, of two different political theories. Deleuze does not make explicit his intention to talk about politics, but it is clear for the reader, because the book analyses concepts such as the law, contracts, anarchy and institution. *Coldness and Cruelty* therefore deserves more consideration by those interested in the political philosophy of Deleuze and Guattari. It is not, as popular use might lead us to believe, only *Anti-Oedipus* and *A Thousand Plateaus* that can help us discover the political potential of Deleuze's philosophy, but also his book on Sade and Masoch. In particular, this chapter focuses on the Marquis de Sade rather than Masoch, as Deleuze links him to anarchist political thought. The aim of this discussion is to show the relation that Deleuze establishes between anarchy and institutions. Starting from this connection, a new vision of anarchy emerges – one that is opposed to a government based on law but is, at the same time, different from the idea of an anarchist regime characterised by chaos and disorder (which, at any rate, is a false or dogmatic image of thought to begin with).

## Must We Take Sade Seriously?

This question references an essay by Simone de Beauvoir, published in 1951, with the title 'Must We Burn Sade?' The question is not an ironic one; in fact, it corresponds to a serious examination by many critics who read Sade. The Marquis de Sade, as is well known, was a member of the French aristocracy who became famous as a writer of novels and stories that celebrated libertine sexuality. Because of the pornographic, violent and blasphemous content of his work, as well as his scandalous conduct, Sade was often accused of immorality and was, eventually, incarcerated. During the thirty-two years he spent in prison, all his books were censored, while many were actually burnt, which may be one of the reasons that Sade's work was overlooked, even after his death.

Attention to his literary production re-emerged in the twentieth century, especially after the first publication of *The One Hundred and Twenty Days of Sodom* in 1904 (1990). This book has a curious history as it is connected to an important event of the French Revolution, namely Bastille Day (14 July 1789). Sade had in fact been imprisoned in the Bastille since 1784 and was transferred to a lunatic asylum near Paris because of his misconduct only a few days before the storming of the Bastille. At that time, he was forced to discontinue writing *The One Hundred and Twenty Days of Sodom* – a novel he considered his masterpiece. The manuscript, which was caught up in the storming of the Bastille, remained hidden until 1904 when the German psychiatrist Iwan Bloch published the book. For this reason, it was really only during the twentieth century that Sade's image was rehabilitated by, for example, the interpretations of Apollinaire, Bréton and Heine. Nevertheless, because much of his work was taken up by psychoanalysts, Sade became a symbol of pathology. According to Deleuze, however, reading Sade's work only through the lens of pathology does not allow one to take Sade seriously, in the same way that the censorship of the eighteenth century failed to. Deleuze, therefore, wrote *Coldness and Cruelty* in order to show that Sade does more than exalt violence; he also has a distinct political strategy. Deleuze is not the only author who, starting from the 1950s, has tried to read Sade from a new perspective. After the Second World War, many philosophers, like Adorno and Horkheimer, Klossowski, Blanchot, de Beauvoir, Bataille, Lacan, Barthes and Foucault, began to be interested in Sade for his theories and his political agenda.

Deleuze defines Sade's political views as 'an institutional model of anarchy' (Deleuze 1991a: 87). Even before Deleuze's reading, Sade was considered close to an anarchist or revolutionary position and, besides, many of the elements that Deleuze uses in his reading of Sade (like the comparison with Kant, the transgression of law, the irony and the creation of a cruel and libertine society) are also emphasised by other interpreters. I argue, however, that Deleuze comes to an original conclusion because he is able to read these elements in a different way through some of the key concepts of his thought. These original elements, which are schematically mentioned here, concern three aspects in particular. First, the relationship between Sade and Kant is not understood as an encounter but, on the contrary, as a real *renversement* (reversal). Second, Sade's critical strategy linked to crime and violence is not seen as a symbol of mere destruction or personal revolution but as a *pars destruens*, so that the destruction is followed by a positive and social moment of reconstruction. Finally, the reading of Sade's cruel and libertine vision of society is seen to follow a naturalistic approach, rather than an anthropological one. The latter view makes the Sadean libertine appear an apathetic and indifferent man – which Deleuze does not reject (Deleuze 1991a: 29) as he considers this apathy a functional element for the *pars destruens*. But it is the naturalistic point of view which shows us the Sadean construction of an anarchy as permanent revolution. In my analysis of these three points, I reconstruct not only the Deleuzian interpretation of Sade, but also Deleuze's ideas around what anarchist political organisation might look like.

## Sade against Kant

Sade is the protagonist of the ironic overthrow of modern law. This, for Deleuze, is a Kantian construction: the German philosopher has created, in the *Critique of Practical Reason*, a new image of law, which is founded on itself. This law is a pure form, without materiality and without object. Kant can, therefore, be considered the father of the modern image of law, which is universal and indeterminate. This law, not having content, is a pure obligation, a pure duty with a pure certainty of punishment. In the world governed by universal and formal law, it is actually possible to obey only by way of 'an indefinite prolongation', which, according to Deleuze, 'rather than leading us to a paradise above, already installs us in a hell here below. Rather than announcing immortality, it distills a "slow death", and continuously defers the judgment of the law' (Deleuze 1998: 33).

According to Deleuze, Sade's critique is directed, in particular, against the first characteristic of modern law; that is, its independence from all the other principles. Hence, Sade's challenge is to show that the law is not a first principle and that it cannot be founded on itself. His criticism, moreover, does not simply consist of adopting 'irrational' or 'illegal' conduct, which would constitute a mere negation of Kant's moral law, but proceeds through a rational and philosophical demonstration. Many interpreters, in fact, have drawn attention to the argumentative nature of Sadean discourse that is seemingly in contrast with the violence and wildness of the erotic scenes. Roland Barthes, for example, in his analysis of the Sadean language of crime, refuses to define Sade in terms of his eroticism, because of the prevalence of a strong rationality in the organisation of the crime that is subjected 'to a system of articulated language' (Barthes 1989: 27). Foucault, too, in the lectures he gave on Sade in 1970, shows the role and the importance of his rational and philosophical discourse (Foucault 2013). Sade's writing, in fact, unleashes desire from the repression of power through this kind of discourse, rather than through the description of the erotic scenes. In these treatises, the libertines attempt to justify their conduct in front of their victims. This emerges as a 'perverse' rationality which, in turn, reverses the law and common sense, showing the appropriateness and naturalness of libertine behaviour. This 'improper' use of reason has led many to think that there is a connection between Sade and Kant, especially because his *The Philosophy in the Bedroom* was published in 1795, only eight years after the *Critique of Practical Reason*. Sade, in fact, seems to construct an answer to Kantian theory, because he uses reason in order to give logical coherence to his reversed morality. In this way, he shows that reason has aims other than Kant's categorical imperative. Among the most significant interpretations of the relation between Sade and Kant is that of Adorno and Horkheimer, as well as the famous essay by Lacan, 'Kant with Sade'. But, as we will see, Deleuze proposes a new point of view which differs from these preceding perspectives.

Adorno and Horkheimer dedicate to Sade the second excursus of their masterpiece, *Dialectic of Enlightenment*, titled 'Juliette, or Enlightenment and Morality' – a reflection on the Sade's role in the history of Enlightenment. They argue that even though Kant made a rigorous effort to construct a scientific system of pure reason, Sade is closer to attaining it because, in order to be coherent, the system has to be neutral in relation to all values and aims. Consequently, according to Adorno and Horkheimer, it is Sade who embodies the spirit of the Enlightenment. Sade, in particular through the character of Juliette, is an example of what an Enlightenment thought has to be: namely, indifferent to every sentiment, compassion, religion, value or virtue. Adorno and Horkheimer therefore read Sade's work as the complete realisation of a coherent and universal system of pure reason; in short, Sade seems to go beyond Kant because he does what Kant was not able to do.

Lacan proposes a very different interpretation of the relation between Sade and Kant in 'Kant with Sade', published in 1963 (Lacan 1989). According to Lacan, Kant, in his formulation of moral law, regrets the lack of a phenomenal object, which he had to sacrifice for a universal system. Sade tries to reformulate the Kantian law using as universal imperative the libertine principle 'I have the right to enjoy your body'. The libertines would want to submit everyone to this principle and their discourse serves to persuade their victims. Moreover, the place of law is taken by desire, which becomes as unconditional as Kantian morality was and establishes itself as a rigorous law. Sadean characters, in pursuing desire, therefore submit themselves to libertine law. This renders Sade *with* Kant, according to Lacan, and is supported also by the fact that both the submission to moral law and the submission to desire produce the same feeling – pain (Lacan 1992: 80). This, says Lacan, basically means that in order for the Sadean project to 'combine the crime with the law' (Sade 2012), it would have been drawn up in accordance with Kantian moral law. Consequently, Sade constitutes a sort of parody of Kant.

In *Coldness and Cruelty*, Deleuze quotes neither Adorno and Horkheimer nor Lacan for the simple reason that he proposes an entirely new point of view, in which Sade is against Kant. Deleuze does not read Sadean irony as a kind of caricature of Kant; for him, Sade's work has to be taken seriously, because it does not represent the simple replication of the Kantian system. Sadean irony is a movement that brings Kant to the extreme and this operation, for Deleuze, is intentionally paradoxical. Hence, the paradox is part of the critique and does not compromise its efficacy. To put it differently, Sadean irony does not want to replicate or continue Kantian theory but comes out against the moral law of Kant and, in this, Sade's desire refuses to assume the form of a law, instead taking the form of anarchy. Adorno and Horkheimer also used the term 'anarchy' to describe Sade's political praxis, but they conceive of anarchy in its pejorative sense as chaos and disorder (Adorno and Horkheimer 2002: 92). Deleuze, instead, uses the word in a positive sense: anarchy as a system capable of accepting reality because it renounces universality and thereby shows itself to be more flexible than the law. Consequently, while Adorno and Horkheimer see in Sade the triumph of the general and the universal, Deleuze considers his anarchic project the singularisation of *a* life.

## The Irony Between the Critical and the Clinical

At this point, we have to ask how the ironic reversal of Kant works in concrete terms. As I have said before, Sade's critique is opposed to the first characteristic of modern law, namely its role of first principle and its capacity to legitimate itself. Irony, therefore, can be defined as the movement of thought, which starts from below and moves higher in order to go beyond the law and its false independence. 'Transcend the law toward a higher principle' thus means at the same time, 'bypass the law as a merely secondary power' (Deleuze 1991a: 86). It is only in this way that the Sadean critique becomes concrete. If we demonstrate that there is a principle higher than the law, then the law has to be demoted to second position. This operation thus invalidates the law's power in so far as this is appropriate only for a first and universal principle. Without this condition, the law loses its force because real power has to depend on the highest principle and cannot be based on second nature. Here Deleuze introduces an important distinction between first nature/higher principle and second nature, which is associated with the contingency and uncertainty of the human condition. The law is placed in second nature and is consequently considered to be an 'artifice'. This characteristic is what prevents the law from becoming a first principle: the law cannot be autonomous or founded on itself, because it is produced by something else. Deleuze writes: 'Sade's answer is that in all its forms – natural, moral and political – the law represents the rule of secondary nature which is always geared to the demands of conservation' (1991a: 86). The Law is thus a rule that cannot be universal because it is linked to the precarious condition of humanity. It will never be everybody's law, yet it will always be somebody's law, usually someone who wants to impose rules.

In the Deleuzian reading, moreover, Sade seems to draw nearer to Nietzsche, because he sees the law mainly as the product of the union of the weak. In reality, it does not matter if the law expresses the point of view of the strongest or of the weak because, in every case, it deals with a particular point of view and not with a universal one. But, Deleuze adds, it seems that the union of the weak encourages the development of tyranny which Sade strongly denounces. The tyrant really needs the union of the weak in order to obtain power and this power is always obtained with the complicity of slaves. Tyranny is the symbol of a usurped power – its mystification – which itself is born from another powerful mystification: the law. As Sade writes in *Juliette*: 'Tyrants are never born in anarchy, they only flourish in the shadow of the laws and draw their authority from them' (Sade 1969, quoted in Deleuze 1991a: 86–7). It is thus the Law that gives birth to the tyrant and is always the cause of injustice. It not only deceives us, but through its presumed universality also becomes unconditional and thus more dangerous. This is the reason why Deleuze underscores Sade's aversion to tyranny:

> Sade's hatred of tyranny, his demonstration that the law enables the tyrant to exist, form the essence of his thinking. The tyrant speaks the language of the law, and acknowledges no other . . . The heroes of Sade are inspired with an extraordinary passion against tyranny. (Deleuze 1991a: 87)

In fact, the characters of Sade, unlike tyrants, speak another language entirely, the libertine one, which does not have anything to do with the discourse of law – the 'order-word', as Deleuze and Guattari call it in *A Thousand Plateaus* (Deleuze and Guattari 2005: 75–110). Whereas the law claims a false rationality that functions through obfuscation, Sade proposes a counter-langauge that has nothing to hide and it is for this reason that the libertines do not conceal their 'crimes'. It might appear paradoxical that Sade's heroes, who commit the worst injustices, do not tolerate any usurpation of power. Moreover, this concerns Sade himself who was accused of many crimes, yet could not bear the violence of the Terror, which he openly criticised, despite this costing him his freedom and leading to a new period of imprisonment. As González-Torre points out in his essay on Sade, the difference is that the crimes of Sade and those of his characters are born from a natural impulse, while what cannot properly be accepted by a libertine is the violence of the law or as a consequence of the law (González-Torre 2006: 100). Sade, therefore, criticises Robespierre's conduct, but supports the French Revolution, which culminated in the killing of Louis XVI. The difference is that, in the case of the Terror, the violence was committed with the approval of the law and was directed at the construction of a tyrannical power. In the case of the Revolution, however, the crime was against laws and power and, above all, was directed by the idea of equality. As Klossowski affirms, this equality, for Sade, has nothing to do with the birth of a Republic. What interests him, rather, is that a fraternity is born from a patricide. This means that it is the crime itself that creates a common goal among the citizens and sets them against the injustices of the law. This critique against tyranny emerges especially in the famous pamphlet 'Yet another effort, Frenchmen, if you would become republicans', read by Dolmancé in *Philosophy in the Bedroom*, where we find an explicit invitation addressed to the French people to free Europe from the real tyranny (Sade 1965).

The Sadean critique of the law exposes the law as belonging to second nature and the artifice and contingency of humanity. But the element of protest in Sade is not an original element of the Deleuzian reading; many other commentators have underscored the presence of rebellion in his work. Most interpreters, however, read this as a failure. For example, Simone de Beauvoir, who recognises the Sadean critique of the law and common values, still argues that he does not move beyond an aristocratic vision of society. According to her, the only solution to the abstraction and universality of the law he offers is an individual revolution (de Beauvoir 1990). The crimes in Sade's writings are thus only reflective of a personal rebellion, which Sade undertakes as an individual, but this, she holds, does not have any social value. Klossowski, on the other hand, attributes the failure of the Sadean critique to the absence of a positive proposal. He thus sees Sadean immorality as a strategy that conducts 'society ineluctably into its own destruction' (Klossowski 1991: 62). There is no room for any constructive element. Even Georges Bataille seems to agree with this perspective when he affirms, in his *Literature and Evil*, that Sade did not determine any political position and, on the contrary, pursued a state of disorder, excess and frenzy, which reflected his state of mind (Bataille 2001).

In his own reading, Deleuze does not find a purely destructive intent in the Sadean critique of the law; that is, he does not see in Sade's work only a negative *reaction* against law. Sadean irony – as a form of excess that goes beyond the limits of law – cannot, however, be aimed only at the removal of the power of the law (the 'critical', in other words) if it is to have a positive aim. Deleuze argues that Sade's irony contains in itself a positive strategy that is not critical, but defined as 'clinical'.

## The Concept of 'Institution'

By now it should be clear that I see a positive and creative project in Sade's work. Such a positive element is born from the division between first and second nature. The first person to point out this division was Klossowski in his essay, 'Éléments d'une étude psychanalytiques sur le Marquis de Sade' (Klossowski 1933). Deleuze, who drew on the work of Klossowski, returned to this idea of a first nature, which Sade discovers beyond the law. He writes: 'The transcendence of the law implies the discovery of a primary nature which is in every way opposed to the demands and the rule of secondary nature' (Deleuze 1991a: 87). This primary nature is neither the law, nor the Good, as the latter would render Sade's critique slave to Plato's insistence that the Good is a first (transcendent) principle. Sade, instead, distances himself from both ancient and modern law, because he identifies first nature with the idea of Evil. It is really through this idea of an absolute Evil as superior principle that Sade completes the reversal of Platonism, Kantianism and, in general, of the dogmatic image of the law. But what does it mean to submit to such an absolute principle?

According to Deleuze, the creation of a 'higher, impersonal model is rather to be found in the anarchic institutions of perpetual motion and permanent revolution' (Deleuze 1991a: 87). Here we see a reference to the concept of *institution*, although *Coldness and Cruelty* is not the first place where Deleuze discusses this concept. He had already addressed institutions in his monograph on Hume (Deleuze 1991b) and then in the introduction to *Instincts and Institutions*, a collection of short texts by different authors, edited by Deleuze in 1955 (Deleuze 2004: 19–21). In these texts, Deleuze was in search of a nomadic space that had to be constructed in opposition to the government space, already delimited by a hierarchic power. Actually, a nomadic space cannot be occupied by laws and borders, but has to be administrated by institutions.[1] Deleuze uses Hume's theory in particular to define institutions as an 'organized systems of means' that is always positive in so far as an organism produces institutions in order to satisfy its tendencies and needs (2004: 19). This idea of giving primacy to institutions rather than laws implies an implicit critique of modern contractualism, which considers the human as essentially egoistic. According to this perspective, humans would be *homo homini lupus* without the law because their self-centredness would force everyone into permanent war. Laws are necessary, therefore, to create a peaceful society. According to contractualism, laws and contracts are indispensable, yet they also constitute the limitations of human nature and thus embody the negative aspect of the social body. According to Hume, on the contrary, men [*sic*] enter into society motivated not by egoism, but by sympathy (Hume 1739: II, XI). This sympathetic relation allows for a positive concept of society in that it expresses the creative capacity of humans. This means that the essence of society is no longer based on a limitation, but on invention, namely the creation of institutions, which provide a positive model of action (Deleuze 1991b: 49). In this way, the social fabric is no longer identified with a lack or need, but rather with a creative practice (De Sutter 2009). Institutions are thus produced by human imagination, born from the capacity for creative power (*pouvoir*). But these institutional procedures are not created in order to answer general and universal needs, but to attend to particular tendencies which, rather than individuate, singularise life. Deleuze, following Hume, thus argues that the primary determination of society is institutions, rather than laws and contracts.

I want to underscore here that this Deleuzian idea of institution is influenced not only by Hume, but also by Maurice Hauriou (as pointed out in Dosse 2010: 113). In *Instinct and Institution*, Deleuze quotes Hariou (Hauriou 1896, 1925), a French jurist of the early twentieth century who is considered to be the father of institutionalism. Deleuze considers him an ally in the support of the primacy of institutions over laws and contracts because Hauriou defines the concept 'institution' as an idea of *enterprise* which has to be realised (Hauriou 1933: 96) and distinguishes two types of institutions: 'person institutions' and 'thing institutions'. The first type refers to personified institutions that realise themselves in a constituted body (a State, an association, a labour union). These person institutions internalise the members of the group, becoming a sort of moral person. The thing institutions, on the other hand, are part of a social body, but they do not give life to a corporation because they borrow the power from the social body in which they are born. This means, according to Hauriou, that person institutions propose principles of action, while thing institutions are only limitations. Hauriou's differentiation reflects the Humean one between institution and law: the contract, being a limitation, represents abstract laws or the norms of juridical positivism. Institutions, being positive actions, come before these abstract norms and this primacy is linked to the idea of a positive society, which is not based on the limitations of power. We can see from this that institutionalism is an important step in the development of Deleuzian political philosophy, because it implies a concept of human capacity and of society. As Guillaume Sibertin-Blanc points out: 'Institution, the "real enterprise", is understood as a creation and an assemblage of action, while law implicates a subjective interpretation as duty or interdict. Law is reflective, institution makes a move' (Sibertin-Blanc 2006: 67, own translation).

We see now that when Deleuze defines Sadean anarchy in terms of institutions, he considers it as a positive form of social organisation. This implies, first of all, that it does not concern an individual or a personal revolution, because an institution always has a social and community value. Second, Sadean anarchy is not reducible to chaos, because it is really an organisation. It also differs from the law in that it does not aim for universality, but instead aims at singularising life as *a* life, not *the* life (Deleuze 2007: 385). As François Ost underlines in his book on Sade and law: 'Any idea of general law has been blocked . . . Difference, caprice, singularity are the elements which make law. It is detail that makes passion, and not its reproducible and generalizable abstraction' (Ost 2005: 186–7, own translation).

On this point, Deleuze seems to be in complete disagreement with Blanchot, who thinks that the only alternative strategy proposed by Sade is the formulation of a universal system that is a kind of 'Declaration of Erotism Rights' (Blanchot 2004: 20). If what Blanchot says is true, the Sadean critique of the law would be a failure because, instead of proposing something completely new, it would simply establish another legislative system, which would assume the point of view of the libertines, rather than that of the tyrant or slaves. In this case, Sade's strategy would not constitute a reversal, but a simple replication. However, according to Deleuze, there is a strong opposition between the law and anarchist institutions, as the latter are not only aimed at singularisation rather than universalisation, but also a form of auto-organisation (immanent), rather than one based on a higher order (transcendent).

This definition of anarchy as a form of auto-organisation means that it is really a political system and not mere chaos. To think anarchy in terms of institution means, in other words, to make it a political and social organisation which, in Sade, has a preference for immorality (in favour of a situational ethics), the absence of laws and atheism, instead of the false values and rigid juridical order of laws and religions.

## An Anarchic Naturalism

A question remains: How does anarchy justify its own statute of political organisation? The first answer lies in identifying anarchist institutions with the libertine societies described by Sade in his work. According to this view, it is the isolation of libertine societies that made the survival of anarchy possible. Barthes and Foucault seem to agree with this anthropological reflection when the former underscores the loneliness of the libertine in the execution of crimes (Barthes 1989: 16), and the latter defines Sade's eroticism as conforming to disciplinary societies (Foucault 1996: 818). It is true, after all, that we can find in Sade many descriptions of libertine societies, all of which are always isolated and organised in terms of their procedures for selecting victims, for executing crimes and, finally, for the division of class. The libertines are, in fact, always rich and belong to the upper class. Moreover, a number of accounts reveal their contempt for the lower classes. These libertine societies can not, therefore, be considered in terms of the positive proposal of Sade while considered only from an anthropological point of view. Ultimately, the libertine communities are 'outlaw' communities only because they are situated in isolated places where the power cannot find them. Accordingly, they do not constitute a new model of society. The libertine coexists with law and they are only a private or personal line of escape that is entirely artificial and, as such, belongs, like laws, to second nature. If the political conception of Sade stops at such an anthropological description of libertines' private community, his critique would be a failure, because it would not entail any consequence for said society.

Deleuze's hypothesis is different. For him, anarchy does not coincide with the libertine societies but, on the contrary, with a form of auto-organisation. Moreover, anarchist institutions are not justified on the basis of an anthropological point of view because, according to Deleuze, they 'cannot be equated either with tyranny or with a combination of whims and arbitrariness' (Deleuze 1991a: 87). The institutions of permanent revolution constitute an 'impersonal' model, and this clearly shows that they do not concern humankind – that is, second nature – but instead concern first nature, which I earlier defined as an impersonal force. This idea of an impersonal and necessary first nature, opposed to a personal and contingent second nature, is indeed the element that defines Sade's naturalism. Furthermore, Deleuze finds the same naturalism in Spinoza, so connecting the two authors. In fact, in the first pages of *Coldness and Cruelty*, Deleuze writes: 'In Sade we discover a surprising affinity with Spinoza – a naturalistic and mechanistic approach imbued with the mathematical spirit' (1991a: 20).

Deleuze connects Sade to Spinoza because both authors are concerned with first nature as immanent and impersonal (this despite the fact that they are given opposite values by the authors; first nature is God in Spinoza and Evil in Sade). They also describe the passage from second to first nature in similar ways. There is, in fact, in Spinoza, the theorisation of a state of nature in which everyone enjoys his own natural rights, that is, his *potentia*, and in which there are not universal and general laws (Spinoza 2002). According to Spinoza, it is only in the second moment that the civil state is born in order to establish laws and coercive rules. Spinoza finally hypothesises the possibility of making a leap from civil state to a state of reason in which there is no need for laws. Laws are now replaced by the auto-organisation of a political community in which every member can really enjoy of his/her *potentia*. This political community had been defined by Deleuze – not by chance – as an anarchy (Deleuze 1980). This definition has a strong Sadean echo as it is also necessary for Sade that a leap be made from the world of laws and coercive power towards an anarchist state which can, finally, destroy the limitations of law's order. In other words, Deleuze reads Sade starting from his naturalism, which proposes neither a mere transgression of the law nor an individual and personal revolution (even if this is also desirable for Sade) but, on the contrary, a complete reversal of laws (Deleuze 1991a: 86). This reversal is not merely a temporary action because it is aimed at institutionalising anarchist political organisation. The difference between Sade and Spinoza is in the conception of this political organisation. In both cases, anarchy aims to realise first nature, but for the author of *Ethics*, this realisation always implies an increase of the *potentia* of everyone, while for Sade it coincides with the achievement of an absolute Evil. In this way, the Deleuzian concept of anarchy, obtained from his reading of Sade and Spinoza, is directed at the constitution of a 'community of bodies' (Jallon 1997) or, rather, of an 'auto-poietic' organisation that is not composed of a union of obedient subjects but, on the contrary, of a multitude of desiring and often cruel bodies. Deleuze's challenge is to consider the latter not as 'dangerous individuals' but as the rich and vital excess of society. This perspective implies the refusal of one of the most important concepts of modern political philosophy – the social contract. As Ost writes: 'The social model based on contract and sacrifice has been reversed into a negative utopia, that of the despotic counter-society marked by the sign of privilege. The libertine, without faith and without law, doesn't swear; he blasphemes' (Ost 2005: 15, own translation).

## Conclusion

The contract is a mystification, like law, because it is an instrument used to give all the power to the tyrant and to make slaves of all the other contractors. The refusal of laws and contracts is a political strategy that is developed and made more concrete by Deleuze in the books written with Guattari after May '68, which moved Deleuze definitively 'into politics' (Deleuze 1995: 170). But the political direction taken in

*Anti-Oedipus* and *A Thousand Plateaus*, especially the critique of the capitalist State and the proposal of a nomadic war machine, had been prepared, I argue here, by Deleuze's analysis of the institution in his writings of the 1950s and in *Coldness and Cruelty*. It is particularly in this book that the refusal of law and hierarchical power becomes clear, as well as the link between this refusal and anarchy. According to Deleuze, we cannot limit ourselves by disobeying laws in order to critique them; rather, we have to substitute them with positive models of action which indicate what we can do, and not only what is forbidden. These positive models of action are called institutions and they do not meet the needs of (human) power (to oblige, to prohibit), but those of nature (to satisfy instincts). For this reason, a political regime full of institutions and lacking in laws coincides with anarchism. Thus, there is in Deleuzian anarchy some typical elements of anarchism, like the naturalism present also in Bakunin, and the rejection of a sovereign and other hierarchies that characterises Proudhon's thought. However, Deleuze's originality consists in a positive definition of anarchist society: it is not only stateless or leaderless, but also creative. Indeed, society is composed not of individuals, but of singularities and fluxes of desires and anarchism is the regime that allows a free circulation of these.[2] In other words, nomadism will become the synonym for anarchism in Deleuze's later works. Nomadism, like anarchism, deterritorialises the rigid and static boundaries of the State and, in so doing, constructs a new kind of smooth space (Deleuze and Guattari 2005: ch. 14). However, the political figure of the anarchic nomad that is explained in *A Thousand Plateaus* finds its ontological foundation in Deleuze's work of the 1950s and 1960s because, as Deleuze says in his course on Spinoza,

> There is a fundamental relation between Ontology and a certain style of politics . . . What appears to me striking in a pure ontology is the point at which it repudiates the hierarchies . . . It is anti-hierarchical thought. It is almost a kind of anarchy. There is an anarchy of beings in being. (Deleuze 1980)

According to Deleuze, political anarchism must be based on an ontological anarchy: a pure ontology of immanence, the affirmation of the univocity of being that is at the same time a nomadic distribution and crowned anarchy (Deleuze 1994: 37). Sadean anarchic institutions, when seen as the right of community, and when understood as the realisation of *potentia*, or the 'auto-poietic capacity' of the multitude,[3] allows Sade's irony to become a positive model of action intended not as a laugh but, on the contrary, as a political weapon, directed against tyranny and the law. This understanding of instutions, I believe, offers a very contemporary understanding of anarchist praxis as we find it in the world today, bringing together the series Deleuze *and* Sade *and* anarchism.

## Notes

1. It should be noted that the French term *institution* used by Deleuze and Guattari does not mean the same as the English one. Whereas the English term is associated with hospitals and mental institutions (which *institutionalise* patients, for example), the French term implies an action as well as oppositional action (Ayme 2009: 113). The French term means in fact the dissemination of certain social relations that are not necessarily imposed from above, but that could also come from opposition movements. A good example of what 'institution' means here is the work made on this concept by Félix Guattari, in particular in his essay 'Transversality'. Guattari deals with institutional practices and institutional groups with patients (Guattari 2015) and transversality is conceptualised as a critique of the psychoanalytic notion of transference, and in particular of the dual analytic relation between analyst and analysand. Transversality favours instead a more collective psychotherapy, which becomes institutional.

2. Posing passions, desires and their satisfactions as the natural engine of society, which have to be freed from the restrictions of the power and the corruption of civil society, is an element that unites Sadean irony with the other political strategy against law present in *Coldness and Cruelty*: the humour of Sacher-Masoch. Despite all the differences between the two critical strategies, humour too – no longer through a transgression of laws, but through an excess of zeal in their application – can contribute to a sort of anarchy, but this time it will be a utopia. Humour creates a new now-here (this is the meaning of utopia), which is the product of the second nature (mankind). Thus, there is a proliferation of personal and private contracts, which mocks the mystification of the social contract. In this sense, an anarchic utopia of liberation of the positive (and no longer cruel, as in Sade) human nature, could be found in the humour of Rousseau (Deleuze 2004: 52–5) and in the passionate attraction analysed by Charles Fourier, at least in the way in which René Shérer reads the political perspective of this latter (Shérer 1970).

3. We follow, in this case, the concept of 'right of the multitude', proposed by Andalgiso Amendola, who starts from the Deleuzian idea of institution, in order to think this right as the autopoietic capacity of the subjectivity. Moreover, this latter is conceived as an excess, which is not willing to submit itself to power (Amendola 2012: 96–7).

## References

Adorno, T. and M. Horkheimer (2002), *Dialectic of Enlightenment*, Stanford: Stanford University Press.

Amendola, A. (2012), 'Autopoiesi del sistema, autonomia dell'eccedenza', in S. Chignola (ed.), *Il diritto del comune: Crisi della sovranità, proprietà e nuovi poteri costituenti*, Verona: Ombrecorte, pp. 65–97.

Ayme, J. (2009), 'Essai sur l'histoire de la psychothérapie institutionnelle', *Institutions: Revue de la Psychothérapie Institutionnelle*, 44: 111–53.

Barthes, R. (1989), *Sade, Fourier, Loyola*, Berkeley and Los Angeles: University of California.

Bataille, G. (2001), *Literature and Evil*, London: Marion Boyars.

de Beauvoir, S. (1990), 'Must We Burn Sade?', in D. A. F. Sade, *The One Hundred and Twenty Days of Sodom*, London: Arrow Books, pp. 3–64.

Blanchot, M. (2004), *Lautréamont and Sade*, Stanford: Stanford University Press.

Deleuze, G. (1980), *Cours sur Spinoza*, Vincennes, 12 December, http://www.web deleuze.com/php/texte.php?cle=23&groupe=Spinoza&langue=2 (last accessed 1 April 2018).

Deleuze, G. (1991a), *Masochism: Coldness and Cruelty*, trans. J. McNeil and A. Willm, New York: Zone Books.

Deleuze, G. (1991b), *Empiricism and Subjectivity. An Essay on Hume's Human Nature*, trans. C. Boundas, New York: Columbia University Press.

Deleuze, G. (1994), *Difference and Repetition*, trans. Paul Patton, New York: Columbia University Press.

Deleuze, G. (1995), *Negotiations*, trans. M. Joughin, New York: Columbia University Press.

Deleuze, G. (1998), *Essays Critical and Clinical*, trans. M. Greco and D. Smith, London: Verso.

Deleuze, G. (2004), *Desert Islands and Other Texts*, trans. M. Taormina, New York: Semiotext(e).

Deleuze, G. (2007), *Two Regimes of Madness*, trans. A. Hodges and M. Taormina, New York: Semiotext(e).

Deleuze, G. and F. Guattari (2005), *A Thousand Plateaus: Capitalism and Schizophrenia*, trans. B. Massumi, Minneapolis: University of Minnesota Press.

De Sutter, L. (2009), *Deleuze: La Pratique du droit*, Paris: Michalon.

Dosse, F. (2010), *Gilles Deleuze and Félix Guattari: Intersecting Lives*, New York: Columbia University Press.

Foucault, M. (1996), 'Sade, sergent du sexe', in M. Foucault, *Dits et Écrits II*, 1976–1988, Paris: Gallimard, pp. 818–22.

Foucault, M. (2013), *La Grande Étrangère*, Paris: Éditions de l'École des hautes études en science.

Freud, S. (1975), *Three Essays on Sexual Theory*, New York: Basic Books.

González-Torre, A. P. (2006), *La sombra de la illustración: Tres variaciones sobre Sade*. Santander: Servicio de Publicaciones de la Universidad de Cantabria.

Guattari, F. (1991), 'The Schizo Chaosmosis', in É. Alliez and A. Goffey (eds), *The Guattari Effect*, London: Continuum, pp. 17–24.

Guattari, F. (2015), *Psychoanalysis and Transversality: Texts and Interviews 1955–1971*, trans. A. Hodges, Los Angeles: Semiotext(e).

Harris, E. and L. Lauwaert (2015), 'The Enjoyment of Pure Reasoning. Gilles Deleuze on Marquis de Sade', *Philosophy Today*, 59(2): 191–206.

Hauriou, M. (1896), *La Science sociale traditionnelle: Cours de science sociale*, Paris: Larose & Forcel.

Hauriou, M. (1925), *La Cité moderne et les trasformations du droit*, Paris: Bloud & Gay.

Hauriou, M. (1933), 'La Théorie de l'institution et de la fondation: Essai de vitalisme social', in M. Hauriou, *Aux Sources du droit: Le Pouvoir, l'ordre et la liberté*, Paris: Bloud & Gay, pp. 89–119.

Hume, D. (2003) [1739], *A Treatise of Human Nature: Being an Attempt to Introduce the Experimental Method of Reasoning into Moral Subjects*, London: Dover.

Jallon, H. (1997), *Sade: Le Corps constituant*, Paris: Éditions Michalon.

Klossowski, P. (1933), 'Éléments d'une étude psychanalytique sur le Marquis de Sade', *Revue française de psychanalyse*, Paris: Denoel et Steele, pp. 458–74.

Klossowski, P. (1991), *Sade My Neighbor*, Evanston: Northwestern University Press.

Krafft-Ebing, R. (1939), *Psychopathia Sexualis: A Medico-Forensic Study*, London: William Heinemann.

Lacan, J. (1989), 'Kant with Sade', *October*, 51: 55–75.

Lacan, J. (1992), *The Ethics of Psychoanalysis 1959/1969: The Seminar of Jacques Lacan. Book VII*, New York: Norton.

Ost, F. (2005), *Sade et la loi*, Paris: Odile Jacob.

Sade, D. A. F. (1965), *Justine, Philosophy in the Bedroom, and Other Writings*, New York: Grove Press.

Sade, D. A. F. (1969), *Juliette, or Vice Amply Rewarded*, New York: Lancer.

Sade, D. A. F. (1990), *The One Hundred and Twenty Days of Sodom*, London: Arrow Books.

Sade, D. A. F. (2012), *Aline et Valcour*, UK: Emereo.

Shérer, R. (1970), *Charles Fourier ou la Contestation Globale*, Paris: Seghers.

Sibertin-Blanc, G. (2006), 'Politique et clinique: Recherche sur la philosophie pratique de Gilles Deleuze', PhD thesis, Charles de Gaulle University – Lille III.

Spinoza, B. (2002), 'Ethics', in B. Spinoza, *Complete Works*, Indianapolis/Cambridge: Hackett.

# PART III

# RELAYS OF A DIFFERENT KIND

# Chapter 9

# Who's Afraid of the Big Bad Wolves?: Coming to Terms with Deleuze

*Jesse Cohn*

I want to explain how I moved from a sharp mistrust of Deleuzian philosophy to a place where, as Wittgenstein might have said, I now no longer see certain problems as problems (and new problems have replaced them). This drama has five acts, the first of which we shall call 'Universal Wolves'.

## Act I: Universal Wolves (1990–95)

My first glimpse of 'the Idea', as the old anarchists called it, at a May Day picnic in St. Louis (Figure 9.1), was no more innocent than anybody else's, as I had marinated since birth in the usual hegemonic prejudices. What prepared me to refuse the Hobbesian blackmail that makes almost everyone afraid, like Shakespeare's Ulysses, to even *imagine* the undoing of hierarchies? 'Take but degree away,' he warns, 'And, hark, what discord follows':

> Force should be right; or rather, right and wrong,
> Between whose endless jar justice resides,
> Should lose their names, and so should justice too.
> Then every thing includes itself in power,
> Power into will, will into appetite;
> And appetite, an universal wolf,
> So doubly seconded with will and power,
> Must make perforce an universal prey,
> And last eat up himself.
>
> Shakespeare, *Troilus and Cressida* I, iii, 562–3, 569–77

I was not scared of the universal wolf. A century after Peter Kropotkin reminded the Western world of what, according to Deleuze and Guattari, '[e]very child knows' – that is, 'that wolves travel in packs', that the

Figure 9.1 May Day flyer (St. Louis, 1990).

world is formed by cooperation – I knew it for certain (Kropotkin 1902; Deleuze and Guattari 2005). Maybe, perversely, my own social 'degree' helped: as an able-bodied, (mostly) straight, white college boy from the suburbs, I had the luxury to be philosophical, and I found it hard to believe that behind the apparent benevolence of most adults I met, *homo homini lupus* ('man is a wolf to man'). My own experiences had been a blend of comfortable nurturance (growing up in a happy, middle-class family) and lonely idiosyncrasy (coming of age as a weirdo egghead). Loneliness could have disposed me to pessimism, but happiness doubtless furnished me with a store of optimism. So when, at the age of nineteen, I laid hands on *The Essential Works of Anarchism* (Shatz 1971), I was doubtless ready for something that could make sense of my experiences of separateness and togetherness alike.

It was, as Deleuze might have said, a good encounter. The summer before my junior year of college, I found the paperback anthology (born the same year I was) while on a road trip with friends, and I couldn't put it down for the rest of the trip. I began connecting every new bit of knowledge to this framework. It all came together in the spring of my senior year (1994), when, studying for Postcolonial Lit, I found a piece from *The Atlantic* in the library: Robert D. Kaplan's cover article, 'The Coming Anarchy: How Scarcity, Crime, Overpopulation, Tribalism, and Disease Are Rapidly Destroying the Social Fabric of Our Planet' (Kaplan 1994).

Kaplan's article visited the scene of Postcolonial Lit, but there, instead of the struggles of men and women to construct new worlds out of the wreckage of empire, Kaplan saw a 'symbol' of what might become of the empire itself, 'an eerie taste what American cities might be like in the future'. 'In Abidjan', I read, 'restaurants have stick- and gun-wielding guards who walk you the fifteen feet or so between your car and the entrance.' *Crimes against brunch!* If something in Kaplan's tone reminded me of Kurtz's histrionics in Conrad's *Heart of Darkness* – 'The horror! The horror!' (1997/1899 – the whiff of colonialism only got stronger as I read on: 'Though the French are working assiduously to preserve stability, the Ivory Coast faces a possibility worse than a coup: an anarchic implosion of criminal violence', he warned. '[I]t is Thomas Malthus, the philosopher of demographic doomsday, who is now the prophet of West Africa's future. And West Africa's future, eventually, will also be that of most of the rest of the world.' The global future à la Kaplan was a nightmare of 'overpopulation, unprovoked crime, scarcity of resources, refugee migrations, the increasing erosion of nation-states and international borders' – in short, 'anarchy' (Kaplan 1994: 45–9).

And so I was inspired to write my first anarchist critique of anything.

First of all, I noted, Kaplan's nostalgia for Empire encouraged us to forget how brutal that order was and still is. The 'nation-states' and 'borders' imposed on the world by the Western powers had never meant peace or stability for those on the other side of the process. His account of 'scarcity' failed to describe an Africa where farmers planted cotton for export right through years of famine, in a world producing sufficient grain to feed every mouth while millions starved; the irrationality was coded into capitalism, which put profit ahead of human needs, then blamed the poor for their own misery (Lappé et al. 1979: 13). Calling Malthus a 'prophet' erased the historical origins of his population economics, helpfully reconstructed by Alan Ryan in a review-essay from the previous year: 'He had no basis for his calculations, and wrote his *Essay on the Principles of Population* (1798) to attack William Godwin', whose declaration that 'man is not originally vicious' had offended his sense of Original Sin. In Malthus's mathematicised mythology, human lust (never mind the possibility of birth control, another 'vice') doomed us to war and poverty (Ryan 1993: 21; Godwin 1971/1793: 40). The argument had been reprised a near century later by Peter Kropotkin and Thomas Huxley: Huxley's image of life as a 'Hobbesian war of each against all' appeared as a mere fig leaf for Victorian industrialists' greed before Kropotkin's account of evolution as driven by a cooperative 'Mutual Aid instinct' (Kropotkin 1902: 78). As for 'unprovoked' criminality, the Spanish anarchists had affirmed that 'social injustice is the main cause of crime' (Guérin 1971: 122–3). And calling the inevitable results of a brutally unequal system 'anarchy' was an insult to anarchism, which meant not mere disorganisation but 'organization . . . established freely, socially, and, above all, from below' (1971: 43).

A few themes emerged from this critique:

1. Using an English major's basic tool kit, placing text in historical context to reveal political subtext, one could detect, behind false claims to objectivity, the specific agendas of specific people with specific interests at work.
2. Accounts of possibility, necessity and morality were inseparable. Ascribing a *necessary* character to something, making alternatives appear *impossible*, ends up dignifying it as a positive *good*. Descriptions of what *is* may always carry the prescriptive force of an *ought*.
3. Rhetoric attributing social problems to nature was a mask for theology.
4. Ideas of 'human nature' were central to all of this, all the more so when tacit.

But what did this centrality imply? Marshall Shatz asserts that '[a]mong the central tenets that virtually every subsequent anarchist will reiterate' was Godwin's 'abiding faith in human nature' (Shatz 1971: 3). This judgement is echoed nearly everywhere in the secondary literature: 'classical libertarian thought', writes Noam Chomsky, is founded on 'deeper assumptions about human nature' (Guérin 1971: xii). For George

Woodcock, too, 'the idea common to most anarchists' is 'that society is a natural phenomenon . . . and that man is naturally adapted to observe its laws without the need for artificial regulations' (Woodcock 1962: 201). Surely all these scholars couldn't be wrong?

One entry in Shatz's anthology raised these questions for me in a particularly sharp way: Herbert Read's 'Existentialism, Marxism and Anarchism' (1949). Read is jousting with the hot philosophies of his day: Jean-Paul Sartre's existentialism and Georg Lukács's Marxism. While Sartre posits 'freedom as the foundation of all values' (Sartre 1975: 366), Lukács's demand for commitment is unsatisfied by assurances that existentialists may also embrace humanist values; wasn't Heidegger left 'free' to embrace fascism, as indeed he had? Sartre, Read notes, 'does not make very clear what would happen supposing he could not persuade his fellow-men to agree on certain lines of conduct, or certain values' (Read quoted in Shatz 1971: 520). Without belief in 'a given and fixed human nature', have we any common ground, or are private beliefs all that is left (1971: 527)? For Sartre, wishing to anchor values in 'human nature' is irresponsible; after the death of God, 'We are alone, without excuse' (527).

Marx's work, tracing supposedly timeless ideas and institutions back to historical and material origins, appealed to me. Howard Richards's *Letters from Québec* (1987) demonstrated Marxism's versatility in incorporating elements of newer theories (Richards 1996). Yet the element of economic reductivism seemed to persist, no matter how often the critique of capitalism was updated to include, for instance, sexism (as a 'vertical class' system), racism (as a 'psychological wage' paid to white workers), heterosexism (as a by-product of the bourgeois family) and so on (Lippard 1984: 96; DuBois quoted in Roediger 1991: 12; D'Emilio 1992: 11). Every epicycle added to the Ptolemaic system of historical materialism made the whole more cumbersome and rickety; why not dispense with the search for a 'centre' from which all domination supposedly springs in favour of the ethical stance of anarchism, opposing domination in all its forms? And wasn't the lack of such an ethical principle at the heart of the repellent betrayals of party Marxism? Read didn't need to convince me of that.

What occupied more of my concern, as I passed from college to graduate school, was what Read called 'the abyss of nothingness', 'the nihilism which is the philosophical disease of our time', lately renamed 'postmodernism'. A comic strip that ran in the college newspaper towards the end of my senior year aptly parodies my muddled impression of the phenomenon (Figure 9.2). How could my classmates deny the existence

Figure 9.2 Kate Garduño, 'Pomo Dino', *The Earlham Word*, 22 April 1991, p. 12.

of universal values? How could Foucault spout such moral and episte-mological relativism in his 1971 debate with Chomsky, as represented in archival footage from *Manufacturing Consent: Noam Chomsky and the Media* (1992) and in Jim Miller's sensationalist biography, *The Passion of Michel Foucault* (1993)? Science, human rights, culture – all were just an arena for the will to power. 'I'd never met anyone who was so totally amoral', marveled Chomsky, speaking for me as well (Chomsky quoted in Miller 1993: 201). As for Deleuze and Guattari, minor characters in *The Passion of Michel Foucault* – I had absolutely no idea what to make of them. In Miller's representation, their thought became a blur of transgressive, sadomasochistic imagery: vague visions of 'cruelty' cracking subjectivity open like a piñata, releasing a shower of senseless 'intensities' and 'multiplicities' (Miller 1993: 432n17). Surely here was Ulysses' image of 'discord' come to life: 'every thing includes itself in power' seemed the postmodern thesis. Quoth Pomo Dino: 'No truth, no essence, no progress, no liberation, and no mercy!' (Figure 9.2).

Sir Read to the rescue. If certain French thinkers had perhaps unwisely peered into the abyss, a renewed humanism (with antecedents in the naturalist philosophy of Lucretius) offered an 'antidote' to the gloom, 'an affirmation of the significance of our human destiny': a vision, inspired by the scientific investigation of a majestic natural world, of 'man ... stand[ing] on the apex of this complex structure, its crown of perfection, alone conscious of the coherence of the Whole'. Grounding values in a 'biological' freedom' that is 'germinatively at work in all living things', he writes, 'the anarchist rejects the philosophical nihilism of the existentialist' in favour of 'the consciousness of an overriding human solidarity' – Kropotkin's mutual aid instinct (Read quoted in Shatz 1971: 532–3, 536, 534).

This kind of argument was being repeatedly reiterated, in the 1980s and early 1990s, by Murray Bookchin (indeed, Read had been one of Bookchin's early guides to anarchism (Bookchin 1993: 53). *The Ecology of Freedom* (1982) writes large Read's bio-freedom as the 'potentiality, direction, meaning, and self-realization' implicit in the natural world which ultimately comes to unfold and express itself in humanity (Bookchin 1982: 34). *Re-enchanting Humanity* (1995) replays Read's pronouncement of humanity's meaning and mission against the 'nihilistic reaction' most dramatically represented by the 'radical relativism' of postmodern theory (Bookchin 1995a: 174–8). No wonder I received Bookchin's *Social Anarchism or Lifestyle Anarchism* (1995b) as a vindication of my kind of anarchism: resolutely committed to 'the social', to 'objective reality' and to 'ethical criteria and ideals beyond personal satisfaction' (Bookchin 1995b: 53).

This early education in anarchism made it difficult for me to come to terms with Deleuze, later – and yet it seems to me now that it announced in advance what those terms might be.

## Act II: Unexpected Fecundity (1996–2003)

'To the poststructuralists,' wrote Andrew M. Koch in 'Poststructuralism and the Epistemological Basis of Anarchism' (1993), 'the ideal speech situation will produce skewed languages speaking at one another, neither "truth" nor consensus' (Koch 1993: 338). In the autumn of 1997, midway through grad school, I found myself in a series of skewed conversations, disembodied voices talking past one another. How could Koch call himself an anarchist while maintaining that 'consensus without deception or force' (perhaps the shortest possible description of anarchy as a social system) was 'impossible' (1993: 343)? That same semester, Joff Bradley launched his own provocation: 'Is an anti-humanist anarchism a coherent idea or is anarchism necessarily humanist? Can there be real dialogue between anarchism and Deleuze and Guattari's anti-Oedipal schizoanalysis?' (Bradley 1997). I could only echo Herbert Read in reply: 'anarchism is a humanism' (Cohn 1997). Joff went on to post a sort of manifesto, 'The Possibility of an Antihumanist EcoAnarchism' (2000), declaring that 'the question of rational dialogue, for those who have ears to listen, between PS [poststructuralism], social and deep ecology and anarchism ought to be posed' (Bradley 1997).

I did not yet have ears to listen.

My education in theory had been largely conducted outside of academia, in online conversations where I sought remedies for my confusion. In college, I had discovered *Science Fiction EYE* (1987–97), which introduced me to a perception of 'the postmodern', not as an idea to be validated or refuted but (in the words of one of Bruce Sterling's columns) as 'a certain sensibility', 'the way that living in the late twentieth century makes you feel' (Sterling 1989: 80). Through reviews and ads, I cottoned on to books published by RE/Search, Autonomedia and Semiotext(e) which trafficked in this sensibility in ways that were recognisably critical and anti-authoritarian. Were they really, as Bookchin insisted, mere simulations of rebellion, bourgeois titillation? Were they without an ethic?

Here was Rolando Perez's *On An(archy) and Schizoanalysis* (1990), proposing that Deleuze and Guattari's 'constant questioning of all values' was a process 'ending . . . in a certain "ethical an(archy)"'. If this 'structureless, noncoded, non-inscribed morality, or perhaps more appropriately "immorality"' (Perez 1990: 18) sounded too similar to the kind of DIY value system Read had found wanting in Sartre, it also sounded similar to the kind of 'amoral responsibility' championed in one of the more striking manifestos published in *Science Fiction EYE* (Wilson 1991). Inspired, perhaps, by Nietzsche's observation – 'what does art do? Doesn't it praise? Doesn't it dignify? Doesn't it select? Doesn't it have preferences?' (Nietzsche 2005: 204) – Peter Lamborn Wilson proposed that texts, without endorsing 'any code of "received values"', can 'create a new set of values centered on life rather than on meaningless abstractions, or on nothing at all', representing life in ways that expressed *these* values (Perez 1990: 18). All of this seemed to coincide neatly with some academics' arguments about the ethical character of the kinds of theory that they preferred to call 'poststructuralist'. Thus, Simon Critchley's *The Ethics of Deconstruction: Derrida and Levinas* (1992) argued that we should understand the work of the poststructuralists *as* a kind of ethics – ultimately, as an anarchist ethics (Critchley 1992: 1).

It was Steve Robinson, a big-hearted Aussie anarchist working on Derrida, who got me to see how this might work out in practice. How, I asked Steve, could he be an anarchist and endorse this obscurantist theory which openly declared that 'there is nothing outside the text'? He explained it as a matter of 'looking at a text (let's say a social interaction) and spotting the moment when "power" tries to efface itself . . . and disappear into the "metaphysical realm", thus making itself "immune" from criticism' (Robinson 1997). Later, I would hear echoes of this in William Spanos's indictment of 'inquiry . . . [which] proceeds from *above* (*meta-ta-physika*): from a fixed transcendental vantage point – a "Transcendental Signified" or "center elsewhere", in Derrida's terms, which is beyond the reach of free play' (Spanos 1993: 142). And this, in turn, suggested James C. Scott's critique of the manner of 'seeing like a State' inscribed into the grid layout of modern cities like Manhattan or Chicago, maximally intelligible 'from above and from outside . . . a God's-eye view, or the view of an absolute ruler' (Scott 1998: 57). When Ronald Creagh shared Scott's book with me on a visit in the summer of 1999, I realised that I had already encountered this critique of 'metaphysical' planning and thinking in Daniel Chodorkoff's contrast between socially/ecologically grounded strategies of community development and the 'war on poverty model' in which 'outsiders delivering services' operate as generals with a synoptic map of the 'battlefield' (Chodorkoff 1990: 69).

My education in a deconstructive ethics took another step forward in the spring of 2003, when I read Gareth Gordon's thesis, 'Horizons of Change: Deconstruction and the Evanescence of Authority' (2003), as the first US bombs were falling on Iraq. Gordon's readings of Derrida's 'Force of Law' and *The Gift of Death* spoke to my anger and sorrow, as the lives of uncounted others were sacrificed to the murderous abstractions of 'security' and 'rights'. Gordon wove connections between the ethical core of deconstruction – respect for otherness as that which forever escapes the all-governing eye – and paradigmatic statements of the anarchist tradition, from Bakunin's affirmation of a 'life' that can never be captured and fixed in advance by 'science', to Proudhon's fidelity to 'universal movement' and 'the fecundity of the unexpected' against the desire for some 'ideal perfection or final state' (Gordon 2003). His rejection of the Hegelian *Aufhebung* (overcoming) of contradictions suggested a deconstructive distrust of the way in which Hegel 'determines difference as contradiction only in order to resolve it', a dialectic carried forward in the bestowal of Marx's blessing upon the levelling of all cultural differences by Capital: 'The problem', for Proudhon, 'is not to bring about their fusion, for this would be death, but to establish an equilibrium between them – an unstable equilibrium, that changes as society develops' (Derrida 1982: 43; Proudhon 1970: 229).

My first publication, a critique of Pat Murphy's 1999 *The City, Not Long After*, is marked by this growing interest in deconstructive concepts, particularly the Levinasian notion of 'the trace of the other': 'for every pair of opposed terms, neither term can exist apart from its partner . . . none can free itself from the trace of its "other" and become completely self-contained' (Derrida 1991: 103; Cohn 1999: 123). While affirming Murphy's impulse to 'take [her] desires for reality', I argued that she had *too* carefully insulated her utopia from the 'trace' of its traumatic origins, rendering it too remote for us to entertain as a possibility. This raised a wider question: if utopia can never be free of the trace of its other, have we not simply reached a conservative conclusion? Instead, I proposed

> a utopian fiction which acknowledges the necessity of the trace can instead choose to conceive of trace as memory ... we can imagine a future of untrammeled pleasure in which horror exists only as a thing which from we have learned in order that we might not be forced to repeat it' (Cohn 1999: 123–4)

Deconstructive ethics suggested an anarchist aesthetic.

Here, then, were the ways in which I learnt to understand deconstruction as (an) anarchist:

1. Read the declaration that 'there is nothing outside of the text' not 'simplistically forwards' (to mean 'there is nothing real except books') but 'backwards ... to show that the concept of textuality extends to cover everything of which we can have a concept' (Gordon 2003: 2.1).
2. Refuse to think deconstruction without a recognition of the 'undeconstructible' – death, the future, justice; locate a 'responsibility without limits' in the recognition that there is something 'unknowable' in the other which is nonetheless real (Gordon 2003: 2.1).
3. Watch for the 'violent hierarchy' of binary oppositions; show the mutual imbrication of the terms, each of which bears 'the trace of the other' (Derrida 1982: 41).
4. Insist on the immanence of power and meaning, tracking down and blocking recourse to transcendence.

## Act III: Uncommon Ground (2004–7)

As important as my encounter with Derrida and Levinas was for my education, it was hard to shake the feeling that deconstruction remained perpetually susceptible to a kind of textual idealism (as Richard Rorty claimed in its favour; Rorty 1982: 140). I could not have predicted in advance, however, that I would follow the trajectory described by John Protevi, 'turn[ing] away from a postphenomenological stance in which the real is only a retrojected effect of entering signifying systems' in favour of 'a Deleuzean neo-materialism ... allow[ing] for a productive engagement with contemporary scientific findings and, most important, for a productive engagement with political practice' (Protevi 2009: vii–viii). This would retain 'the refusal of any transcendence, any all-encompassing system that claims, from the "heights" of its external perspective, to know and define the *raison d'être* and the meaning of each person and thing' (Colson 2001: 187).

The really indigestible aspect of what had come to be known, by the early 2000s, as 'postanarchism' was the almost compulsory disavowal of the supposed essentialism of 'classical' anarchism.[1] Shawn Wilbur and I wrote (2003) that while '[a]narchists can indeed usefully take several things from poststructuralism', we nonetheless saw 'a number of serious problems with postanarchism's manner of wedding poststructuralism to anarchism'; notably, the postanarchists' representation of 'classical anarchism' seemed disastrously reductive (Cohn and Wilbur 2003). We were not alone in observing that the conceptions of nature and the human subject afforded by the anarchist tradition were far from the simplistic Rousseauvian cliché replicated across the postanarchist literature.[2] Ultimately, I argued that notions of 'essentialism' and 'representation' as such were too broadly defined to be useful (Cohn 2006: 40–4). Refusals of essentialism and/or representation *tout court* invariably ended up in something like the nihilistic slough to which Read had raised his objections half a century earlier, or at best in a self-negating muddle.

And this is what made it difficult for me, at first, to understand what Daniel Colson was saying.

In his *Petit lexique philosophique de l'anarchisme: De Proudhon à Deleuze* (Colson 2001), Colson was clearly contributing to the postanarchist literature, but in a way that nobody else, to my knowledge, had really attempted. This was a rereading of the anarchist tradition with the revisionary imagination and ambition of an Antonio Negri, demonstrating, in a way I had been unable to do, the real richness of our resources. We had inherited a philosophy of radical immanence, grounded in and arising out of workers' movements, for which the historical becoming of collectivities was more real than static identities, but which owed nothing to the dialectics of Marx or Hegel.

Over the course of a half-year sabbatical in 2007, I trained myself to read both Colson and Proudhon, slowly translating both. This is when I began to think of myself, in Deleuze's word, as a 'relay' – transmitting knowledge between languages, between times, between traditions and perspectives (Day 2005: 10–11). An interrupted transmission had prevented us from reading Proudhon for ourselves; seen afresh, he appeared not as just another humanist, but as the utterly strange thinker who declared 'war' not only 'on God himself' but on 'the God-Humanity', indeed, on 'all the absolutes that have been produced' (Proudhon 1930:

3.249). And if Proudhon could afford such surprises, what was just as surprising, for me, was the Deleuze to whom this Proudhon gestured – a Deleuze who, while affirming an 'absolute *subjectivism*', could forcefully reject relativism and assert the primacy of the ethical; a Deleuze who could speak of everything in terms of 'Nature', but who was in no way embarrassed by any essentialist baggage (Colson 2001). What had I been missing? What had I been misreading?

In the process of publishing my first book (2003–6), I was gently and generously called to order, with respect to my reading of Deleuze and Guattari, by one of the manuscript's reviewers: Todd May. In particular, I had too quickly and superficially identified their accounts of reading as 'appropriat[ion]' or 'possession' (for example, in *Nietzsche and Philosophy*; Deleuze 1983: 3) with the comparatively crude instrumentalism of theorists such as Stanley Fish and Richard Rorty, for whom 'all anybody ever does with anything is use it' – indeed, a reader 'simply beats the text into a shape which will serve his own purpose' (Rorty quoted in Cohn 2006: 26).[3] For the Deleuze of *Spinoza: Practical Philosophy*, this image of the reader as autonomous subject manipulating the passive textual object is left behind in favour of a relational, ethical conception: reading as 'no longer a matter of utilizations or captures, but of sociabilities and communities', an art of determining 'whether relations (and which ones?) can compound directly . . . to form a new, more "extensive" relation' (Colson 2001: 81). This sounded a lot more like Levinas's ethical relationship to the other than Rorty's bullying.

To better understand this account of reading and semiosis, I turned to the work of other theorists who had paid attention to the philosophical sources of Deleuze-Guattarian ontology. Steven Best and Douglas Kellner's *Postmodern Theory* (1991), which had long ago served as my (very inadequate) introduction to this territory, had presented this as a disguised and self-contradictory form of 'essentialism' (Best and Kellner 1991: 106–7). Michael Hardt, however, seemed untroubled by identifying *Anti-Oedipus* as making, from its very first sentence, 'a properly ontological claim, a claim about the nature of reality' (Hardt 2017); a 'vitalist ontology', for Iain MacKenzie (MacKenzie 1996: 1240). What did this mean? Manuel DeLanda clarified: 'Although many relativists declare themselves "anti-essentialist", they share with essentialism a view of matter as an inert material . . . The world is amorphous, and we cut it out into forms using language.' Deleuze rejected this 'linguistic relativism which does not really break with essentialism' (DeLanda 1999).

Here was a reminder of something I had found puzzling about Bradley's Deleuzian essay – which, had I paid it more attention, might have steered my thought down a different path earlier. He had suggested that there was a ground for a comparative encounter between Deleuze/Guattari and Bookchin, and his name for that ground, following Patrick Hayden (2009/1997), was 'naturalism'. 'The term *naturalism*', Hayden acknowledges, 'is rarely, if ever, encountered in the writings of post-structuralists, and even then usually appears only as an object of hostile interest'; indeed, I had used this term to name one of the ontological tenets of representationalism that ought to be challenged, namely, 'the notion that things have natures that predestine or predict their behavior', and with a similar understanding, Colson flatly asserts that 'anarchism is not a naturalism' (Hayden 2009: 23; Colson 2001: 260). Bradley, however, follows Hayden in distinguishing between 'naturalism' as a recourse to 'predetermined orders of "natures" or invariant essences', on the one hand, and a more defensible 'version of naturalism compatible with the critiques of essentialism and dualism addressed in [Deleuze's] numerous publications'. Rather than positing a false world of transitory 'appearances' and a real world of unchanging 'essences', Hayden's Deleuze witnesses a single corporeal world constituted by 'real conditions of material difference and processes of becoming' (Hayden 2009: 23).

Intriguingly, Hayden acknowledges another source of inspiration for Deleuze that jogged my memory: the Epicurean philosopher and proto-scientist Lucretius. Hadn't Read, in that same essay that had so absorbed me years before, invoked Lucretius' naturalism as an 'antidote to the existentialists'? Indeed, Deleuze and Read seem to value Lucretius for some of the same reasons: his account of a wondrous, self-sufficient natural world is a way of mobilizing both 'science and pleasure' to ward off the abyssal 'fear of Acheron', to 'deprive the negative of all its power', 'to denounce everything that is sadness, everything that is the cause of sadness, and everything that needs sadness to exercise its power' (Deleuze 1990: 278). For Read, too, Lucretius joins an immanentist tradition 'constituted by the critique of negativity, the cultivation of joy, the hatred of interiority, the exteriority of forces and relations, the denunciation of power': an anarchist tradition (Deleuze 1995: 6).

## Act IV: The Possibility of Other Worlds (2004–17)

I wrote my first book, following the line of thought I'd first traced in my dissertation (1999), as a riposte to the postmodern theory then hegemonic in my corner of academia and to the varieties of post-situationist primitivism that had become one of the dominant strains in US anarchism.

The common thread between the two was anti-representationalism. Extending a *critique* of representation into an all-encompassing *refusal* of representation as such, these theorists had, I felt, painted themselves into a corner: a self-refuting scepticism on the one hand, a valorisation of mindless action on the other. My hope was that a return to social anarchist principles would clarify the proper targets for a critique of representation, which – hadn't Derrida said as much? – could not, in any case, be transcended. Equipped with more careful criteria, we could deconstruct the dominant discourses while simultaneously building up our own structures of signification, making better representations.

This argument parallels the critique Eduardo Colombo launches at Colson's *Petit lexique* in an exchange published in the French anarchist journal *Réfractions* (2002). Colombo identifies a 'constant slippage from force to action, from action to meaning, and vice versa, as a consequence of the conceptual preeminence of power' (Colombo 2002: 130). This, in turn, signals a dangerous 'slide into irrationalism':

> If an idea, a project, is the mere 'product of a material arrangement of forces . . . forces themselves made up of other forces, etc.', we rapidly slide into irrationalism. Ideas without action are degraded, made inert; action without ideas is blind, inconsistent. (Colombo 2002: 128)

For Colombo, the importance of language and the symbolic in constructing a world of domination also pointed to the central place they must have in the struggle to imagine and create a world of freedom (Colombo 2006: 16). In contrast to Colson, then, Colombo proposed to 'privilege signification . . . above force or power', using the tools of hermeneutics, psychoanalysis and ideological critique (2002: 132). In this, he follows Cornelius Castoriadis's understanding of 'autonomy' as 'self-legislation or self-regulation', 'consciousness's rule over the unconscious', as opposed to 'heteronomy, that is legislation or regulation by another' (Castoriadis 1987: 102). From this standpoint, as Colombo writes elsewhere, '"postmodern" theories' of all kinds can appear only as '[t]he dispossession of human beings as intentional agents of action in the real world . . . a straight-out repudiation of any pretension of supporting a revolutionary project' (Colombo 2008). Like ideologies, mythologies and complexes of all kinds, Deleuzian anti-humanism presents itself to Colombo as yet another 'dispossession of human power'.

Colson's response (2002), which took me a long time to understand fully, helpfully restates a key element of Deleuze's ontology. Following Spinoza's rejection of Cartesian mind–body dualism in favour of a dual-aspect monism for which thought and extension are but two attributes of a single universe, Deleuze and Guattari (2005/1987) propose that 'all reality has two distinct and yet indissociable aspects: a discursive aspect, the world of expression, language and signs, and a "machinic" aspect, the world of contents, the body, reality, and forces' (Colson 2001: 273–4). It is not a question of privileging one over the other, then: 'every force has a signification and that every signification is the expression of a force'. Colombo's theory then risks 'reaffirming a hierarchical dualism' between signification and force, theory and practice, idea and action (Colson 2002: 144, own translation).[4]

Like Colombo and Castoriadis, and with equal force, Colson warns of the tendency for signs to become autonomous from their creators and referents, so that 'symbolic power then comes to complete the work of oppression, to consecrate a dispossession, by conferring absoluteness upon what is created by human beings' (Colson 2001: 317). As Proudhon says: 'By [an] optical illusion of the intellect, man projects what is within himself outside of himself, and makes of his own Justice an idol that is no longer himself' (Proudhon 1930: 1.489, own translation). Like them, too, Colson accords an 'essential role' to signification and the symbolic in the process of emancipation from oppression: it is through them that the entities which Deleuze and Guattari call *agencements* ('assemblages' or 'arrangements') and which Proudhon calls 'collective beings' come into existence, associating with one another, producing a 'collective force' and 'collective reason' irreducible to the sum of the entities thus connected (Colson 2001: 316–17).

Here, Deleuzian ontology makes another important difference. If the critique of representation which Colson, Colombo and I share is concerned to prevent representations and representatives from drifting away into the heaven of transcendence, another variety of theory which has been acquiring prominence in US academic discourse takes for granted the intractability of representations, the 'primacy of the signifier' and 'the impossibility of the Real' (Lacan 2006: 391; Zupančič 2000: 235). From Chantal Mouffe to Slavoj Žižek and the postanarchist Saul Newman, Lacanian theorists have proceeded from a 'basic claim', as Andrew Robinson puts it, 'that identity – whether individual or social – is founded on a lack', and that '[t]herefore, social relations are always irreducibly concerned with antagonism, conflict, strife and exclusion' (Robinson 2005: n.p.). Here, it seems, we have fallen back, not only into Sartre's abyss but (Newman's apologia notwithstanding) into Hobbes's dogma of *homo homini lupus*. Since I agree with Robinson that this doctrine of 'constitutive lack' is far more an obstacle than an aid to political action and social transformation, I find it newly helpful to try to think through Deleuze's concept of desire as world-creating, because:

- desire powers imagination, opening dimensions of possibility within the actual (and the other within the self);
- desire motivates action and, conversely, the stagnation of social movements is marked by a kind of deficit of desire (Gibson-Graham 2006: 11, 13);
- desire brings us into relationship with others (it is inherently *social* in character);
- desiring relationships may be constituted on the basis of mutual recognition, without domination and violence (Graeber 2011: 494).

## Act V: Transversal Wolves (2016–?)

It is the possibility of mutual recognition without mastery or slavery that seems to be systematically obscured within the kinds of theoretical discourse founded on Hegel's dialectic of master and slave (particularly, though not solely, as mediated by Alexandre Kojève), which, as David Graeber remarks, 'has made it difficult for future theorists to think of this kind of [social] desire without also thinking of violence and domination' (Graeber 2011: 494). 'Whereas, in the theory of desire as lack, the encounter with the other becomes impossible,' Colson argues, 'the libertarian conception of desire and its power continuously make possible an encounter with the totality of other collective forces' (Colson 2001: 181).

This question of how 'collective forces' might form and meet seems vital now, as we find ourselves in a moment of heightened social crisis and contestation reminiscent of the 1960s. In a retrospective analysis of their experience as 1960s radicals, Gina Rosenberg and Chris Shutes regret having dismissed many 'actually very radical' movements as merely 'spectacular', that is, a surrogate for real social transformation, because they seemed to be only 'partial revolts' rather than addressing the totality (Rosenberg and Shutes 1974: 18). Yet the dynamics of revolt which engulfed the United States (and much of the rest of the world) in the 1960s seemed to obey the logic neither of the 'partial' nor of the 'total'. Rather, each newly emerging social protagonist seemed to find its voice by *analogy* with others, so that black power, women's liberation, gay rights, the American Indian movement and a score of other forces stood to one another not as parts to whole nor as parallel equivalents, but each as *singular* in a way that was also, in spite of very real tensions and conflicts, in a relation of *affinity* to all the others. All of these 'partial revolts', in the words of Rosenberg and Shutes, were also simultaneously 'absolutely "total" rebellions, which somehow concerned absolutely everybody' (1974: 18).

In this respect, Deleuzian thought might also yet come to the aid of an anarchism still struggling to come to terms with what are often called 'identity politics'. If anarchism was always theoretically better suited to the new social movements than Marxism – positing 'a multitude of power relations and not . . . a first principle or a determining totality', as Colson notes, it is not constrained to regard economic class as the fundamental structure of power, to relegate all other struggles to the status of epiphenomena or matters to be sorted 'after the revolution' (Colson 2001: 59)[5] – it was the reformist dialectic of 'recognition' which ensured that the proliferation of desires that erupted in the mid-twentieth century did not threaten the structures of Capital and the State.

A Deleuzian analysis of these 'molecular' movements, rather than dismissing them as mere 'partial revolts', might argue, with Richard J. F. Day, that they have been recuperated via another kind of master–slave dialectic, ensnared in a politics of 'recognition'. By offering 'the gifts of *recognition* and *integration* to subordinate identities and communities', the State acts as an 'apparatus of capture', trapping the desires animating social movements so that they *behave* in a Lacanian manner, producing 'an endless repetition of a self-defeating act that only perpetuates the conditions that give rise to its own motive force' (Day 2005: 14–15, 78–9, 137). Rather than mourning the demise of a unified revolutionary subject or casting about for replacements (like the 'multitude'), we could instead focus on blocking processes of conformist 'subjection' (the production of docile bodies and identities) and identifying and facilitating processes of radical 'subjectification' (the production of rebellious individuals and groups) (Angaut 2010: 29–37). Jasbir Puar's suggestion that we rethink identities and their intersectionality in terms of assemblage/*agencement* is promising in this respect (Puar 2012: 49–66).

Complementary to the project of reimagining desire in positive terms is the ongoing renaissance in studies of *affect* to which Deleuze and Guattari have contributed. Here, I see some affinities with the Anglo-American stream of affect theory. Both attempt to go beyond the repressive hypothesis – indeed, beyond much of psychoanalytic doctrine, 'displacing the Freudian emphasis on oedipality and repression' which has done so much to distort and misrepresent experiences of (for example) queerness and disability;[6] both are attentive to the body, refusing to textualise it away, to treat it as undifferentiated *hyle* (matter without intrinsic form), and therefore unafraid of and curious about the biological and natural frameworks within which mental and social life unfold;[7] both are wary of the negative affects of 'mastery, melancholia, and moralism' and the abstract negativity that is tasked with historical labour by the Hegelians.[8] Taken together, I think these constitute the bases for an alternative to the entire apparatus of ideology critique exemplified in Žižek's work, a 'paranoid theoretical stance' par excellence (Gibson-Graham 2006: 10).

A Deleuzian anarchism could help us to re-engage in the unfinished (and never-finished) process of seeking coherence in oppositional milieus, or, in common Anglo-American anarchist parlance, *getting our shit together*. Some of Colson's analyses of the 'micropolitics' of the movement indicate the difficulty of this task, providing a glimpse into the affective vicissitudes of this milieu. Anyone who has spent time in this environment might recognise the phenomenon named 'locking horns' – 'useless' arguments between comrades driven by 'macho hypersensitivity' and the wish to 'have the last word' (Colson 2001: 248–9). Another series of entries describe 'common notions' and collective ethical practices enabling the negotiation of these difficulties. Together with entries describing broader ethical and ontological notions, these can help us to think through some concrete problems faced by radical groups and communities.

It immediately clarifies the anti-fascist practice of denying fascists a 'platform': rather than feeling constrained to defend the 'right' of white supremacists to 'speak' in public, we can identify this as a case of 'ideomania' (a 'fetishized, autonomized perspective, detached from its conditions of production, intent on applying itself as it is, absolutely, everywhere and in all circumstances') and think about intervention or non-intervention in terms of 'local', immediate, pragmatic, concrete effects (Colson 2001: 153). 'No-platforming' is then not a matter of a transcendent Kantian rule but a decision about what is good *for* a particular community in which we are implicated, with the recognition that 'every force has a signification and that every signification is the expression of a force' (Colson 2002: 144).

However, Deleuzian analyses might be deployed in ways that obscure rather than clarify. A discouraging example appears in Dupuis-Déri's (2009) examination of the case of a dispute around feminism during a three-day festival of lectures and discussions held by the La Gryffe anarchist bookstore in Lyon in 1998. A group calling itself the Collectif des femmes, des féministes et des lesbiennes de l'action féministe lors des journées libertaires du 8, 9 et 10 mai 1998 à Lyon ('Collective of Women,

Feminists, and Lesbians for Feminist Action at the Libertarian Days of 8–10 May in Lyon') had disrupted a plenary to protest the monopolization of speech by male comrades. An extremely regressive sexism was the immediate response to this intervention, as the Collective were called 'poor little idiots [*pauv' connes*]' and 'lesbians' – and later treated with condescension, powered by a certain 'universalist argument' that treated their concerns, all too predictably, as *merely* particular.

This disqualifying discourse is clearly expressed in the writing of four men, members of La Gryffe, signatories of a text (Daniel et al. 1998) denouncing the direct action of the Collective of Women, Feminists and Lesbians. If several passages of this text are pro-feminist, the signatories nevertheless regret that the feminists and lesbians practised 'a kind of secession or separation, leaving . . . only one division, seen [by them] as determining and primary: the relations between men and women' (Dupuis-Déri 2009: 197–8). It seems likely that the 'Daniel' signing this article, 'Anarchie et mouvement des femmes' (Anarchy and the Women's Movement), published in the bookstore's journal, *La Griffe*, is Daniel Colson, a longtime activist with La Gryffe (Daniel et al. 1998). Yet how can this be the same Daniel Colson who so clearly articulates the Deleuzian bases for practising exactly this 'kind of secession or separation' in the *Petit lexique*?

In his entry on '*non-mixité*' or 'separatism' (which is directly and uniquely cross-referenced with 'anarchy'), Colson begins by dismissing the response of 'a great number of anarchists' to 'feminists' demand to meet on their own, to constitute themselves as autonomous groupings': such 'experimentation with the various methods of association and disassociation' merely expresses the vital plurality and autonomy of forces seeking their own emancipation. Several key Deleuzian concepts are mobilised in this argument: the valorisation of the micropolitical (or molecular) over the macropolitical (or molar), singularity, becoming-minor, the assemblage/*agencement*, rejecting the organ-isation of the body politic and so on. It is, as Colson demonstrates, a very traditional anarchist argument as well: the concept of 'worker separatism' is founded in Proudhon's work, along with the principle of free 'association' and 'disassociation', part and parcel of the theory of federation as well as that of 'revolt' or 'rupture' (Colson 2001: 41–4, 119, 177–80, 292). How can he dismiss the women's action as 'separatism'?

The article to which 'Daniel' is a signatory is multiply authored, but there is a recognizably Deleuzian element in certain passages. Thus, the authors of 'Anarchie et mouvement des femmes' concede, in terms very similar to those Colson would use in the entry on separatism just three years later, that anarchists have 'always' recognized the necessity of 'fully autonomous specific groupings . . . to allow every struggle and every movement to do all that they are capable of without being cut off from or hindered by other struggles and movements, however different or conflicting' (Daniel et al. 1998, own translation) 'To do all that one is capable of' or 'to go to the limits of one's capacity [*aller jusqu'au bout de ce qu'on peut*]' is a Deleuzian formula, appearing first in *Difference and Repetition* (1968), that recurs frequently (at least thirty occurrences, with variations) throughout the *Petit lexique*; it always signals the wider significance of singular, molecular revolts, the strange way in which each 'monad' immediately connects to all the others, 'somehow concern[ing] absolutely everybody'.[9] In Deleuze-Guattarian terms, it is a formula for 'transversality' – the unity of the absolutely singular, separate and incommensurable, the 'trans-monadic axis' or 'horizontalness' which stands as a challenge to abstract, metaphysical 'universality', 'the traditional vertical stance of thought' (Guattari 1996: 167, 174). The power of women, of feminists, of lesbians to withdraw from the conversation dominated by male anarchists in order to talk among themselves is, as Daniel et al. acknowledge, the *guarantee* of 'the paradoxically conflictual unity of all these struggles . . . And that is why a number of the signatories of this text were still surprised that libertarians can dispute the need for women to come together and to group independently' (Daniel et al. 1998, own translation).

Quickly, however, this grand gesture is turned back on itself, as the concept of transversality is deployed *against* the protest: if the Libertarian Days, La Gryffe itself and the anarchist movement as such include sexists as well as feminists, women as well as misogynists, this is to be expected, because '[a]ll these views are also contributing to compose the libertarian movement and we believe each of them, because of its own transversality, is necessary to the other, in an overall movement that remains largely to be invented' (Daniel et al. 1998). In this argument, transversality operates in a manner remarkably similar to legalistic liberal concepts: for example, the principle of 'free speech' which insists (separating 'speech' from 'action', signs from forces) that if X has a right to speak, so does Y, and so does Z, ad infinitum, regardless of the gap between this representation of equal rights and the material experiences of intimidation, terror and domination for which it serves as rhetorical decor. This is a very far cry from the anarchist understanding of equality that informs Colson's *Petit lexique*, which, far from presenting 'a mere relativism or a liberalism in which all things are equal since anything is just as valid as anything else . . . presuppose[s] a continuous evaluation of the emancipatory or oppressive quality of actions, perspectives, and standpoints' (Colson 2001: 112–13). The spectre of liberal relativism is precisely what the authors of 'Anarchisme et mouvement des femmes' imagine as 'transversality': a *refusal to judge* (or, significantly, a refusal by anarchist men to judge other anarchist men). In the name of 'plurality', then (or is it laissez-faire?), they offer an a priori excuse for extending tolerance to all forms of domination: anarchism 'does not identify with the struggle of women, or with any other particular struggle, but with the union and confrontation of all struggles against domination'. In other words, just because anarchism does not reduce all struggles to one single contradiction, these men allege, it cannot specifically commit to feminist principles. And just because of this non-commitment, and in the name of an 'open' and 'inclusive' political project, it is 'inevitable' that some of those present will be non-feminist, or indeed *anti*-feminist: 'What did the feminist comrades who agreed to participate in the event expect? Ideological unanimity and politically correct speech? An a priori prioritisation of problems? A liberated zone free from domination, an oasis of egalitarian and transparent relations?' (Daniel et al. 1998).

The demand to be included, to open up the space of discussion for women, to overturn the hierarchy of speakers and spoken-to/spoken-of, is deftly turned into a demand for the exclusion of others, for ideological closure, for a place atop a hierarchy of concerns. It is an astonishing feat of rhetoric, almost enough to make one miss the way in which, as Dupuis-Déri notes, '[t]his declaration deeply contradicts a very long-standing anarchist tradition according to which militant organizations must incarnate the principles of anarchism – the very principle of prefiguration which distinguishes anarchism' (2009: 198). The policy of 'inclusion' promoted by the members of La Gryffe rather recalls the crude means–ends calculations by which, as Rebecca Winter notes, 'sexual violence survivors have been sacrificed at the altar of "movement building"' (Winter 2014: 16–17). Difficult as it may be, it is certain that the will to egalitarian relations in the future presupposes the effort to create egalitarian spaces in the present. Perhaps this is even what Critchley means by the infinite, unfulfillable, but by no means dispensable, demand of ethics (Critchley 2007: 10).

What does all of this mean for the possibilities of a Deleuzian anarchism and for the ongoing project of *getting our shit together*? Transversality worthy of the name is difficult to achieve, even if we attend nice liberal-arts colleges where difference is typically represented as enjoyable. We need common notions, shared symbols and ethical practices that help us recognize and avoid bad encounters which decrease our power; spaces facilitating good encounters that let us unfold our powers and do all that we are capable of.

But the 'continuous evaluation of the emancipatory or oppressive quality of actions, perspectives, and standpoints' (Colson 2001: 112–13) this requires is no picnic. As attested by the ongoing, intractable disputes around 'call-out culture' – and the ongoing reality of oppressive behaviors and structures within every corner of radical life – the micropolitical question of whom to trust, to work with, even to tolerate, does not allow of any definitive or universal answers. If I have reached for deconstructive tools in response to the discourse of 'Anarchisme et mouvement des femmes', I don't think that rigorous discursive critique of this kind is sufficient, for want of a better word, to keep us honest. As much as I want to help develop a more articulate ethics – for example, of the sort pioneered by Philly's Pissed in response to sexual violence in the punk scene (Winter 2014: 102), so that our responses may become more coordinated and less improvisational – I have to admit that Colson's Deleuzian ethics of constant qualitative evaluation – a kind of affective smell-test: what is the 'feel' of this room tonight, of that person's gestures, of this organization's culture? – is probably indispensable.

The Acheron that haunts me, these days, is no longer the abyss of epistemological or moral nihilism. It is the rising temperature, the rising oceans, the rising cruelty of neoliberalism, the rising tides of misogyny and neo-Nazism. In Portland, Oregon this week (26 May 2017), fascists celebrate a senseless murder on a train by a man screaming racist and nationalist obscenities – a 'lone wolf', as the media cliché has it, in a perennial untruth about the associative capacities both of fascists and of wolves. The alienation generated by the 'planetary/patriarchal work & war machine' (Figure 9.1) has created good soil for the growth of international fascist rhizomes: from Portland to Poland, they are assembling, linking up, finding their own horrific affinities.

The mimetic force of the negative affects is hard to resist, and there are now even a number of Deleuzians who, reading his philosophy of radical affirmation against the grain, argue persuasively that we ought not to resist them (for example, Culp 2016). I have come to better understand the costs of suppressing negative emotions and the value of engaging with them. Having considered structural racism a more fundamental source of oppression than conscious racist ideology, I grossly underestimated the threat posed by organised white supremacism in the United States, which will consolidate its new foothold in public space if not resisted with force. Nonetheless, I continue to believe that the cultivation of the 'warlike' posture in our milieu has helped maintain the centrality of the young, able-bodied, usually white and male protagonist dubbed 'Anarchist Action Man' (Coleman and Bassi 2011: 20–224) and that we would do well to cultivate some more traditionally feminine skills: education, healing, listening, caregiving, '[c]reating intimacy, communities & freedom' (Figure 9.1). My studies of anarchist resistance culture increasingly incline me to think of what we need to do as creating what Stevphen Shukaitis calls 'a sustainable culture of . . . affective resistance' (Shukaitis 2011: 46). This immense labour of caregiving absolutely must be shared by men, as women have sustained the world this way far too alone for far too long.[10] As Juan Duchesne-Winter suggests, rather than focusing all our attention on the 'front' facing the armored enemy, we need to put more energy than before into the 'rearguard', where street medics tend to the wounded, prison-support organisers and media and legal teams do their work, children and elders are cared for, food is prepared and shelter arranged (Duchesne-Winter 2010: 229).

It is in the spaces created by this work of mutual aid – a classical anarchist concept/practice par excellence which is mysteriously absent from the *Petit lexique*[11] – that we may more fully pursue the kinds of separation and connection which constitute an emancipatory transversality, not through liberal *inclusion* but through radical *implication*: the process which produces subjectivity, folding the world inward to make a little pocket within it which is itself also a world, withdrawing into an inside that is composed of outsides, each implicated in the folds of other rebel subjectivities.[12] Linked together, each a relay of the others, these pockets of anarchy could form a 'world in which many worlds fit' (Nail 2012: 168–9) which might deserve the name 'Deleuzian'.

## Notes

1. See Gordon (2003: 4.1), Newman (2000: n.p.; 2001: 38), Koch (2005: 131), May (1994: 61), Call (2002: 14), Mueller (2003: 122–49), Critchley (2009: 276), Day (2005: 95).
2. See Miller (1984: 76), Hartley (1995: 145–64), Morland (1997: 8–23).
3. See also Deleuze and Guattari: 'reading a text is never a scholarly exercise in search of what is signified, still less a highly textual exercise in search of a signifier. Rather it is a productive use of the literary machine' (Deleuze and Guattari 1983: 106).
4. And indeed, in the *Petit lexique*, Colson indicts Castoriadis as the 'totally Sartrean' thinker of 'an abstract emancipation, thought in a dualist manner (through the distinctions between the instituting and the instituted, autonomy and heteronomy), in the manner of a creation *ex nihilo*' (Colson 2001: 171).
5. See also Shannon and Rogue (2009), Bookchin (1989: 259–74).
6. Kosovsky Sedgwick and Frank (2003: 98), Deleuze and Parnet (2007: 77–8), Siebers (2008: 34–52).
7. Kosovsky Sedgwick and Frank (2003: 93), Gibson-Graham (2006: 1–2).

8. Gibson-Graham (2006: 7), Colson (2001: 92–3).
9. Colson (2001: 22, 25, 28, 43, 49, 70, 79, 81, 89, 90, 94, 95, 98, 117, 138, 149, 153, 166, 173, 174, 181, 245, 253, 254, 256, 275, 292, 302).
10. I am obliged to Aura Bogado for some recent conversation that has stirred and added to my thoughts about this.
11. See Stocker (2001: 30–55). My thanks to Josh Lukin for pointing this essay out to me.
12. Deleuze (2006: 80). My thanks to Andrew Culp for discussing Deleuze's elusive concept of 'implication' with me.

# References

Angaut, J. (2010), 'La construction du "sujet révolutionnaire" ou la dislocation du marxisme', *Réfractions*, 25: 29–38.
Best, S. and S. Kellner (1991), *Postmodern Theory: Critical Interrogations*, New York: Guilford Press.
Bookchin, M. (1982), *The Ecology of Freedom: The Emergence and Dissolution of Hierarchy*, Palo Alto: Cheshire Books.
Bookchin, M. (1989), 'New Social Movements: The Anarchic Dimension', in D. Goodway (ed.), *For Anarchism: History, Theory, and Practice*, London: Routledge, pp. 259–74.
Bookchin, M. (1993), *Deep Ecology and Anarchism: A Polemic*, London: Freedom Press.
Bookchin, M. (1995a), *Re-enchanting Humanity: A Defense of the Human Spirit Against Antihumanism, Misanthropy, Mysticism, and Primitivism*, London: Cassell.
Bookchin, M. (1995b), *Social Anarchism or Lifestyle Anarchism: An Unbridgeable Chasm*, Oakland: AK Press.
Bradley, J. (1997), post to RA-L, 29 September 1997.
Bradley, J. (2000), 'The Possibility of an Antihumanist EcoAnarchism', RA-forum.
Call, L. (2002), *Postmodern Anarchism*, Lanham, MD: Lexington Books.
Castoriadis, C. (1987), *The Imaginary Institution of Society*, trans. K. Blamey, Cambridge, MA: MIT Press.
Chodorkoff, D. (1990), 'Social Ecology and Community Development', in J. P. Clark and M. Bookchin (eds), *Renewing the Earth: The Promise of Social Ecology: A Celebration of the Work of Murray Bookchin*, London: Green Print.
Cohn, J. (1997), post to RA-L, 2 October 1997.
Cohn, J. (1999), 'An Exemplary Failure: Pat Murphy's *The City, Not Long After* and the Dilemmas of Anarchist Utopian Fiction', *Anarchist Studies*, 7(2): 105–10.
Cohn, J. (2006), *Anarchism and the Crisis of Representation: Hermeneutics, Aesthetics, Politics*, Selinsgrove, PA: Susquehanna University Press.
Cohn, J. and S. Wilbur (2003), 'What's Wrong with Postanarchism?', *Theory & Practice*, Institute for Anarchist Studies, pp. 157–70.
Coleman, L. and S. Bassi (2011), 'Deconstructing Militant Manhood: Masculinities in the Disciplining of (Anti-)Globalization Politics', *International Feminist Journal of Politics*, 13(2): 204–24.
Colombo, E. (2002), 'À propos du *Petit lexique philosophique: De l'anarchisme* de Daniel Colson', *Réfractions*, 8: 130, translation mine.
Colombo, E. (2006), 'El anarquismo ante la crisis de las ideologías', *Acción Directa*, 1(1): 16, translation mine.
Colombo, E. (2008), 'The Revolution: A Concept Dissolvable in Postmodernity', trans. Helen Arnold, *Research on Anarchism Forum*.

Colson, D. (2001), *Petit lexique philosophique de l'anarchisme: De Proudhon à Deleuze*, Paris: Librairie Générale Française.

Colson, D. (2002), 'Réponse de Daniel Colson à Eduardo Colombo', *Réfractions*, 8: 144, translation mine.

Conrad, J. (1997) [1899], *Heart of Darkness: Complete, Authoritative Text with Biographical, Historical, and Cultural Contexts, Critical History, and Essays from Contemporary Critical Perspectives*, Boston and New York: Bedford/St. Martin's.

Critchley S. (1992), *The Ethics of Deconstruction: Derrida and Levinas*, Oxford: Blackwell.

Critchley, S. (2007), *Infinitely Demanding: Ethics of Commitment, Politics of Resistance*, London: Verso.

Critchley, S. (2009), 'Mystical Anarchism', *Critical Horizons: A Journal of Philosophy and Social Theory*, 10(2): 272–306.

Culp, A. (2016), *Dark Deleuze*, Minneapolis: University of Minnesota Press.

Daniel, Fred, Jean-Luc, and Jean Pierre [no surnames] (1998), 'Anarchie et mouvement des femmes', *La Griffe* 11, translation mine.

Day, R. J. F. (2005), *Gramsci Is Dead: Anarchist Currents in the Newest Social Movements*, London: Pluto Press.

D'Emilio, J. (1992), 'Capitalism and Gay Identity', in J. D'Emilio, *Making Trouble: Essays on Gay History, Politics, and the University*, New York: Routledge.

DeLanda, M. (1999), 'An Interview with Manuel DeLanda', *Switch*, 5(1), http://switch.sjsu.edu/archive/web/v5n1/deLanda/index.html (last accessed 15 August 2018).

Deleuze, G. (1983), *Nietzsche and Philosophy*, trans. H. Tomlinson, New York: Columbia University Press.

Deleuze, G. (1990), *The Logic of Sense*, trans. M. Lester and C. Stivale, New York: Columbia University Press.

Deleuze, G. (1995), *Negotiations*, trans. M. Joughin, New York: Columbia University Press.

Deleuze, G. (2006), *Foucault*, trans. S. Hand, London: Continuum.

Deleuze, G. and F. Guattari (1983), *Anti-Oedipus: Capitalism and Schizophrenia*, trans. R. Hurley, M. Seem and H. Lane, Minneapolis: University of Minnesota Press.

Deleuze G. and F. Guattari (2005) [1987], *A Thousand Plateaus*, trans. B. Massumi, Minneapolis: University of Minnesota Press.

Deleuze, G. and P. Parnet (2007), *Dialogues II*, trans. H. Tomlinson and B. Habberjam, New York: Columbia University Press.

Derrida, J. (1982), *Positions*, trans. A. Bass, Chicago: University of Chicago Press.

Derrida, J. (1991), '"Eating Well": An Interview', in E. Cadava, P. Connor and J.-L. Nancy (eds), *Who Comes After the Subject?*, New York: Routledge, pp. 96–119.

Duchesne-Winter, J. (2010), 'Literary Communism: A Manifesto of the Rearguard', *Journal of Latin American Cultural Studies: Travesia*, 19(3): 225–36.

Dupuis-Déri, F. (2009), 'L'Anarchisme face au féminisme: Comparaison France-Québec', in O. Fillieule and P. Roux (eds), *Le Sexe du militantisme*, Paris: Presses de Sciences Po.

Gibson-Graham, J. K. (2006), *A Postcapitalist Politics*, Minneapolis: University of Minnesota Press.

Godwin, W. (1971) [1793], *Enquiry Concerning Political Justice*, in M. S. Shatz (ed.), *The Essential Works of Anarchism*, New York: Bantam.

Gordon, U. (2003), 'Horizons of Change: Deconstruction and the Evanescence of Authority', thesis, RA-Forum.

Graeber, D. (2011), 'Consumption', *Current Anthropology*, 52(4): 489–511.

Guattari, F. (1996), 'Ritornellos and Existential Affects', trans. J. Schiesari and G. van den Abbeele, and 'Microphysics of Power/Micropolitics of Desire', trans. J. Caruana, in G. Genosko (ed.), *The Guattari Reader*, Oxford: Blackwell, pp. 158–71.

Guérin, D. (1971), *Anarchism: From Theory to Practice*, trans. M. Klopper, New York: Monthly Review Press.

Hardt, M. (2017), 'Reading Notes on Deleuze and Guattari, Capitalism & Schizophrenia', Duke University, http://people.duke.edu/~hardt/Deleuze&Guattari.html (last accessed 15 August 2018).

Hartley, D. (1995), 'Communitarian Anarchism and Human Nature', *Anarchist Studies*, 3(2): 145–64.

Hayden, P. (2009) [1997], 'Gilles Deleuze and Naturalism: A Convergence with Ecological Theory and Politics', in B. Herzogenrath (ed.), *An (Un)likely Alliance: Thinking Environment(s) with Deleuze/Guattari*, Newcastle upon Tyne: Cambridge Scholars.

Kaplan, R. (1994), 'The Coming Anarchy: How Scarcity, Crime, Overpopulation, Tribalism, and Disease Are Rapidly Destroying the Social Fabric of Our Planet', *The Atlantic*, 273(2): 44–76.

Koch, A. (1993), 'Poststructuralism and Epistemological Basis of Anarchism', *The Philosophy of the Social Sciences*, 23(3): 263–305.

Koch, A. (2005), *Knowledge and Social Construction*, Lanham, MD: Lexington Books.

Kosovsky Sedgwick, E. and A. Frank (2003), 'Shame in the Cybernetic Fold: Reading Silvan Tomkins', in E. Kosovsky Sedgwick, *Touching Feeling: Affect, Pedagogy, Performativity*, Durham, NC: Duke University Press.

Kropotkin, P. (1902), *Mutual Aid: A Factor of Evolution*, New York: McClure, Philips & Co.

Lacan, J. (2006), *Écrits: The First Complete Edition in English*, trans. B. Fink, New York: Norton.

Lappé, F., J. Collins and C. Fowler (1979), *Food First: Beyond the Myth of Scarcity*, New York: Ballantine Books.

Lippard, L. (1984), *Get the Message?: A Decade of Art for Social Change*, New York: Dutton.

Lukács, G. (1973), 'Existentialism', in *Marxism and Human Liberation: Essays on History, Culture and Revolution*, trans. H. F. Mins, New York: Delta.

MacKenzie, I. (1996), 'Deleuze and Guattari's Poststructuralist Philosophy', in P. Dunleavy and J. Stanyer (eds), *Contemporary Political Studies*, Exeter: Political Studies Association, pp. 1234–41.

*Manufacturing Consent: Noam Chomsky and the Media* (1992), film, directed by Mark Achbar and Peter Wintonick.

May, T. (1994), *Political Philosophy of Poststructuralist Anarchism*, University Park: Pennsylvania State University Press.

Miller, D. (1984), *Anarchism*, London and Melbourne: J. M. Dent.

Miller, J. (1993), *The Passion of Michel Foucault*, London: HarperCollins.

Morland, D. (1997), 'Anarchism, Human Nature and History: Lessons for the Future', in J. Purkis and J. Bowen (eds), *Twenty-First Century Anarchism*, London: Cassell, pp. 8–23.

Mueller, T. (2003), 'Empowering Anarchy: Power, Hegemony, and Anarchist Strategy', *Anarchist Studies*, 11(2): 122–49.

Nail, T. (2012), *Returning to Revolution: Deleuze, Guattari and Zapatismo*, Edinburgh: Edinburgh University Press.

Newman, S. (2000), 'Anarchism and the Politics of Ressentiment', *Theory and Event*, 4(3).

Newman, S. (2001), *From Bakunin to Lacan*, Lanham, MA: Rowman & Littlefield.

Nietzsche, F. (2005), *The Anti-Christ, Ecce Homo, Twilight of the Idols, and Other Writings*, trans. J. Norman, Cambridge: Cambridge University Press.

Perez, R. (1990), *On An(archy) and Schizoanalysis*, New York: Autonomedia.

Protevi, J. (2009), *Political Affect: Connecting the Social and the Somatic*, Minneapolis: University of Minneapolis Press.

Proudhon, P. (1930), *De la justice dans la révolution et dans l'église*, Paris: Rivière, translation mine.

Proudhon, P. (1970), *Selected Writings of Pierre-Joseph Proudhon*, trans. E. Fraser, London: Macmillan, translation mine.

Puar, J. (2012), '"I Would Rather Be a Cyborg Than a Goddess": Becoming-Intersectional in Assemblage Theory', *PhiloSOPHIA*, 2(1): 49–66.

Read, H. (1949), *Existentialism, Marxism and Anarchism*, London: Freedom Press.

Richards, H. (1996), *Letters from Québec: A Philosophy for Peace and Justice*, San Francisco: International Scholars Publications.

Robinson, S. (1997), email to the author, 18 December 1997.

Robinson, A. (2005), 'The Politics of Constitutive Lack: A Critique', *Theory & Event*, 8(1).

Roediger, D. (1991), *The Wages of Whiteness: Race and the Making of the American Working Class*, London: Verso.

Rorty, R. (1982), *Consequences of Pragmatism: Essays: 1972–1980*, Minneapolis: University of Minnesota Press.

Rosenberg, G. and C. Shutes (1974), *Disinterest Compounded Daily*, Berkeley: Point-Blank.

Ryan, A. (1993), '"Twenty-first Century Blues", review of *Preparing for the Twenty-first Century* by Paul Kennedy', *New York Review of Books*, 40(9): 20–3.

Sartre, J. (1975), 'Existentialism Is a Humanism', trans. P. Mairet, in W. Kaufmann (ed.), *Existentialism From Dostoevsky to Sartre*, New York: New American Library, pp. 345–69.

Scott, J. (1998), *Seeing Like a State: How Certain Schemes to Improve the Human Condition Have Failed*, New Haven, CT: Yale University Press.

Shannon, D. and J. Rogue (2009), *Refusing to Wait: Anarchism & Intersectionality*, Fordsburg, South Africa: Zabalaza Books.

Shatz, M., ed. (1971), *The Essential Works of Anarchism*, New York: Bantam Books.

Shukaitis, S. (2011), 'Nobody Knows What an Insurgent Body Can Do: Questions for Affective Resistance', in J. Heckert and R. Cleminson (eds), *Anarchism & Sexuality: Ethics, Relationships and Power*, New York: Routledge, pp. 45–66.

Siebers, T. (2008), *Disability Theory*, Ann Arbor: Michigan University Press.

Spanos, W. (1993), *Heidegger and Criticism: Retrieving the Cultural Politics of Destruction*, Minneapolis: University of Minnesota Press.

Sterling, B. (1989), 'Slipstream', *Science Fiction EYE*, 5.

Stocker, S. (2001), 'Problems of Embodiment and Problematic Embodiment', *Hypatia*, 16(3): 30–55.

Wilson, P. (1991), 'Amoral Responsibility', *Science Fiction EYE*, 8.

Winter, R. (2014), 'Silent No Longer: Confronting Sexual Violence in the Left', *The Platform*, 1.

Woodcock, G. (1962), *Anarchism: A History of Libertarian Ideas and Movements*, Cleveland: Meridian Books.

Zupančič, A. (2000), *Ethics of the Real: Kant, Lacan*, London: Verso.

Chapter 10

# Deterritorialising Anarchist Geographies: A Deleuzian Approach

*Alejandro de la Torre Hernández and Gerónimo Barrera de la Torre*

## Diasporas

It has been established in anarchist studies that the spread of anarchist philosophy and its political practices were based on migratory waves and diasporas of militants who disseminated their ideology throughout the world. These dispersions made possible the construction of a cosmopolitan narrative of resistance and social struggle, based on worldwide networks of militants, made public through the anarchist press (Anderson 2013; Zimmer 2015).

Although there exists no history of a centralised anarchist structure or political party that exercised control and dictated the organisation of its followers, it is still possible to reconstruct this diaspora by tracing the histories of exiled anarchists, particularly through the newspapers they produced. These served as propaganda, mechanisms of sociability, means of political articulation and a way to survive. In many aspects, these anarchist newspapers, together with their affinity groups, can be considered the main type of political unit of the anarchist movement at the turn of the century. Thus, they functioned concurrently as a means of expression, a way to ensure solidarity and organisational unity, and a resource that created a cohesive nexus among communities of readers who were often geographically distant from each other, but united by a common language, ideology and shared political culture.

For the purposes of historical inquiry, these newspapers are key elements for understanding the material dimension of the links between anarchist communities. It is in the tangibility of these newspaper-objects that we find strengths and weakness of the anarchist movement. On a symbolic level, the newspaper can be read as a synecdoche standing for the modern city, comprised of a barrage of images, labyrinths of messages, guides for foreigners and an overwhelming succession of events

(Fritzsche 2008: 27–62). Thus, the anarchist press develops its own 'transnational city', made up of communities of readers defined by their mobility and international dispersion. Our engagement here explores two scales: the anarchist Spanish-speaking networks and the subjects that nourished them. To avoid fixed, linear and transcendental accounts, we think through the performativity entangled in the emergence and configuration of such networks. We also think about subjectivation – the plane of thought that anarchist correspondents, as wandering rebels, navigate by continually becoming.

These publications, which were gradually weaving networks of communication and exchange, reached maturity – at least as far as Spanish anarchist newspapers are concerned – towards the second decade of the twentieth century, but their gestation is located in the last two decades of the preceding century. Through this set of publications, distant anarchist communities, characterised by their transnational status and nomadic, international experience, could be contacted. We see how, for example, suffering under capitalist exploitation in large urban centres, Spanish migrants settled in the ports of America, Mexican workers in the United States and Italian propagandists on the shores of the Rio de la Plata as full-time propagandists and wandering prophets of the social revolution. Thus, one primary objective of the publications' web was to bring these heterogeneous sets of wandering anarchist communities into contact.

Here we embrace the complex, fluid, multifarious and decentred configuration of networks as assemblages, emergent and contingent, without structures or model. Images of roots, branches, cephalopods, webs and even archipelagos or constellations come to mind as we try to imagine the physiognomy and *geographicity* of these protean networks of relationships, encounters and disagreements, amputations and regenerations. As the work of Deleuze and Guattari does not have a sustained discussion on anarchism, we think, in this chapter, about how Deleuze-Guattarian ideas overlap, intersect and augment the historical Spanish-speaking anarchist movement. This is an open interpretation and, as such, may lead to alternative ways of rethinking the complex networks of the international movement. We hope that it exposes the movement's tensions and conflicts, thus eluding narrow visions centred on teleological and cause–effect explanations. We suggest that readers think through rhizomatic horizons about how anarchists actualise anarchy in its multiplicity, contingency and continuous difference/differentiation. Always unfinished, these networks fold and unfold, sometimes towards openness, sometimes aimed at fixing their horizons. It is in the intensities, we hope to show, that the continuous struggle to keep connections alive, communications open and thoughts receptive, are reflected. These intensities also reflect the different flows that stabilised and neutralised multiplicities according to axes of subjectification (Deleuze and Guattari 2005: 12). Deterritorialisation and reterritorialisation were key in maintaining such openness, working against hierarchical ideas and formations through experiences of territories and landscapes. We are not suggesting here that there is a 'positive' effect intrinsic to such processes of anarchist subjectivation, but pointing to the capacity these can have in maintaining and navigating the multiple lines of transcendence and fixation.

The anarchists' migratory mobility is attributable to many causes. At the end of the nineteenth century, when global voyages increased as a result of technological advancements, economic migration and political persecution became leading factors in the mobility of anarchist militants from every continent. These waves of dispersion, as far as Spanish-speaking anarchism is concerned, are marked by social struggles. In fact, it is difficult to follow the flow of Atlantic anarchism if we ignore specific incidents. We may think here of the suppression of the Jerez de la Frontera uprising, Cuba's independence wars, the Montjuich affairs, the political persecution of opponents of the Porfirio Díaz regime in Mexico, the application of Residence and Social Defence Laws in Argentina, the Tragic Week of Barcelona and other historical processes. These, coupled with the slow and constant migration motivated by economic factors, also led to the migration of anarchist militants. Such oppressive cycles, combined with the will to spread anarchist thought and practices, and spark a social revolution, produced a peculiar diaspora, characterised by the absence of a 'promised land' or homeland to return to in a geographical sense (contrary to the classical model of diasporas). Thus, the 'return' of the anarchist diaspora is accomplished in time – the creation of the future – rather than in space.

The main nodes of anarchist Spanish-speaking press networks can be found in cities such as Barcelona, New York, Havana and Buenos Aires. These are points on the map where important communities of anarchist readers were based and where much of the source material of influential anarchist propaganda was created and then spread to different regions of the globe. The importance and density of these networks are not negligible, neither are the quantity of newspapers and the scope of their distribution. From the 1880s until the beginning of the First World War, these networks were made up of numerous anarchist publications that were distributed throughout the continents.[1] Nevertheless, as with any network, these anarchist communities were 'selective' in certain ways as particular connections were established through language, political culture or personal relations. At the same time, these networks continuously sought to increase their scope.

In the following two sections, we look first at the forms of connections in Spanish-speaking anarchist networks which roughly form two 'layers' (although this can, of course, be thought of differently). The first addresses the unfolding of interconnections and will be followed by reference to newspapers as material indications. Maps and visual representations as used here are cartographic demonstrations of change and intensity, open to the multiple dimensions and intersections in their construction. We follow Deleuze and Guattari when they assert that 'the map is open and connectable in all of its dimensions; it is detachable, reversible, susceptible to constant modification' (Deleuze and Guattari 2005: 12). Imagining this network can also lead to imagining an atlas of fantastic confines or maps of imaginary roads from the alternative deterritorialisations glimpsed by the many anarchisms. The protean networks with which we work always risk conforming to mere images, rooted in stabilised and organised arborescent reproductions. In that sense, we acknowledge Deleuze and Guattari's characterisation of a map as 'always detachable, connectable, reversible, modifiable' (2005: 21).

The second aspect centres on 'becoming anarchisms', unfolding against and entangled with multifarious hierarchies, located in the subject's movement, but also outside the individual, in the materiality of migration, travelling, deportation and exile. Drawing on the priority of space/territory/landscape in Deleuze-Guattarian thought, we approach the contradictory and heterogeneous contexts in which subjectivities and their networks emerge. Space acquires a central place here as we map the ways in which performances and experiences in these spaces allowed for new and renewed conceptions of what it means to be an anarchist. As Deleuze and Guattari state, 'thinking takes place in the relationship of territory and the earth' (Deleuze and Guattari 1994: 87). Space is considered to be the grounding of thought, not as an object of reflection, but as a precursor for constructing concepts, posing questions and, ultimately, providing a territorial analysis of collective and individual identities (Sibertin-Blanc 2010: 226). In this sense, Deleuze and Guattari embrace space as an inextricable part of their ontology by acknowledging its relevance at the individual and collective levels. Movements of deterritorialisation and reterritorialisation provide some paths for thinking about interactions and the exchange of anarchist ideas in different geographies, moments and circumstances. This perspective aids us in circumventing essentialist identities as subjectivity is analysed in terms of continual variation and becoming. Our approach thus relies on the idea that essential identities are fictions and, in order to avoid reifying anarchists and their wandering communities, we emphasise their extrinsic relations (Janz 2001). Because there 'is always a risk of restoration, and sometimes a proud affirmation of transcendence' when speaking of utopias (Deleuze and Guattari 1994: 100), we put into question the performance of anarchist ideas. Thus, we follow Deleuze and Guattari in working against fixed identities, and against essentialist conceptions of logic and ontological identity.

The networks of communication and exchange are evidence of the fluidity of thought and practice of historical anarchism. As we argue, Deleuze's perspective engages geocultural multiplicities, thus acknowledging their geographical spatiality and the continual fluctuation between movement and rest as an integral part of subjectivities and ideas (Sibertin-Blanc 2010: 233). Hence, 'individuals and groups are always grasped within a multiplicity of territorial arrangements, which conditions their identities internally' and 'marks them with ambivalence at all times' (2010: 236, own translation). The fluidity of these networks is reminiscent of nomadism. But, as Deleuze and Guattari state, there are no perfectly smooth or striated spaces and, as nomadism is a theoretical model and praxis rather than a concrete figure, we conceive of anarchists and their communities as movements that create new spaces and territories against reactionary processes, against the State and other forms of dominating striated spaces (Deleuze and Guattari 2005: 351–423). As 'nomads', they were combative but also fragile. Unlike nomads, they *arrived*, they moved and rested, they were *en route* as well as *rooted* (Saldanha 2017). What we emphasise, in other words, is the Deleuze-Guattarian idea that space is central to processes of subjectivation. We are also aware of the 'selectivity' of the anarchists' networks. Often dominated by men, it is mostly male experiences that are depicted in this chapter. One of the main limitations of our analysis is that even when women participated in such networks, it was mostly marginal. While anarchism characterises itself as being against *all* forms of domination, the masculinism of the networks represented here betrays the gendered nature of historical anarchism.

Deleuze and Guattari's ideas have been introduced and reworked in geography (for example, Haesbaert 2011, 2013 in terms of territorialisation, and Bonta and Protevi 2004 in terms of geophilosophy), creating new avenues for spatial–temporal analyses and possibilities for engagement with social movements from territorial or conservation perspectives. Although we are not using these sources in depth, we consider these conversations relevant to understanding anarchism both as a complex set of networks and as a polyphonic movement. We connect this contribution to the growing work on anarchist geographies and geographers (see Ince 2012; Pelletier 2013; Ince and Barrera 2016; Springer 2016; Ferretti 2017). Furthermore, we emphasise the reterritorialised condition of anarchist thought and, at the same time, the subsequent reterritorialisation through episodes of movement and rest that respond to concrete spatial circumstances. It bears noting that our perspective does not pretend to be the only possible or most accurate approach for exploring these networks; we simply offer a different approach to these past encounters in order to illuminate some aspects of contemporary anarchist movements. This is a creative interpretation of ideas and concepts through historical and geographical processes that configured and expanded anarchist networks throughout the world.

## Nodes

To show the density and complexity of these newspaper networks, we examined the exchange relationships of four newspapers, two in Barcelona and two in New York, corresponding to different periods. What we construct with this numerical and visual analysis is a cartography that avoids the centrality of the State and hegemonic notions of national territoriality; maps that grasp the mobility and fluidity of links within and outside of the networks of presses and their multiple possibilities for contact. As Deleuze and Guattari put it, 'The map does not reproduce an unconscious closed in upon itself; it constructs the unconscious'; here 'the maps have to do with the performance' of such networks (2005: 2, 12). We consider a double movement where networks as constellations defined and were defined by (1) individuals in (2) their continual and creative movement. Far from defining such wandering rebels as 'nomads', we consider anarchists' efforts as an example of nomadic thought against hierarchical organisation and domination. The emphasis is thus on praxis and assemblages in and between territories, rather than discrete, rational individuals. Always unfinished, renewed spaces are created and smoothed to be open-ended, directed against hierarchies and in opposition to 'the State and the worldwide axiomatic expressed by States' (2005: 422). Ambiguities are always present; we not only acknowledge them but also bring them to the fore as we are interested in what such thought might unfold.

In this context, the notion of territory remains a frame of reference, although it is used expressly to indicate the fluidity and mobility of anarchist networks. Mapping guided by such critical concerns, as Matthew Farish points out, 'is useful not only to interrogate the official histories of colonialism, but also to challenge the unquestioned colonialism still persisting within hybrid postcolonial states' (Farish 2009: 453). This exercise in cartography thus allows us to include the 'hidden forces' that act not only on space itself – and are usually represented in canonical maps – but also in the social phenomena that take place within it. These maps function as a 'theatre of operations' (to using James Corner's expression) in which the cartographer can combine, connect and explore the multiplicity of flows that unfold on the map (Corner 2002: 214). In short, a cartographic representation allows us to mould notions of territory and space according to the semi-nomadic routes of anarchist militants and the flows of information and cultural exchange that circulated through their communication networks.

  *El Producto*r, one of the founding journals of Barcelona's anarcho-collectivist propaganda, and one of the most representative publications of Spanish anarchism in the so-called classical period, refers to about 450 other newspapers from five continents (Figure 10.1). Of these, a

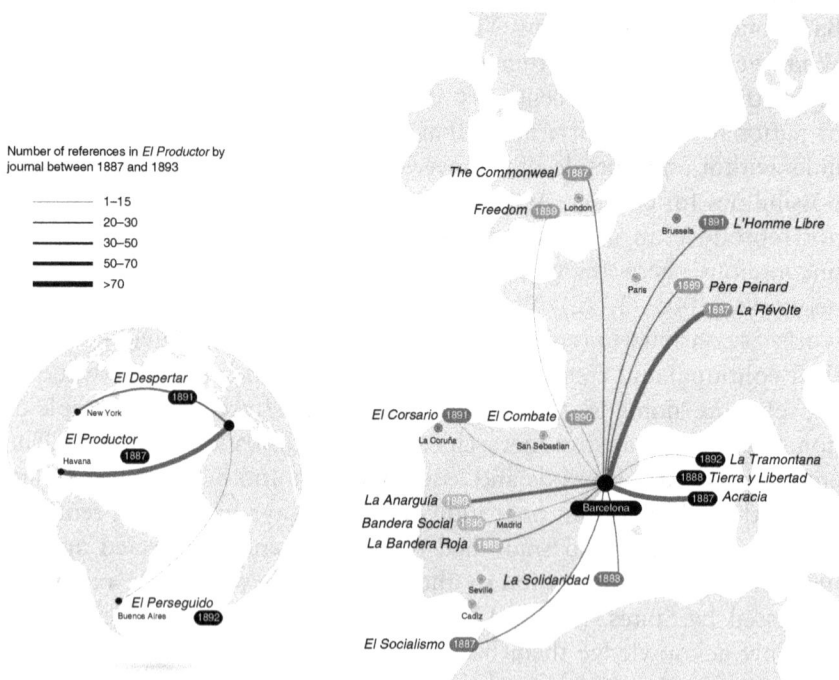

Figure 10.1 Map showing the number of references in *El Productor* (Barcelona), by journal, 1887–93.

little more than 200 were openly anarchist newspapers with which the publishing group of *El Productor* maintained editorial exchange relations. In the course of the six years in which the weekly newspaper was published (1887–93), one can see the formation of a solid core of anarchist publications with which *El Productor* cultivated close ties. This consists of a nucleus of over fifty publications, highlighting a significant number of newspapers written in Spanish both inside and outside of the Iberian Peninsula. It also reveals the systematic exchange with other publications in Italian, French, English, Portuguese and German.

In this set, we found a number of radical socialist and anarcho-communist newspapers with which *El Productor* had strong theoretical and tactical discrepancies but, despite such differences, they did not fail to play an important part in the interweaving of their political relations. In this sense, the discussions of *El Productor* with *La Controversia* (Valencia), *El Perseguido* (Buenos Aires) and *Tierra y Libertad* (Gracia) were important in terms of (1) labour organisation in the fight against capitalism; and (2) economic organisation of the future society. The main core of publications was formed by *La Révolte* (Paris), *La Anarquía* (Madrid), *Acracia* (Barcelona), *El Productor* (Havana), *El Despertar* (New York), *El Socialismo* (Cádiz), *El Corsario* (La Coruña), *La Bandera Roja* (Madrid), *Père Peinard* (Paris), *La Solidaridad* (Seville), *L'Homme Libre* (Brussels) and *The Commomweal* (London).[2]

On the other side of the Atlantic, in the pages of *El Despertar* (New York), we trace a long and hazardous trajectory throughout the crucial decade of 1892–1902 and find reference to about 240 newspapers of anarchist orientation. Of these, twenty-two publications formed the core with which the New York newspaper maintained close relations of exchange. In particular, links were sustained with *El Corsario* (Corunna), *El Esclavo* (Tampa), *El Productor y Ciencia Social* (Barcelona), *La Idea Libre* (Madrid), *La Questione Sociale* (Buenos Aires), *El Derecho a la Vida* (Montevideo), *Les Temps Nouveaux* (Paris), *El Perseguido* (Buenos Aires), *La Questione Sociale* (Paterson – with whom *El Despertar* shared typographic workshops), and *El Productor* and *El Nuevo Ideal* (Havana). The links maintained between these newspapers were based above all on solidarity: the reciprocal collection of economic resources, the redistribution of printed materials in the respective areas of influence of each newspaper, the reprint of texts and informative notes, and so on (Figure 10.2).

With the arrival of the twentieth century, we see a number of substantial changes in the structure of this network. The main transformation was reflected in a decrease in the total number of newspapers

Number of references in *El Despertar* by journal

30
20
10
0

1891
1892
La Anarquia
El Productor (Barcelona)
1893
El Productor (Havana)
A Propaganda (Lisbon)
1894
El Corsario
El Derecho a la Vida
La Idea Libre
El Perseguido
1895
Ciencia Social
La Questione Sociale (Buenos Aires)
1896
La Questione Sociale (Paterson)
1897
Les Temps Nouveaux
1898
1899
El Esclavo
1900
La Revista Blanca
1901
El Nuevo Ideal
1902

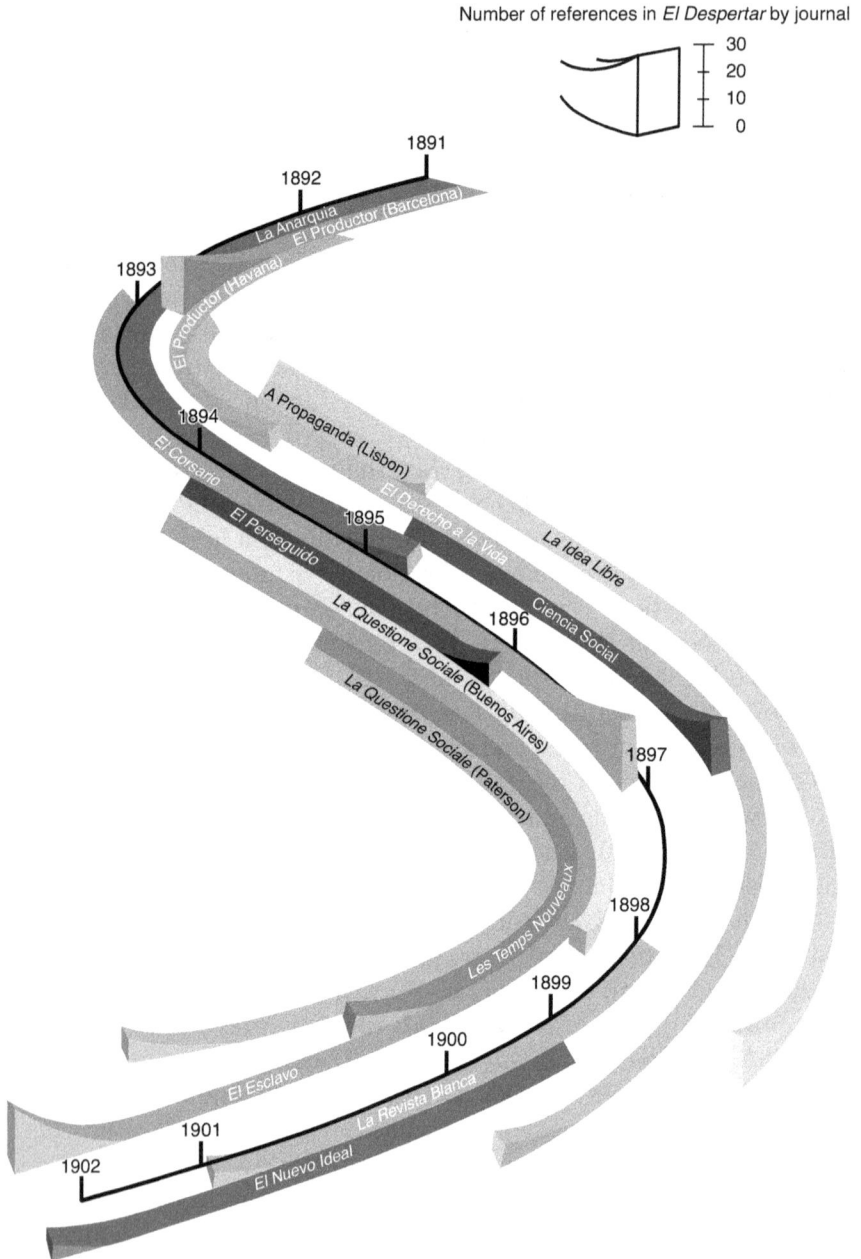

Figure 10.2 Relations between *El Despertar* (New York) and other publications, 1891–1902.

that were published, but their circulation was more stable; they got more regularity for longer periods and a bigger print run – in short, fewer newspapers, but more solidly established. *Cultura Proletaria* and its mutation, *Cultura Obrera* (New York), for example, maintained frequent exchanges with only twenty or so publications from 1910 to 1917. The main ones were *Regeneración* (Los Angeles), *Tierra y Libertad* (Barcelona), *¡Tierra!* (Havana), *La Voz del Obrero* (Corunna), *Fuerza Consciente* (New York and subsequently San Francisco) and *La Protesta* (Buenos Aires). This structural change may be due to repressive waves against the anarchist press, coupled with the reconcentration of migratory flows of anarchist militants in specific points of the globe. Also, because of the economic and political difficulties involved in the publication of a newspaper, many collectives and anarchist groups opted to use the existing newspapers rather than launching their own publication. Through them, they could participate in news, debates, solidarity campaigns and cultural practices. This process would result in a certain type of centralisation of the press networks, generating a few nodes of greater influence and distributive capacity, instead of a wider dissemination of small newspapers of lesser scope and duration.

The numerical data from *Cultura Obrera* create an image of a less geographically extended publication network, as well as a smaller number of publications, but it is important to observe that this division of the press network consisted of more consolidated publications. For that very reason, they were of a noticeably more regular presence during longer and more stable periods, although with a geographical scope apparently less extensive. This time period of 'maturity' of the international anarchist press networks was characterised by the stabilisation and strengthening of anarchist publications in different regions of the globe. This transformation is indicated by the fact that a handful of well-established newspapers served as a link between smaller publications or groups, and between these and other newspapers or groups capable of wider international distribution.

Back in Barcelona, one of the newspapers that *Cultura Obrera* maintained a close relationship with, namely *Tierra y Libertad*, gives a clear indication of the reach of the anarchist press at the beginning of the twentieth century through its network of contacts (Table 10.1). This weekly anarchist publication, which was active from 1904 to 1913, refers to 353 anarchist-oriented newspapers published in America, Europe, North Africa and Asia. *Tierra y Libertad* established relations with a core group of forty newspapers. These relations included editorial exchanges, political dialogues, reprints of writings and participation in

Table 10.1 Distribution of newspaper *Tierra y Libertad*, Barcelona, 1904–13.

| Location | Period | Number of references |
|---|---|---|
| Barcelona | 06/01/1905–24/12/1913 | 152 |
| Madrid | 15/11/1906–31/12/1913 | 119 |
| Seville | 06/01/1905–31/12/1913 | 113 |
| Valencia | 15/11/1906–24/12/1913 | 96 |
| Bilbao | 24/02/1905–24/12/1913 | 95 |
| Zaragoza | 06/01/1905–19/11/1913 | 85 |
| La Línea | 06/01/1905–31/12/1913 | 84 |
| Mexico [Los Angeles] | 17/05/1911–17/09/1913 | 82 |
| The vast majority of references to Mexico are not related to sending the newspaper to Mexican territory, but rather to the mediation in sending economic resources to the leadership of the Mexican Liberal Party, whose headquarters was in Los Angeles. | | |
| Havana | 16/02/1905–31/12/1913 | 79 |
| Sabadell | 29/11/1906–10/12/1913 | 78 |
| Malaga | 06/12/1906–31/12/1913 | 77 |
| Corunna | 06/01/1905–17/12/1913 | 75 |
| Alicante | 10/01/1907–12/11/1913 | 74 |
| Santander | 24/02/1905–31/12/1913 | 74 |
| Castro del Río | 10/01/1907–12/11/1913 | 72 |
| Jerez de la Frontera | 15/11/1906–26/11/1913 | 70 |
| Logroño | 28/03/1907–02/12/1913 | 69 |
| San Sebastián | 04/04/1907–31/12/1913 | 69 |
| Ferrol | 06/01/1905–12/11/1913 | 68 |
| Azuaga | 24/02/1905–10/12/1913 | 67 |
| Buenos Aires | 18/04/1907–24/12/1913 | 67 |
| Cordoba | 14/02/1907–19/11/1913 | 67 |
| Palamós | 10/01/1907–24/12/1913 | 67 |
| Cullera | 13/12/1906–24/12/1913 | 63 |
| Tarrasa | 20/12/1906–31/12/1913 | 61 |
| Alcoy | 06/12/1906–12/11/1913 | 60 |
| Gijón | 13/12/1906–24/12/1913 | 60 |
| Nerva | 06/01/1905–10/12/1913 | 60 |
| Huelva | 15/11/1906–22/10/1913 | 58 |
| Mahón | 06/01/1905–19/11/1913 | 58 |
| Bordeaux | 03/01/1907–24/12/1913 | 56 |
| Vilasar de Dalt | 29/11/1906–19/11/1913 | 56 |
| Aznalcóllar | 15/11/1906–31/12/1913 | 55 |
| Valladolid | 18/04/1907–19/11/1913 | 54 |
| Algeciras | 06/01/1905–17/12/1913 | 53 |
| San Feliú de Giuxols | 06/01/1905–17/12/1913 | 53 |
| Villanueva y Geltrú | 09/05/1907–31/12/1913 | 53 |
| Elche | 04/07/1907–29/01/1913 | 51 |
| Dowlais | 06/01/1905–22/10/1913 | 50 |
| Medinasidonia | 24/02/1905–05/11/1913 | 49 |
| Riotinto | 29/11/1906–10/12/1913 | 49 |
| Baracaldo | 06/01/1905–26/03/1913 | 47 |
| Paris | 20/12/1906–31/12/1913 | 47 |
| Cadiz | 13/12/1906–24/12/1913 | 46 |
| Murcia | 20/12/1906–02/12/1913 | 46 |

**Distribution by country** (in this period *Tierra y Libertad* was distributed in 931 cities and villages):
Spain: 687 places; France: 77; North America: 44; Antilles: 35; South America: 32; Central America: 15; North Africa: 10; Great Britain: 7; Central Europe: 6; Italy: 6; Portugal: 5; Oceania: 3; North & East Europe: 2; Not located: 2
Source: Own elaboration database. This information comes from the administrative sections of *Tierra y Libertad*, which produced a *lugares census* to which the newspaper was sent, both inside and outside the Iberian Peninsula.

solidarity campaigns. The main exchanges during this period focused on the discussion of issues relevant to anarchism, such as the Russian and the Mexican Revolutions, the strengthening of anarcho-syndicalism, the rise of militarist tensions in Europe, as well as the deportation of militants from Spain, Cuba, Brazil and Argentina. The main publications, in order of frequency, are: *Regeneración* (Los Angeles), *¡Tierra!* (Havana), *La Voz del Cantero* (Madrid), *La Protesta* (Buenos Aires), *Solidaridad Obrera* (Barcelona), *El Provenir del Obrero* (Mahón), *Salud y Fuerza* (Barcelona), *Acción Libertaria* (Gijón/Madrid), *Escuela Moderna* (Valencia), *Renovación* (Costa Rica), *El Único* (Panama) and *Cultura Obrera* (New York). We also found a set of thirty newspapers with which exchanges were less frequent. *Freedom* from London, *Les Temps Nouveaux* and *La Bataille Syndicaliste* from Paris, and *L'Universitá Popolare* from Milan stand out.

## Networks

This transnational framework of anarchist publications provided the material basis for the elaboration of a political culture based on an international struggle. Together, they helped create a set of historical and geographical milestones that strengthened the idea of a borderless social struggle against capital and authority. That is, they constructed an anarchistic consciousness that emphasised the global dimension of social confrontation. In the minds of those participating in the cultural rituals of the anarchist communities in different locations, a symbolic geography took shape, one that united the oppressed throughout the world, linking the historical struggles of the 'militant proletariat' with ongoing and intensified struggles in the present. In this sense, an atlas of social struggle can be traced so that it maps the Commune of Paris – an experience understood as a revolutionary *event* in the Deleuze-Guattarian sense, and as an extension of the 'unfinished' revolution of 1789 – alongside the brutal struggle and later martyrdom of the Chicago anarchists, the fierce repression of the Andalusian peasants of Jerez, the Cuban war, the bombs of Barcelona and the Montjuich processes, the migratory tragedy of the persecuted anarchists in the Río de la Plata, the Tragic Week (once again in Barcelona) and the Revolution of Mexico.

However, this symbolic geography and collective consciousness was not universal and was not imposed as a single, unified definition of anarchism, anarchists or anarchy. Rather, this cartography can be seen to represent heterogeneous instantiations of a larger movement that is characterised by the lack of rigid and hierarchical organisation so that subjects, ideas and even the map are constantly shifting. In a Deleuzian sense, anarchist collectives and subjects should be seen as processes of becoming, as part of relational and continual variation. Thus, we suggest that instead of privileging identity, we should consider difference and destabilisation as inseparable from anarchists' subjectivation as their movement and change are concomitant components of their collective consciousness (Lorraine 2005). Both difference and destabilisation are present, but not necessarily at the same time, often alternating in contradictory and complex arrangements. That is, the dynamic processes to which anarchists were (and remain in different ways) subjected to, their repeated relations of movement and rest, and the journeys they undertook to spread a common politics became a form that generated (re)new(ed) thought. These relations with different milieus thus invented thresholds where different notions of space, time, identity and anarchy emerged, transformed by deterritorialising movements.

On the one hand, the deployment put into operation by the anarchist press networks leads us to an image of a world interconnected by a particular sense of geographical contiguity. Cities as distant as São Paulo become joined to Geneva, Los Angeles and Havana which, in turn, are adjoined to Barcelona and Buenos Aires who seem to be neighbouring cities. It is an image of the world already outlined by Walter Benjamin in his appreciations of a sailor's life, in his unique work *One Way Street*:

> Thus, on the high seas the sailor lives in a city where, in the Cannebière of Marseilles, a bar of Port Said is in front of a Hamburg brothel, and the Castel dell' Ovo in the Naples' Bay is located in the Plaza de Cataluña of Barcelona. (2010: 86)

On the other hand, this world of diluted territories and anarchist journeys brings about the experience of uprootedness. The Catalan anarchist Pedro Esteve referred to this as:

> Sad, and pleasant at the same time, is the life of the revolutionary propagandist. The desire to propagate the ideal, the demands of the struggle, the persecutions, sometimes take him from one side to another, from here an intense affection, from there a pleasant memory, from there a bitter misfortune, from every place retains something that widens or compresses the heart, which gives life to feelings, to intense sensations, which must be drowned, not infrequently, just spawned. (1900: 82–3)[3]

This kind of testimony is frequent in the recollections of the correspondents and libertarian militants, almost to the point of constituting an autonomous literary genre, centred on the vicissitudes of the immigrant's life, the semi-nomadic revolutionary, sometimes emphasising in lyrical overtones the troubles of a struggle that was born from perpetual movement. The Cuban tobacco worker Marcelo Salinas, who was based in Tampa and then travelled to New Orleans, New York, Corunna, Madrid, Barcelona and Havana, evokes in a poem this atmosphere:

> Starving brothers, lost in the world,
> Without homeland, no friends,
> No bread and homeless
> To cease in your breasts the groan,
> It's time of combat, it's time to fight.
> . . .
> Wandering rebels; despised bohemia,
> Which goes from pole to pole singing freedom,
> Lift up the hearts! And in this great parade,
> Let's form the world fraternity of the free.[4]

The author of these lines, a 'wandering rebel' himself, took part in a cultural practice that would become a political tradition of Spanish-speaking anarchism, namely reading aloud in the tobacco workshops. This performance, both recreational and instructional, is part of the network of the exchange for solidarity and other cultural goods. Although it transcends materiality and extends the network beyond the newspaper as an object to a dimension that cannot be represented carto-graphically, it updated the connections between those who participated in the network.

As Tamsin Lorraine argues, the nomad style of subjectivity depicted by Deleuze 'consists in the unfolding of patterns that are not referred to an external plan of organisation or conventional notions of space and time, but rather evolve from the force of patterns immanent to the individual in its specific milieu' (Lorraine 2005: 171). This idea reflects what we have been arguing about anarchist transnational net-works very closely but, as Deleuze states, the idea of nomads is a way of thinking, a way of 'privileging flow ontologically' (Saldanha 2017: 46). Furthermore, 'truth nomads' are abstract constructions (Deleuze and Guattari 2005: 351–423), so anarchist militants should rather be understood as semi-nomads, or contradictory nomads that, as the Deleuze-Guattarian concept suggests, struggled to construct their own kinds of space; spaces that escape the State, that obstruct the expansion of the State and capitalism or, in Deleuzian words, disrupt striated space. What we want to emphasise is how anarchists, in their 'escape' to different worlds – even if for short periods of time such as when a news-paper was read aloud in a factory – maintained a constant flight from the State, and other forms of coercive power relations were performed to construct new spaces and territories. But then again, we must not universalise these correspondents and anarchist militants because even though they were not 'becoming *rooted*' by nationalism or localism, they were also not endlessly '*en route*' (Saldanha 2017: 57). Neither of these states were thus discrete conditions of their identity, both as individuals and in groups. Moreover, because different intensities were experienced and created at different times, these semi-nomads sometimes navigated diluted territories. It is productive to think of these links and nodes as ever-changing and differenc/tiating all the time. Following this ongoing transformation, it is difficult to establish fixed norms that describe how these networks work. As the singular examples examined in the previous section show, the Spanish-speaking network changed and mended, its nodes temporarily *rooted* ultimately wove together in variable and diverse forms, and the connections were not fixed but part of ongoing processes, always alive.

It seems as if the network of anarchist communications not only puts into circulation a rebellious culture, but also *a will to deterritorialise*, to subvert the logic of nation-state, to remap according to the bias provided by migrations and rebel experiences. These ongoing processes show a complex and contradictory relation between the development of anarchism, on the one hand, and the deterritorialisation processes of the State and capitalism to prevent their expansion, on the other. There is a double and permanent movement between deterritorialisation and relative reterritorialisation that is far from being linear or teleological; rather, it represents how anarchism actualised in specific space-times. Thus, to better understand the Spanish-speaking anarchist networks, it is necessary to have a vision of the world that acknowledges and values contexts (Haesbaert 2011: 89). Every migrant anarchist/ic community takes something from its place of origin, bringing with it certain tensions, conflicts, ideas and projects. Some disputes travelled through the networks, following migration patterns. At the same time, these conflicts and the ideas that underpin them changed according to different deterritorialisation and reterritorialisation patterns within a particular territory and context. We may think here, for example, of the dispute over the Mexican Revolution between anarchist communities in Brazil. These communities were mostly made up of Italian migrants that followed two main branches of anarchism. The first was located in São Paulo and is known as the branch of Barre, Vermont, which followed Luigi Galleani and expressed their views in the newspaper *La Battaglia*. This branch of anarchism supported unfavourable views about the Mexican Liberal Party (PLM in Spanish), led by Ricardo Flores Magón and supported from the USA by *Cronaca Sovversiva*. The other branch settled in Río de Janeiro and articulated their views in the newspaper *A Guerra Social* while maintaining close relations with Helvetian anarchism (whose newspaper was *Il Risveglio*) and the more 'flexible' anarchist French press, *Le Libertaire* (Paris), where *Regeneración*'s information (the PLM main publication) was translated to Portuguese.

In accordance with its own views on heterogeneous potentiality, we see from these accounts that as anarchism expanded, it did not unfold as a homogeneous movement against the ongoing development of State power and capitalism or towards a predefined outcome and 'promised land', but as living networks and entangled assemblages of communities. This does not mean that the latter was chaotic, rather it actualised in multiple ways. Thinking otherwise, or defining anarchism in a cause–effect manner, would be a reductionist approach, foreclosing the possibilities of various intersections, contexts, emotions, geographical origins, and so on – even contradictory ones. The blooming of these rhizomatic anarchist networks offers a very different view to that of capitalist expansion and the frenzied optimism of capitalist development and progress. It may be tempting to think of anarchism as belonging to specific spaces, or as unfolding according to fixed patterns (contra the frantic State and capitalist expansion), but it would be more rigorous to think of anarchism as an intersection of flows, ideas, praxis and so on. These were influenced by a number of known and unknown circumstantial factors, such as exile, persecution and migration, all entangled with a kind of 'apostolic' will to spread anarchy throughout the world. Accordingly, anarchism is the multiple and differentiated response to the construction of a hegemonic world order.

Struggles against the oppression of private property, capitalist expansion and State-instituted spaces led to ongoing practices of alternative social organisations, which can productively be thought of in terms of the distinction between smooth and striated spaces (Buchanan and Lambert 2005: 5). Although these two spaces are only 'distinguishable on the conceptual plane' for the reason that 'no real space is perfectly smooth or perfectly striated' (Saldanha 2017: 107), the 'promised future' of anarchist endeavours (as opposed to a promised land) is clearly a constant movement towards non-striated spaces. As Deleuze and Guattari argue, it is not the case that the striated is 'bad' and the smooth 'good', but rather about the passage between these two abstract forms of spatiality. Hence, shifts and fluidity are at all times disrupting stable identities or reactionary identities. The movement of these semi-nomadic anarchist correspondents across multiple smooth and striated spaces allowed striated spaces to be smoothed and striated again in different ways so that striation can be said to enable 'new kinds of smoothness' (Saldanha 2017: 107). That is to say, their journeys always required them to deal with a multiplicity of territories and, at the same time, to experiment along lines of flight in order to escape the State apparatus and other forms of domination (which was not always successful). These multiple, conflicting and ceaselessly becoming identities were affirmed in difference rather than the imposition of new hegemonic patterns and, as such, are more in line with a never-ending transformation. As Jesse Cohn and other authors have argued, the role of the vagabond (the *trimardeur*, the *linyera*) has been and continues to be crucial in the transmission of anarchist culture, its literature and its poetic (affirmative) power. Having no firm ties to the world of work and social conventions, these sorts of *lumpenproletarians* can easily become full-time propagandists (Cohn 2014: 96). This is true also of sea workers, characterised by uprootedness and the absence of a native settlement. It is worth remembering that the New York newspaper *Cultura Obrera* achieved much of its worldwide distribution in the mid-1910s thanks to the work of stokers, engineers and port stevedores, making the circulation of the anarchist press a deterritorialisation practice par excellence.

The rhizomatic networks that we follow through the Spanish-speaking newspapers is based on encounters, revealing a multiplicitous cartography. Maps tend to present particular worldviews (coloniality has a long history of this), but here the maps *traverse* the world. In other words, there is a constant flow of communities linked by encounters. These networks mirror each other through distorted and lengthened reflections and connective series: Barcelona *and* Havana *and* Key West *and* Tampa *and* New York *and* San Francisco *and* Los Angeles *and* Havana (again) *and* Costa Rica *and* Barcelona (again) *and* Marseilles *and* Panama *and* São Paulo *and* Montevideo *and* Buenos Aires *and* Lima *and* Iquique *and* Antofagasta *and* Veracruz *and* New York *and, and, and* . . . Following Deleuze and Guattari's notions of deterritorialisation, we consider these links and the projection of the anarchist network as the development of new encounters where deterritorialisation is never the final phase, but an ongoing process accompanied by reterritorialisations and new lines of flight, interwoven by micropolitics, sedentary lines, 'connections between semiotic chains, organizations of power, and circumstances relative to the arts, sciences, and social struggles' (Deleuze and Guattari 2005: 7). In its different expressions, anarchism is reterritorialised in multiple, even contradictory ways, only to be deterritorialised again. It is in this permanent possibility of new encounters that anarchism as a movement emerged in (pre)existing territories; it is how a multiplicity of anarchisms emerged and continue to emerge.

It is clear that anarchism consists, in part, of large communities of readers, but the intention to 'deterritorialise the reader' is a fundamental aspiration of anarchist literature and propaganda, not only in the sense of territory itself, but also in terms of mobilising readers to question the certainties of their consciousness and surroundings, as well as the spatial and temporal limits of the hierarchies in which they live, thus mobilising them towards revolutionary action (Cohn 2014: 180–1). Rudolf Rocker recalls that Proudhon once said: 'A truly free man is never at all sure if what he [*sic*] claims is really fair. I think this is the best thing that has ever been said about the concept of freedom in general.'[5] Thus, we can understand the latter in terms of absolute and relative deterritorialisation as fundamental in anarchist intentions to liberate the reader and the writer: one related to thoughts, to the possibility of creation when breaking with previous territories to create new ones through which new subjectivities and ideas emerge; the other relative to the socius, to the actual movement of the individuals and collectives around the globe. Absolute and relative deterritorialisation and reterritorialisation act simultaneously, of course, so that the will to deterritorialise anarchist networks and the subsequent reterritorialisation of different territories and thought are always coextensive.

The communities of anarchist and anarchistic readers were, more often than not, effectively deterritorialised by the very trajectories of the individuals and collectives who made them, as well as by the nature of the press networks that were produced, spread and interlinked by these elusive subjects: wandering sailors, vagabonds, homeless bohemians, exiled workers, cursed prophets, revolutionary agitators persecuted by one or more governments, emigrants without a future, but carrying their past and utopia in their luggage.

## Notes

1. Other newspapers with which *El Productor*, a founding journal of Barcelona's anarcho-collectivist propaganda, had frequent relations were (in order of regularity): *Social Demokraten* (Copenhagen), *A Revoluçao Social* (Porto), *Freedom* (London), *Humanitas* (Naples), *Tierra y Libertad* (Gracia), *La Tramontana* (Barcelona), *A Revolta* (Lisbon), *Il Proletario* (Marsala), *Social Demokraten* (Estocolmo), *El Perseguido* (Buenos Aires), *La Questione Sociale* (Florence), *L'Endehors* (Paris), *Ravachol* (Sabadell), *Sempre Avanti* (Livorno), *Die Autonomie* (London), *El Socialista* (Madrid), *Las Dominicales* (Madrid), *El Productor* (Guanabacoa), *El Trabajo* (Guanabacoa), *Le Cri du Peuple* (Paris),

L'*Operaio* (La Spezia), *La Débacle* (Brussels), *La Nuova Gioventú* (Florence), *La Societé Nouvelle* (Brussels), *Le Socialiste* (Paris), *O Protesto Operario* (Lisbon), *The Alarm* (Chicago), *Vorbote* (Chicago), *Die Freiheit* (New York), *Il Grido degli Oppressi* (New York), *La Favilla* (Mantua), *Le Ça Ira* (París), *Arbeiter Zeitung* (Chicago), *Gelichheit* (Vienna), *La Bandera Roja* (La Corunna), *La Revolución Cosmopolita* (Paris), *L'Ordine* (Turin), *Nuova Gazzeta Operaria* (Turin) and *Vorwarts* (Buenos Aires).

2. This core was followed by *Cronaca Sovversiva* (Lynn), *El Dependiente* (Havana), *L'Era Nuova* (Paterson), *Fiat Lux* (Havana), *El Internacional* (Tampa), *Acción Libertaria* (Gijón/Madrid), *El Obrero Industrial* (Tampa), *Les Temps Nouveaux* (Paris), *Pro Vida* (naturist magazine from Havana), *Solidaridad Obrera* (Barcelona), *La Bataille Syndicaliste* (Paris), *Brazo y Cerebro* (New York), *El Libertario* (Gijón) and *El Porvenir del Obrero* (Mahón).

3. 'Triste, y placentera a la par, resulta la vida del propagandista revolucionario. El afán de propagar el ideal, las exigencias de la lucha, las persecuciones a veces, llévanlo de un lado a otro, y de ahí una intensa afección, de allá un placentero recuerdo, de acullá una amarga desventura, de todas partes conserva algo que ensancha o comprime el corazón, que da vida a sentimientos, a sensaciones intensísimas, que hay que ahogar, no pocas veces, apenas nacidas' (Esteve 1900: 82–3).

4. 'Hermanos muertos de hambre, perdidos por el mundo, / sin patria, sin amigos, sin pan y sin hogar / que cese en vuestros pechos acento gemebundo, / es hora de combate, es hora de luchar ... Rebeldes vagabundos; bohemia despreciada, / que va de polo a polo cantando libertad, / ¡alzad los corazones! y en esta gran parada, / formemos de los libres mundial fraternidad. El canto del trovero rebelde' (*¡Tierra!*, 3 August 1912).

5. Quoted in Meza González (2015: 206).

# References

Anderson, B. (2013), *The Age of Globalization: Anarchists and the Anticolonial Imagination*, New York: Verso.

Benjamin, W. (2010), *Calle de dirección única, en Obras, Book IV, Vol. I*, Madrid: Abada Editores.

Bonta, M. and J. Protevi (2004), *Deleuze and Geophilosophy: A Guide and Glossary*, Edinburgh: Edinburgh University Press.

Buchanan, I. and G. Lambert (2005), 'Introduction', in I. Buchanan and G. Lambert (eds), *Deleuze and Space*, Edinburgh: Edinburgh University Press, pp. 1–15.

Cohn, J. (2014), *Underground Passages: Anarchist Resistance Culture, 1848–2011*, Oakland: AK Press.

Corner, J. (2002), 'The Agency of Mapping: Speculation, Critique and Intervention', in D. Cosgrove (ed.), *Mappings*, London: Reaktion Books, pp. 213–52.

Deleuze, G. and F. Guattari (1994), *What Is Philosophy*, trans. H. Tomlinson and G. Burchell, New York: Columbia University Press.

Deleuze, G. and F. Guattari (2005), *A Thousand Plateaus: Capitalism and Schizoprenia*, trans. B. Massumi, Minneapolis: University of Minnesota Press.

Esteve, P. (1900), *Memorándum. Alos anarquistas de España y Cuba: Memoria de la Conferencia Anarquista Internacional celebrada en Chicago en septiembre de 1893*, Paterson: El Despertar.

Farish, M. (2009), 'Maps and the State', in R. Kitchin and N. J. Thrift (eds), *International Encyclopedia of Human Geography*, Amsterdam: Elsevier, pp. 442–54.

Ferretti, F. (2017), 'Evolution and Revolution: Anarchist Geographies, Modernity and Post-Structuralism', *Environment and Planning: Society and Space*, 35(5): 893–912.

Fritzsche, P. (2008), *Berlín 1900: Prensa, lectores y vida moderna*, Buenos Aires: Siglo XXI Editores.

Haesbaert, R. (2011), *El mito de la desterritorialización: Del "fin de los territorios" a la multiterritorialidad*, Mexico: Siglo XXI.

Haesbaert, R. (2013), 'Del mito de la desterritorialización a la multiterritorialidad', *Cultura y Representaciones Sociales*, 8(15): 9–42.

Ince, A. (2012), 'In the Shell of the Old: Anarchist Geographies of Territorialisation', *Antipode*, 44(5): 1645–66.

Ince, A. and G. Barrera de la Torre (2016), 'For Post-Statist Geographies', *Political Geography*, 55(2): 10–19.

Janz, B. (2001), 'The Territory Is not the Map. Place, Deleuze and Guattari, and African Philosophy', *Philosophy Today*, 45(4): 392–404.

Lorraine, T. (2005), 'Ahab and Becoming-Whale: The Nomadic Subject in Smooch Space', in I. Buchanan and G. Lambert (eds), *Deleuze and Space*, Edinburgh: Edinburgh University Press, pp. 159–75.

Meza González, J. (2015), *Breve introducción a la vida y obra de Rudolf Rocker*, Mexico: Universidad Autónoma Metropolitana.

Pelletier, P. (2013), *Géographie et anarchie: Reclus, Kropotkine, Metchnikoff*, Paris: Éditions du Monde Libertaire.

Saldanha, A. (2017), *Space after Deleuze*, London: Bloomsbury.

Sibertin-Blanc, G. (2010), 'Cartographie et territoires: La Spatialité géographique comme analyseur des forms de subjectivité selon Gilles Deleuze', *L'Éspace Géographique*, 13: 225–38.

Springer, S. (2016), *The Anarchist Roots of Geography: Toward Spatial Emancipation*, Minneapolis: University of Minnesota Press.

Zimmer, K. (2015), *Immigrants against the State: Yiddish and Italian Anarchism in America* (Working Class in American History), Champaign: University of Illinois Press.

# Chapter 11

# 'Visible Invisibility' as Machinic Resistance

*Christoph Hubatschke*

## Prologue

> I am an invisible man. No, I am not a spook like those who haunted Edgar Allan Poe; nor am I one of your Hollywood-movie ectoplasms. I am a man of substance, of flesh and bone, fiber and liquids – and I might even be said to possess a mind. I am invisible, understand, simply because people refuse to see me. (Ellison 2014: 3)

These are the opening words of Ralph Ellison's famous novel *Invisible Man*, published in 1952. This remarkable text is the fictional autobiography of a young black man in New York who discovers his own social invisibility. From his time in school and college, through to different jobs and a short but remarkable career as a spokesperson in Harlem for a somewhat Marxist organisation, he constantly feels unrecognised, used and incapable of having a place, a voice or even a face of his own. Fleeing a society wherein he is a mere shadow, the nameless protagonist hides in a cellar, writing his story and thinking about all the racial discrimination he has faced in his life and about what it means to be invisible – that is, why he cannot have a face of his own. But what does it mean to have a face? Can any face ever be one's own, or is faciality itself always already part of the problem?

## Introduction

In his study on the anarchistic roots of poststructuralism, Todd May (1994) emphasises that it is the critique of representation, the thinking about a new, different politics, without or even against the repressive structures of the State and without the hierarchical and 'pyramidal organization' (Guattari 1984: 215) of parties and political groups, that especially bridges traditional theories of anarchism and poststructuralist philosophy. Gilles Deleuze and Félix Guattari can be seen as two of the key theorists of anarchistic–poststructuralist thinking not only because they share a similar conceptual framework with anarchist theories, but also because they further developed some important anarchistic ideas. In their manifold work, they develop a multiplicity of concepts and notions that are highly apt for political theory, especially contemporary (post) anarchist philosophies. It is specifically their critique of political representation, their prioritising of methods of direct action and their criticism of most forms of hierarchy and the State that resonate not only with political theory, but also with a multitude of different social movements and political struggles. Thinking with and through social movements themselves, it was in particular the events of May 1968 that influenced Deleuze and Guattari's philosophy. As they emphasise again and again in their work, May '68 was an extraordinary 'event', a 'becoming in its pure state' (Deleuze 1995: 171). Attempting to understand what happened in '68, Deleuze and Guattari developed, among others, one concept that seems intrinsically tied to it – the 'machine'. While some aspects of Deleuze-Guattarian political philosophy are widely discussed within contemporary theories of anarchism, very little work has been done on the relation between anarchism and the machine. This seems especially odd because it is precisely the concept of the machine that is at the very core of their thinking about political organisation and also, I argue, their critique of political representation. After a short introduction to some aspects of the machine as a form of non-hierarchical and non-representational political organisation (or, rather, 'movement') and the concept of 'faciality', I analyse methods of non-representation in current social movements, methods that focus on practices of dismantling 'the face' through the specific uses of different masks.

## Machines versus/and Structures

It is no coincidence that the first time Guattari introduces the concept of the machine is in *Machine and Structure*, a text written just after the events of May '68. In the text, which although directly criticising (Lacanian) structuralism was first presented at the Freudian School in Paris in 1969, Guattari discusses the political role of collective desires and how they can be generated and organised in hierarchically structured societies (Guattari 1984: 111). Impressed by the extraordinary revolutionary upheaval of '68, Guattari created the concept of the machine in order to describe a new type of chaosmotic organising: a form of revolutionary politics without a party, without a specified programme and without representation.[1] Guattari's machines, which he and Deleuze developed into the concept of 'desiring-machines' in *Anti-Oedipus*, and 'assemblages' in *A Thousand Plateaus*, work against every form of strict categorisation, organisation, hierarchy and structure. Structure, as Guattari explains, 'positions its elements by way of a system of references that relates each one to the others' (1984: 111). Structure is an enclosed system, determining every aspect of itself and controlling the flows of production as well as subjectivity (112).

Whereas structure determines who is allowed to speak and, resultantly, who gets heard or, in other words, who is 'categorised' as a minority and therefore excluded, the function of the machine is to disturb structure itself by undermining and subverting it, opening it up 'to the exterior' (Sauvagnargues 2016: 195).[2] It is the multitude of heterogeneous machines that contradicts the completeness of a structure and destroys the illusion of a non-exclusive arrangement or organisation, as well as any possibility of fair and authentic representation. For Guattari the idea of the machine is thus deeply connected to the notion of revolution. He notes,

> We may say of revolution, of the revolutionary period, that this is when the machine represents social subjectivity for the structure – as opposed to the phase of oppression and stagnation, when the superstructures are imposed as impossible representations of machine effects. (Guattari 1984: 117)

Building on Marx's famous 'Fragment on Machines' (Marx 1993: 690–712), as well as the works of Italian autonomist Marxists, and inspired by Releaux, Mumford, the historians Vernant, Detienne and Braudel (Sauvagnargues 2016: 198), and the biologists Maturana and Varela, Deleuze and Guattari vastly expand the understanding of the concept 'machine'. For them, machines are much more than simple tools, enormous social mega-machines or mere technical machines; instead, we are confronted with a multitude of different machines, abstract as well as concrete (Guattari 1984: 154). In a word, '[e]verywhere it is machines – real ones, not figurative ones' (Deleuze and Guattari 1983: 1).

Although Guattari introduces the machine as a fairly positive concept in *Machine and Structure*, he is very much aware that the strict dichotomy between machine and structure exists only to make it 'easier to identify [their] peculiar positions', and that 'in reality, a machine is inseparable from its structural articulations' and vice versa (Guattari 1984: 111). In a sense, Guattari has paved the way to getting rid of the notion of structure in favour of complicating the concept of the machine and conceiving of a complex interaction of manifold heterogeneous machines or 'machinic agencements (often translated as assemblages)' (Deleuze and Guattari 2005: 36). For Guattari, however, the machine is not just an analytical tool, it is also a normative programme, as well as a revolutionary organisation. As he emphasises,

> The problem of revolutionary organization is the problem of setting up an institutional machine whose distinctive features would be a theory and practice that ensured its not having to depend on the various social structures – above all the State structure. (Guattari 1984: 118)

For Deleuze and Guattari, the movement of '68 has to be understood as a machine precisely because it tried to constantly work and fight not only against structure, but also against its own structuralisation.[3] One main practice within this struggle was – as Guattari emphasises – the refusal of political representation, of electing spokespersons and thus producing a representative 'face'. Below I argue that this notion of the machine, as theory and practice of non-representational organisation, is not only deeply anarchistic but is also evident in current social movements and strategies of resistance and their refusal of 'faciality' through the use of masks.

## 'All Around Me Are Familiar Faces'

'A horror story, the face is a horror story,' write Deleuze and Guattari in the seventh plateau in *A Thousand Plateaus*, 'Year Zero: Faciality' (Deleuze and Guattari 2005: 168). This horror of the face, the 'inhumanity' of the face, as Deleuze and Guattari emphasise repeatedly, is not the horror of individual or disfigured faces; on the contrary, it is the horror of the process of faciality itself, the horror of *the* Face per se, of the machine of faciality. This abstract machine of faciality reduces everything to the 'white wall/black hole' logic or structure of the face. 'The inhuman in human beings: that is what the face is from the start. It is by nature a closeup, with its inanimate white surfaces, its shining black holes, its emptiness and boredom' (2005: 171). The face is a certain politics, a form of power, which is why every hierarchical organisation, every structure, produces faces. In order to create or 'interpellate' subjects, a face is needed, be it the face of the king, the dictator or, for that matter, the omnipresence of faces in contemporary capitalism, where faciality is once again an integral principle.[4] The only way to politically engage, to speak, to articulate demands, to be a part of political, cultural, economic discussions, to get heard and to be seen, seems to be through 'having' a face, conforming to *the* face. Deleuze and Guattari write:

> The political power operating through the face of the leader (streamers, icons, and photographs), even in mass actions; the power of film operating through the face of the star and the close-up; the power of television … This is an affair not of ideology but of economy and the organization of power [*pouvoir*]. (2005: 175)

Faciality is not simply the driving force of any form of representation; more importantly, it is the very idea of representability itself, of the possibility of representation. Faciality not only demands a reduction to faces or a speaking for others, but is the very basis of the regimes of visibility and sayability: it determines not only who can speak, but also how one speaks. 'The face is a veritable megaphone' (2005: 179). Once everything is reduced to the order of the face, faciality becomes a form of oppression. When Ralph Ellision describes his main character – and therefore minorities – as invisible, as people with 'faceless faces' and 'soundless voices', he is describing the very process of exclusion, of not being recognised as a face, of being categorised as someone who is not allowed to speak, who is not even seen as able to speak (Ellison 2014: 439) – invisible and yet, at the same time, even more visible. Visible as someone who is not the majority, who is not to be seen, heard or included; visible as someone who is not to be represented, but who at the same time comes to represent a different kind of face – a visible target for repression and police targeting, as in racial profiling, for example. The white wall/black hole system is, at its very foundation, a deeply racist and sexist system. 'The face is not a universal. It is not even that of the white man; it is White Man himself, with his broad white cheeks and the black hole of his eyes' (Deleuze and Guattari 2005: 176). Faciality evaluates everything in contrast to a specific norm – white, (cis)-male, adult, heterosexual, ableist and so on.

For Deleuze and Guattari, faciality is the violent concept of racism – racism denoting the inability to conceive of anything 'other'. In the structure of the face, there is no otherness, there are only grades of variation to the norm, the white face.[5] Faciality is therefore always the face of a majority. Minorities in a Deleuze-Guattarian sense can never have a face of their own and are thus always only a deviation from the majority and its abstract face – the white wall/black hole system. This is why minorities cannot be represented in the structure of faciality – they are always the excluded in certain ways, the non-representable. 'Faciality as a concrete machine demonstrates the impossibility, in the field of representation, of any becoming independent of the formalism of contents' (Guattari 1984: 156). Faciality, or representation in general, is not only about the form; it also determines the content, hence the 'indignity of speaking for others' (Deleuze and Foucault 1977: 209). How then is resistance possible? In other words, how can minorities speak when they are invisible, when they cannot be heard? How can minorities organise without representation and without reproducing the logic of faciality themselves?

## Vacuoles of Non-Representation

The logic of the face, as Deleuze and Guattari describe it, is closely connected to how they understand communication. For Deleuze, communication is 'the transmission and propagation of information' and information is 'a set of imperatives, slogans and directions-order-words' (Deleuze 2007: 320). The structure of communication thus has an inherent logic to it which has to do with orders, with being told what to say, what to think and how to behave.[6] Outside of these orders of communication, Deleuze emphasises, there is no real relationality; the hegemonic system can only understand what it can classify according to the logic of the order-word. Both Deleuze and Guattari are convinced that every social movement or form of political resistance therefore has to learn how to speak for itself without representatives and without reproducing the logic of the face or the order-word. This minoritarian speech has to break with norms around how one has to speak and organise. 'We've got to hijack speech,' writes Deleuze. 'Creating has always been something different from communicating. The key thing may be to create vacuoles of noncommunication, circuit breakers, so we can elude control' (Deleuze 1995: 175).

In order to break with faciality and, therefore, with the kinds of subjectivity this produces, minorities have to create vacuoles of non-communication to find 'new languages' and 'a new vocabulary' (Guattari 1984: 221, 109). They have to 'capture the speech' (Certeau 1997), create minor languages (Deleuze and Guattari 1986) by speaking collectively and breaking with informational order-word logic. These speech acts are incomprehensible from the perspective of the majority. They do not follow the rules of proper articulation and may seem like stuttering, but they follow collective desires:

> The social entity is enabled to speak for itself without being obliged to look to representatives or spokesmen to speak for it . . . the movement will always be attentative [sic] to whoever speaks from a position of desire, even, indeed especially, when it means getting 'off the subject'. (Guattari 1984: 220)[7]

To speak for oneself is always an act of desubjectification. To speak is always, as Guattari states, connected to groups, a collective, a heterogeneous movement. It is not the individual's desire, but collective desire that enables speech acts that do not represent something or someone. Not being reducible to one identifiable face, these movements always speak as many:

> Those who act and struggle are no longer represented, either by a group or a union that appropriates the right to stand as their conscience. Who speaks and acts? It is always a multiplicity, even within the person who speaks and acts. All of us are 'groupuscules'. Representation no longer exists; there's only action – theoretical action and practical action which serve as relays and form networks. (Deleuze and Foucault 1977: 206–7)

In order to speak as many, to be groupuscules, to not represent someone, but to act and speak for oneself, to become visible without reproducing the logic of the face, we need what Guattari describes as a collective and always open form of organisation. 'Machines are the form of collective organization which is needed for creating such minor languages, such "collectivities of utterance"' (Guattari 1984: 221). I will now look at some of these machines of collective organisation, machines that refuse representation and break with the abstract machines of faciality.

## Practices of Dismantling the Face

In December 2011, when *Time* magazine revealed its choice for the prestigious Person of the Year award, the magazine cover was fairly atypical. Instead of the usual close-up of the face of an 'important' person, there was a drawing of a protester hiding their face behind a bandana. The person of the year was 'the protester' (Ruiz 2013: 263). But as the different movements did not have any leader, they had to put a masked person on the cover – not a face, a masked face.

This masked figure suggests that contemporary social movements assembled on the streets are, however, not simply masked to hide their identity. Instead, their masks are a political statement. As I argue, eradicating the face is not just a protest strategy or protection from surveillance and police repression; dismantling the face while protesting and fighting on the streets is, in an important sense, also a distinctive form of non-representational politics.[8] To dismantle the face within political movements means to organise in different forms, without spokespersons or representatives. Current social movements – from the Arabic Rebellion (an alternative naming of the 'Arab Spring' which has Eurocentric connotations) to Occupy, from Indignados to Gezi and from the riots in Paris to the struggles in Brazil – refuse to be represented, not only by politicians in liberal democracies, but also by leaders or spokespersons from within their own movements. Squatting in the middle of squares, they are present, visible and loud. Yet many politicians claim that they cannot see them, cannot understand their demands and do not know what they are protesting for or against.

Many of today's social movements are unconcerned with formulating demands that the media and politicians can talk about. Neither are they concerned with sending representatives to media discussions or round tables. Squatting and rioting in the middle of cities, these movements can be understood as machines in Guattari's sense: as collectivities of utterance refusing to structuralise their organisation. Such movements often describe themselves as anti-hierarchical, horizontally organised, anti-representational or even anarchistic (Gerbaudo 2017). These movements cannot and should not be reduced to a face and they eschew leaders and representatives who can speak on their behalf.

The kinds of masks activists use can tell us much about their forms of organising. Simply using masks, however, does not at all presuppose or ensure a progressive and emancipative movement. One can think, for example, of the Ku Klux Klan and their use of a mask that is deeply bound up in faciality – according to the white wall/black hole system. Masks in current social movements are not for disguise since, as James Johnston argues, disguise is used for moving and acting unnoticed. Masks are something different in that they are a 'physical presence'; they 'hide a true identity in a visible way' (Johnston 2001: 96). When wearing a mask you want to be seen – you are not inconspicuous but your face is hidden in plain sight. Masks are a provocation in that, as they do not hide their function of hiding, they are not secret but all the more visible. In what follows, I will briefly introduce three different kinds of masks and three different strategies that are found in current movements and protests, each of which employs the mask to hide the face, but to hide it in plain sight in order to be *visibly invisible.*[9]

## All as None

During the late 1970s in Germany, a new protest tactic emerged and was subsequently adopted, adapted and experimented with all over the world, becoming one of the most prominent tactics of the alter-globalisation movement of the late 1990s and early 2000s and remaining in use today (Katsiaficas 2006). This tactic is, of course, the black bloc, and is closely connected to both the autonomous movement and the squatting scene, reflecting their anarchistic and militant politics. Hiding their faces behind black bandanas, balaclavas or ski masks is an essential part of this approach; individuals dress completely in black and cannot be distinguished from each other, which enables them to remain unidentified and also to commit acts of civil disobedience or militant violence against objects or against the police. Everyone can always take cover in the group, that is, the black bloc.

In *A Thousand Plateaus*, Deleuze and Guattari distinguish between two different kinds of masks, describing the first as follows: 'the mask assures the head's belonging to the body, its becoming-animal, as was the case in primitive societies' (Deleuze and Guattari 2005: 181). The tactic of the black bloc could be understood as this first kind of mask, which dismantles the face for the body to become visible; after all, the militant actions of the black bloc are very physical. This approach dismantles the face completely, reducing each person to an unidentifiable, faceless part of the bloc. The individual protester becomes clandestine, dissolving into the black bloc without being reducible to one face or one leader. The black bloc is not, however, an enclosed community: in theory, anyone wearing solely black can participate and so it becomes a fluid multitude of people which nonetheless is able to present itself as a closed and unified entity, what I call a machinic assemblage. The politics of the black bloc is a becoming clandestine without being invisible; on the contrary, the black bloc is often the most visible and discussed part of a demonstration.[10] As Richard Day notes:

> Perhaps most subversive of all, though, is the challenge that the Black Bloc tactic offers to the monopoly on invisibility and silence, with its active ignorance of the command not only to behave well, but to be available to be *seen* behaving well. (2005: 29)

Another movement that explores these forms of visibility is the Zapatista Army of National Liberation (EZLN). Most Zapatistas wear the infamous black ski masks when they show themselves in public and, although there are speakers within the movement (for example, the anonymous and always masked yet nonetheless 'well known' Subcommandante Marcos), by wearing the masks no one can be identified with any certainty, implying at least some form of equality. Wearing masks is not just a question of protection from state repression but also a visualisation of their grassroots democratic form of organisation.[11] As the EZLN consists primarily of indigenous people, the mask is also a form of protest against the racial exclusion and oppression of indigenous people by the Mexican state. The mask makes it impossible to identify which of the activists has an indigenous background. As a Zapatista saying goes: 'For 500 years our face was forbidden, why do you demand to see it now?' In a state where having an indigenous face makes you a second-class citizen, dismantling the face can be an act of resistance. In a system where a black, disfigured, or any other face outside the norm of the white face, makes you invisible and at the same time very much visible as the target of oppression, covering your face can give you a new form of visibility outside of the logic of faciality.

## All as One

In the vastness of the Darknet and in some obscure and quirky places on the Internet, a movement that questions the logic of faciality began: Anonymous. Formed on the Internet image board *4chan*, Anonymous is a heterogeneous hacker collective without a distinct political agenda.[12] Organised without established hierarchies, anyone can join and, similar to the black bloc, anyone can announce a new operation; however, whether or not the operation will actually take place depends on whether the other activists participate. Anonymous has no official spokespeople; instead anyone can speak as part of the collective, which promotes heterogeneity and at the same time makes Anonymous's political positions nearly unidentifiable. Under the banner of Anonymous, a number of operations were announced that must be categorised as deeply racist, anti-Semitic and sexist. However, there have also been anti-capitalist operations, campaigns for net-neutrality and hacking attacks against corporations and authoritarian leaders, as well as against cults (especially Scientology). A lot of actions have also been undertaken solely for the LULZ (meaning just for 'amusement').

Anonymous has two similar yet different logos, each of which dismantles the face in different ways. The original logo – a man in a suit with a question mark where his face would be – dismantles the face completely. Referencing René Magritte's famous painting *The Son of Man*, the logo illustrates the impossibility of reducing this heterogeneous movement to individual and identifiable faces; on the other hand, however, this logo reduces the movement to a male body wearing Western clothes.[13] The other symbol of Anonymous, namely the Guy Fawkes mask, is much more interesting. While the first kind of mask Deleuze and Guattari describe dismantles the face, the second does exactly the opposite. The second type of mask 'assures the erection, the construction of the face, the facialisation of the head and the body: the mask is now the face itself, the abstraction or operation of the face. The inhumanity of the face' (Deleuze and Guattari 2005: 181). The famous Guy Fawkes mask (which is, of course, not only used by Anonymous but appears at many contemporary demonstrations, and which gained prominence through its use in the Occupy Wall Street movement) is derived from *V for Vendetta*, a graphic novel by Alan Moore. In the novel, an anarchistic superhero who calls himself V re-enacts the gunpowder plot of Guy Fawkes in a futuristic, fascistic Britain. Unlike other superheroes, V uses a cartoonish grinning mask, but not to distinguish himself from others and therefore be identified as a singular hero. Instead, his plan involves everyone being able to put on the mask and act against the government. The mask becomes a symbol of resistance, an 'idea that is bigger than the person' (Call 2008: 162). At the end of the movie adaptation, a large crowd floods central areas of London, with everyone wearing the V mask – many people, but all with one and the same face. However, contrary to what Deleuze and Guattari suggest, this mask – which is of course the face of a white man – perhaps does not reproduce the logic of faciality in the suggested way. In the regime of faciality, where everything is reduced to the face of the white man, wearing this mask, or using it as a logo for online hacker collectives, ridicules this very process. Anonymous presents everyone with the face they are so desperately searching for, but it is a caricature of the white face, a clownish, grinning cartoon and a stiff expression without any movement. The mask presents a face while at the same time showing the artificiality of this very face. Within the logic of faciality, only he who has a white male face is allowed to speak, to be heard. Showing the artificiality of this very logic by ironically disrupting it, the mask reduces everyone to one face, but it is the face of everyone or of no one – a pure artificial face.

## *All in One*

I would like to consider here that there might not only be the two kinds of masks – the ones that dismantle the face and the ones that are the face – that Deleuze and Guattari described. Since 2011, the London-based artist Zach Blas has developed artistic practices against facial recognition software. His ongoing project, *Facial Weaponization Suite*, consists of different artistic projects that involve ways of making the face unreadable or unrecognisable to computer algorithms. One of the pieces is called *Fag Face Mask*.[14] In a video explaining the project, Blas criticises dubious psychological studies that attempt to prove that people are able to recognise the faces of homosexual individuals, even when the faces are shown without hair or any other cultural and technological markings, such as glasses and piercings, and even when they are shown for only a few seconds. Blas rightly observes that the idea behind these and similar studies is that there is something like a 'typical' homosexual face. Homosexuals, like many other minorities, are often seen as different or abnormal, and thus as identifiable.

Blas follows this logic in his art workshops, where the faces of participants are scanned into a virtual 3D model. The models of all the faces are then combined into one model that is eventually printed out as a mask. The *Fag Face Mask* thus combines the faces of several people who identify as queer. Although made from many faces, this mask cannot be reduced to a single face, nor can it be identified as a face by automated facial recognition algorithms. The combination of many faces can, therefore, also dismantle *the* face so that we have a becoming-minoritarian by multiplying, by adding the faces of minorities. As Blas states: 'We propose to start making faces our weapons, we can create many faces and wear them interchangeably . . . we embrace the power of the collective face, we make our faces common with the mask and become a faceless threat' (Blas 2012).

Blas's masks are more than just a way not to be recognised as a face or identified by facial recognition software. These masks also show the potential of what he calls the 'collective face' – a non-face combined of many faces. It is this multitude of faces that overdetermines the logic of faciality itself, creating an indeterminacy that cannot be resolved. There is no 'original' face. This is often the case in social movements such as Occupy or the Indignados, where the movement does not have a few identifiable spokespeople but, on the contrary, lets everyone speak for themselves and provide their own perspective, creating a multitude of faces of the movement. There is not only the possibility of dismantling the face or being the face but, as Blas's work shows, maybe there is also the possibility of creating new kinds of faces that subvert the logic of faciality: collective faces, fabulated faces.

## Fabulating Faces

The movements and practices I have assembled in this text represent just some of the many uses of masks and faces – dismantling practices within current political struggles. These movements cannot be reduced to the faces of leaders. Masked faces, be they black masks, cartoonish grinning white faces or unidentifiable mashups of different faces, refuse to speak as one should speak, refuse to be identified and, consequently, to be represented. The movements and artistic performances discussed in this text speak with many different voices and on different levels. However, although they do not have an identifiable face and do not speak as they are told to, they are not 'unseeable' and silent. Instead, they are what Guattari calls 'collectivities of utterance' (Guattari 1984: 221), not demanding anything specific, not reproducing the logic of faciality – or at least trying to reproduce it as little as possible – but, on the contrary, fabulating their own faces.

Fabulation is an open process of creation, a process of becoming. 'It is the task of the fabulating function to invent a people' (Deleuze 1998: 4). This invention is not a conscious or scheduled one, and cannot be planned. In contrast to the racist hordes marching through more and more cities, chanting 'We are the people'/'Wir sind das Volk' – meaning the people with white faces – the machinic strategies proposed here are not able to name 'their' people or even address them. However, they do not have, nor do they want, such a people, such an ignorant belief in even the slightest possibility of a pure people who see themselves as the face per se – that is, the white face. The people to come are, as Deleuze says, 'bastard people' (1998), always incomplete yet always manifold. The people to come do not have white faces. On the contrary, they do not have faces at all; they are faceless, hiding their faces, dismantling them, masking them.

As I have argued in this chapter, masks are used for far more than disguise or protection. Masks are part of a minor politics, a non-representational or perhaps even anti-representational politics, a politics struggling against the logic of representation and faciality itself. The use of masks can, therefore, be seen as one of many tactics against the movements' own facialisation, or what Guattari called the danger of structuralisation. This is also why the use of masks in current social movements resembles what he describes as the machine as 'revolutionary programme', as a 'machine for institutional subversion' (Guattari 1984: 119). In our capitalist 'societies of control' (Deleuze 1995: 177), especially where the logic of faciality is implemented in algorithms that define what is representable, determine who has access to what and expand the logic of the face, visible invisibility can be a counter-strategy, a becoming visible on new, fabulated terms. As Saul Newman writes: 'Maybe in the society of control, the only way for the people to become visible – to affirm its place at the centre of politics – is to become invisible, to form a singularity that no longer seeks to represent itself' (Newman 2009: 119).

Current social movements hide their faces but not themselves; squatting in squares in the middle of cities they are not 'unseeable' but visibly invisible – which is what Guattari meant when he said, 'after the face, we come to an invisible becoming' (Guattari 1984: 162). As Subcommandante Marcos once stated: 'In order for them to see us, we covered our faces; so that they would call us by name, we gave up our names' (Marcos cited in Nail 2012: 145).

## Epilogue

Let us revisit Ellison's *Invisible Man* one last time. After he has finished writing down the remarkable story of his life, he realises that all of his attempts to obtain a face, represent a face or speak with a voice have failed because there is no face, no voice that can be his own or represent him authentically. He realises that the very attempt to build a face is the problem and that being invisible, being faceless, can be part of a political strategy. He concludes:

> And, as I said before, a decision has been made. I'm shaking off the old skin and I'll leave it here in the hole. I'm coming out, no less invisible without it, but coming out nevertheless ... I've overstayed my hibernation, since there's a possibility that even an invisible man has a socially responsible role to play. (Ellison 2014: 581)

There is a possibility for invisible people, for faceless and speechless minorities, to become revolutionary, to change society – not by becoming majoritarian or believing in representation but, on the contrary, by embracing facelessness and becoming clandestine. Wearing one face for all, wearing many faces at once, or having no face at all, the people to come fabulate their own faces and bodies, become clandestine and, at the same time, more visible than before, or at least visibly invisible.

## Notes

1. 'Chaosmosis' describes processes that instead of oscillating between 'order and disorder', rather find new combinations of the seemingly incompatible (Guattari 1995: 112). 'The machine, every species of machine, is always at the junction of the finite and infinite, at this point of negotiation between complexity and chaos' (111).
2. 'Minority' here should not be understood as a numerical category but rather, as Deleuze and Guattari emphasise repeatedly, as a category of exploitation. Furthermore, it is crucial to distinguish 'minority' as an existing category of domination from 'minoritarian' as 'a potential, creative and created, becoming' (Deleuze and Guattari 2005: 106).
3. For more on the concept of the machine as a social movement, see, for example, Gerald Raunig's (2010) *A Thousand Machines*.

4. 'One might even say that in capitalist systems, based on signifying stratifications and stratifications of subjectivation, no authority could be established without these machines of "faciality"' (Guattari 1984: 156).
5. 'Racism operates by the determination of degrees of deviance in relation to the White-Man face . . . Racism never detects the particles of the other; it propagates waves of sameness until those who resist identification have been wiped out' (Deleuze and Guattari 2005: 178).
6. 'Order-words', however, are much more than just commands, as Deleuze and Guattari make clear when they introduce this term in *A Thousand Plateaus* and discuss the relation between information and noise, and how through order-words what is 'normative' is (re)produced (Deleuze and Guattari 2005: 79).
7. Stuttering is here seen as a creative as well as resisting process, part of a 'minorising' of languages and speech acts: 'Creative stuttering is what makes language grow from the middle, like grass; it is what makes language a rhizome instead of a tree, what puts language in perpetual disequilibrium' (Deleuze 1998: 111).
8. 'Furthermore, the use of masks to cover the faces of protestors and activists is more than simply a defensive gesture against police identification, but points to a new politics of invisibility, where invisibility and anonymity themselves become symbols for resistance' (Newman 2010: 183).
9. Of course, historical as well as current social movements have developed many more kinds of masks than those presented here. Another type of mask would be the jester, for example, present in the connections of carnivals and revolution (Bakhtin 1984), as well as in current forms, as in the CIRCA (Clandestine Insurgent Rebel Clown Army).
10. The black bloc strategy is often criticised from many standpoints. Most relevant are questions concerning race and gender in riots – discussed, for example, in A. K. Thompson's *Black Bloc, White Riot* (2010). The black bloc tactic, at least the criticised aspects of it, are furthermore part of many non-anarchistic groups, including right-wing demonstrations and hooligan groups.
11. For a detailed analysis of the Zapatistas via Deleuze-Guattarian theory, see Thomas Nail's *Returning to Revolution* (2012).
12. For a history of Anonymou, see Gabriella Coleman's *Hacker, Hoaxer, Whistleblower, Spy* (2014).
13. Magritte himself said about this painting, in regard to what I call here the visibly invisible, '[a]t least it hides the face partly well, so you have the apparent face, the apple, hiding the visible but hidden, the face of the person . . . This interest can take the form of a quite intense feeling, a sort of conflict, one might say, between the visible that is hidden and the visible that is present' (Magritte cited in Torczyner 1979: 172).
14. For images and more information see Blas (2012).

# References

Bakhtin, M. (1984), *Rabelais and His World*, Bloomington: Indiana University Press.
Blas, Z. (2012), 'Facial Weaponization Communiqué: Fag Face', http://www.zach blas.info/works/facial-weaponization-suite/ (last accessed 16 August 2018).
Call, L. (2008), 'A is for Anarchy, V is for Vendetta: Images of Guy Fawkes and the Creation of Postmodern Anarchism', *Anarchist Studies*, 16(2): 154–72.
Certeau, M. de (1997), *The Capture of Speech and Other Political Writings*, Minneapolis: University of Minnesota Press.

Coleman, G. (2014), *Hacker, Hoaxer, Whistleblower, Spy: The Many Faces of Anonymous*, London and New York: Verso.

Day, R. (2005), *Gramsci Is Dead: Anarchist Currents in the Newest Social Movements*, London: Pluto Press.

Deleuze, G. (1995), *Negotiations*, trans. M. Joughin, New York: Columbia University Press.

Deleuze, G. (1998), *Essays Critical and Clinical*, trans. M. Greco and D. Smith, London and New York: Verso.

Deleuze, G. (2007), 'What Is the Creative Act?', in G. Deleuze, *Two Regimes of Madness*, trans. A. Hodges and M. Taormina, Los Angeles: Semiotext(e), pp. 312–24.

Deleuze, G. and M. Foucault (1977), 'Intellectuals and Power', in M. Foucault, *Language, Counter-Memory, Practice: Selected Essays and Interviews*, New York: Cornell University Press, pp. 205–17.

Deleuze, G. and F. Guattari (1983), *Anti-Oedipus: Capitalism and Schizophrenia*, trans. R. Hurley, M. Seem and H. R. Lane, Minneapolis: University of Minnesota Press.

Deleuze, G. and F. Guattari (1986), *Kafka: Toward a Minor Literature*, trans. D. Polan, Minneapolis: University of Minnesota Press.

Deleuze, G. and F. Guattari (2005), *A Thousand Plateaus*, trans. B. Massumi, Minneapolis: University of Minnesota Press.

Ellison, R. (2014), *Invisible Man*, London: Penguin Books.

Gerbaudo, P. (2017), *The Mask and the Flag: Populism, Citizenism and Global Protest*, London: Hurst & Co.

Guattari, F. (1984), *Molecular Revolution: Psychiatry and Politics*, trans. R. Sheed and D. Cooper, London: Penguin Books.

Guattari, F. (1995), *Chaosmosis: An Ethico-Aesthetic Paradigm*, trans. P. Bains and J. Pefanis, Bloomington: Indiana University Press.

Johnson, T. (2001), 'Versailles, Meet Les Halles: Masks, Carnival, and the French Revolution', *Representations*, 73(1): 89–116.

Katsiaficas, G. (2006), *The Subversion of Politics: European Autonomous Movements and the Decolonization of Everyday Life*, Oakland: AK Press.

Marx, K. (1993) [1939], *Grundrisse: Foundations of the Critique of Political Economy*. London and New York: Penguin Books.

May, T. (1994), *The Political Philosophy of Poststructural Anarchism*, University Park: Pennsylvania State University Press.

Nail, T. (2012), *Returning to Revolution: Deleuze, Guattari and Zapatismo*, Edinburgh: Edinburgh University Press.

Newman, S. (2009), 'Politics in the Age of Control', in M. Poster and D. Savat (eds), *Deleuze and New Technology*, Edinburgh: Edinburgh University Press, pp. 104–22.

Newman, S. (2010), *The Politics of Postanarchism*, Edinburgh: Edinburgh University Press.

Raunig, G. (2010), *A Thousand Machines: A Concise Philosophy of the Machine as Social Movement*, Los Angeles: Semiotext(e).

Ruiz, P. (2013), 'Revealing Power. Masked Protest and the Blank Figure', *Cultural Politics*, 9(3): 263–79.

Sauvagnargues, A. (2016), *Artmachines: Deleuze, Guattari, Simondon*, Edinburgh: Edinburgh University Press.

Thompson, A. K. (2010), *Black Bloc, White Riot: Anti-Globalization and the Geneology of Dissent*, Oakland: AK Press.

Torczyner, H. (1979), *Magritte: Ideas and Images*, New York: Harry N. Abrams.

# Chapter 12

# Pierre Clastres and the Amazonian War Machine

*Gregory Kalyniuk*

In addressing the relation of Deleuze's philosophy to anarchism, no discussion would be complete without considering Pierre Clastres and his ethnographic research on the stateless peoples of the Amazon basin. A maverick in the field of political anthropology, Clastres was in close contact with Deleuze and Guattari during the composition of *Anti-Oedipus*, and his work forms a key source for both volumes of *Capitalism and Schizophrenia*. Central to Clastres's investigations is his analysis of political power in 'primitive' societies,[1] which he famously characterised as 'societies against the state' or 'societies for war'. Against Hobbes's claim that humanity's state of nature, or the 'war of all against all', was only ever suppressed through the formation of states, and that a society without a state could not even be considered a society, Clastres sought to show how, for Amazonian peoples such as the Guayaki, the Yanomami, the Tupi and the Guarani, the form of political power associated with the state was already understood in its essence, and that these peoples warded off its corrupting influence by becoming societies-for-war. This reversal of the Hobbesian relation between war and state allowed Clastres to go a step further and reverse the relation between war and exchange assumed by his teacher, Lévi-Strauss: 'war implies alliance, alliance entails exchange . . . war is not the accidental failure of exchange, exchange is a tactical effect of war' (Clastres 2010: 270). Finding confirmation for Nietzsche's genealogy of debt among the Amazonians, Clastres was also able to show how it was relations of debt and not of exchange that formed the basis of primitive social organisation. The chief without power was indebted to his people, and the people were indebted to the ancestors and, ultimately, to the earth itself. As we will see, these insights proved to be particularly significant for Deleuze and Guattari in *Anti-Oedipus*. Among the anthropologists who were their contemporaries, Clastres was perhaps the most receptive to their work, with one caveat: he was never fully satisfied with their account of the origin of the state.

Clastres's anarchism makes him unique both as an anthropologist and as a precursor and collaborator of Deleuze and Guattari. After abandoning the French Communist Party in response to the Hungarian Uprising against Soviet occupation in 1956, he soon became a fierce critic of Stalin, totalitarianism and, ultimately, all theories of social progress (Moyn 2004: 57). His path through academia was as tortuous as the development of his political orientation: before Clastres became interested in doing ethnography, he was a student of philosophy who eagerly immersed himself in the works of Nietzsche and Heidegger. Once he completed his studies, he went on to study anthropology under Lévi-Strauss, whose structuralist approach he eventually became critical of after an initial period of enthusiasm. But in his writings, his most vitriolic moments are reserved for Marxist anthropologists, whom he faults for being dogmatic, lacking originality, and awkwardly attempting to conceptualise primitive life in terms of ill-suited Marxist categories, which he dubbed 'ethnomarxism' (Clastres 2010: 221–36). Instead of, for instance, treating religions and myths as if they belonged to the field of ideology, or kinship relations as if they were relations of production, Clastres sought to initiate a Copernican Revolution in anthropology that would put an end to this sort of heavy-handed, Eurocentric theorising, and finally approach the indigenous world on its own terms. It is no surprise that he found it much more fruitful to take the insights he gained studying primitive societies and use them to reconceptualise social systems in the developed world. Against the Marxist contention that the state is an instrument of the rich used to exploit the poor, Clastres sees the relationship between state and class in opposite terms. He argues that, rather than pre-existing the appearance of the state, class divisions are produced by the state machinery, without which there would never have appeared an exploiter or exploited class (Clastres 2012: 17–19). This, of course, makes it all the more difficult for him to theorise the historical origins of the state, since it can no longer be explained as the result of economic transformations.

But Clastres complicates the problem one step further: rather than originating with the appearance of actual state institutions, the state would have already existed in virtual form as a latent social possibility, or what Deleuze and Guattari would go on to christen with the name *Urstaat*. What evidence does Clastres find for this? The chief without power and all of the collective levelling mechanisms that are used to keep him that way stand as proof, in Clastres's mind, that primitive peoples understand what this latent social possibility is and that they will do everything in their power to prevent it from manifesting. But this, he argues, still does not explain the origins of the latent state, nor does it explain what precipitated the political break that would lead to the institutional manifestation of the state. These questions would, as I have already mentioned, become a posthumous cause of disagreement between Deleuze and Guattari and Clastres, whose anarchism prevents him from accepting any theory of economic determinism that would overshadow the human will to be free. Generally speaking, Clastres's own anarchism could perhaps be said to amount to the conviction that we, as state subjects of late capitalist society, may have something important to learn from primitive societies in our struggle against the oppressive exercise of political power – something that would have nonetheless informed the highly unorthodox Marxism introduced by Deleuze and Guattari in *Anti-Oedipus*.

## A Universal History of Contingency

What exactly qualifies the notion of a 'universal history of contingency' that appears in Deleuze and Guattari's *Anti-Oedipus*? How is their theory any different from Hegel's own philosophical understanding of Universal History, and how is it informed by Clastres's account of primitive societies' invention of mechanisms for warding off the state? First, we must understand that because primitive societies had never collectively arrived at the formation of a state, Hegel would have dismissed them for being not only without any genuine history, but also, and contrary to Rousseau, without any freedom. Aside from conceiving of their way of life as being driven solely by irrational, passionate excess, Hegel's teleological view of history would have excluded any consideration of primitive peoples. Clastres, on the other hand, makes a compelling argument for why certain key aspects of the violence characteristic of primitive life not only demonstrate a sophisticated understanding of what state power entails, but also bring into focus the preserving conditions of egalitarian freedom necessary for preventing the latent potential of state power from arising in the social fabric. In the context of a universal history, however, what would contingency have to do with primitive societies' ultimate failure to prevent the emergence of the state and the subsequent passage to the imperial barbarian state that would follow in Deleuze and Guattari's tripartite schema? A provisional answer is to be found, according to Deleuze and Guattari, in what lies outside of the strict social codes that account for the organisation of primitive society, which has less to do with the state form itself than it does with what finally becomes possible in capitalist societies: a full decoding of the flows of desire and an absolute deterritorialisation of the forces of production. Viewed retrospectively in the light of capitalism, primitive coding and despotic overcoding were each, in their own way, focused on concealing their underlying contingency in order to prevent decoding and deterritorialisation from compromising their respective symbolic orders. For the primitive anarchists of the Amazon Basin, it would be a far less familiar image of anarchy that would ultimately lead to their undoing.

Deleuze and Guattari's version of universal history in *Anti-Oedipus* is broken down into three distinct periods: the savagery of what they call primitive societies, the despotism of barbarian empires, and the capitalism of civilised humanity. The form of social organisation corresponding to each period depends upon a particular system of anti-production that organises flows of matter and energy and directs them towards preserving the relations of debt and obligation upon which society is founded. In savage or primitive societies, anti-production organises a social symbolic order around kinship relations, and uses the incest taboo as the impetus for establishing marriage alliances. An important aspect of Lévi-Strauss's structural anthropology, the incest taboo plays a constructive role essential to the organisation of primitive society (Lévi-Strauss 1969: *passim*). It should be noted, however, that for Clastres as well as for Deleuze and Guattari, the primary purpose of kinship structures is to fulfil a debt of social obligation, with the facilitation of exchange only a secondary effect. The mediating role of debt allows for the incest taboo to be further generalised into a taboo that forbids desire from directly accessing the means of life, extending beyond reproduction to include forms of social production as well. One is forbidden to reproduce with immediate family members for the same reasons that one is forbidden to consume the spoils of one's own hunting or gathering: the law of debt must take precedence over all else in order to prevent social disintegration (Deleuze and Guattari 1983: 148). Because it must always mediate access to the means of life through a repressive mechanism that forces desire to substitute its immediate aims on the basis of its social debt, Deleuze and Guattari see primitive society as being fundamentally perverse in nature. In order for primitive society to endure, that which sustains the life of society, or women and nourishment, must circulate freely, and the act of sharing must become an imperative for all.

But marriage alliances and the obligation to be generous only account for how society is organised synchronically. Primitive origin myths support a debt obligation to the ancestors and to the earth itself, which is understood to be the ultimate source of all life and the common ancestor of all filiative lineages. This could be said to account for the diachronic dimension of social organisation, in which the ancestral debt corresponds to a taboo against unmediated communion with the earth. As Nietzsche had intuited in *The Genealogy of Morals*, consciousness of indebtedness to the ancestor lies at the origin of the debtor–creditor relationship, where repayment would have been carried out through the bloodiest of sacrifices (Nietzsche 1967: Second Essay, §19). In primitive societies, according to Deleuze and Guattari, repayment of the ancestral debt involves the creation of a collective memory under the watchful eye of the community – the appreciative eye that grasps 'the terrible equivalence between the voice of alliance that inflicts and constrains, and the body afflicted by the sign that a hand is carving in it' (Deleuze and Guattari 1983: 189). They call this form of writing on the body a 'system of cruelty', or 'cruel mnemotechnics' that implants a memory of death in the initiate. In order to successfully repress 'the great biocosmic memory that threatens to deluge every attempt at collectivity' (1983: 190), the ancestral debt to the earth must be repaid through a torturous initiation ritual in which the primitive law is inscribed into the flesh. The more painful the process, the better it will be remembered, and the more clearly the subject of initiation will understand that they are worth neither more nor less than anyone else. Their organs ultimately cease to be their own as they cease to be a biological organism altogether, to instead become the full body of the earth to which the marked appendages now become attached. As Clastres remarks on the initiation rituals of the Guayaki Indians in a short passage quoted in *Anti-Oedipus*: 'They work the skin, and they scar the earth – and this is one and the same mark' (Clastres 1998: 181; Deleuze and Guattari 1983: 190). The territory to which the 'primitive territorial machine' of the savages is related therefore has more to do with subdividing the bodies of its people, as they become the earth's equivalent through ritual torture, than it does with subdividing the earth itself.

An important focal point in Deleuze and Guattari's theory of universal history is the Oedipalisation of desire. In the context of savage or primitive societies, the system of marriage alliances and ancestral debts acts as the *repressing representation* of desire, while the incest taboo is simply the *displaced represented* of desire in relation to life and the means of life which, in turn, form the immediate object or *representative* of desire (Holland 1999: 73). At this stage, Oedipus is only 'the "baited image" with which desire allows itself to be caught' (Deleuze and Guattari

1983: 166), when in fact the true object of desire is something more far reaching.

The ultimate objective of savage representation is to submit the flows of life to a symbolic social code that puts the life of the society above all else, thus preventing any one individual from appropriating the flows of life as their own and, in so doing, manifesting state power in its embryonic form. At some point in history, however, what Deleuze and Guattari call the Urstaat becomes manifest through symbolic overcoding, and the despotic state is born. Passing from primitive societies to barbarian empires, relations of debt and obligation are redirected from the ancestral body of the earth to the appropriating body of the despot, to whom the imperial subjects are now understood to owe their existence, as to a god. The despot becomes the beneficiary of tributes and forced labour in a society divided into castes, where obedience to the despotic state that rules from above is enforced according to strict legal codes under the threat of death. Writing becomes part of a 'system of terror' through which the law is expressed in the absence of the despotic voice, and the spectacle of cruelty is transformed into a means of punishment to provoke fear and instil a sense of servility. The ancestral debt in the primitive society, whose full repayment through initiation is only possible on account if it being finite, here becomes an infinite debt in relation to a despot who is considered to be everyone's father, and for whom incest now becomes an exclusive and natural right. In the imperial formation, incest is no longer simply the displaced represented of desire as it is in the primitive society, but the repressing representation itself, and the means to overcoding the flows of desire (Deleuze and Guattari 1983: 201). The incest taboo remains the displaced represented of desire, but only for the imperial subjects, while the repressed representative of desire is now the open threat of revolt against the despotic state (Holland 1999: 78). While primitive society is characterised as perverted for forcing desire away from its immediate aims through carefully placed social codes that use Oedipus as a decoy, the despotic state is characterised as paranoid for raising the despot to a transcendent position. Overcoded in the forbidding image of Oedipus, the paranoid despot appears both enviable and vulnerable in the eyes of the oppressed and resentful subjects who may threaten to someday do away with him.

It is only under capitalism, according to Deleuze and Guattari, that Oedipus finally takes centre stage as the representative of desire itself. In capitalist society, relations of debt and obligation are organised according to a process of axiomatisation. In two opposed movements, flows of desire are first decoded or deterritorialised in order to socialise labour and revolutionise the means of production and consumption, and are then recoded or reterritorialised under the guise of private ownership in order to appropriate the resulting surplus-production (Holland 1999: 80–1). This commodification of labour and the limitless production of surplus-value that it brings about manifest what Deleuze and Guattari call 'filiative capital' which, rather than occupying a transcendent position in relation to its subjects as the despot does, becomes immanent to the very process of production by functioning as the creditor of an infinite debt which must be repaid with infinite labour. To be made agreeable to these conditions, capitalist subjectivity is indoctrinated with the ascetic ideal, a task that is fulfilled within the private confines of the nuclear family. Because social production and reproduction are now organised by the market, 'the family becomes a microcosm, suited to expressing what it no longer dominates' (Deleuze and Guattari 1983: 264), or the relations of social reproduction as they exist under the capitalist system. In both the savage and despotic social formations, the aim of desire is never incest itself: for the primitives, incest is a substitute for the means of life as the repressed object of desire while, for the barbarians, royal incest is the divine privilege whose repression of the common man's freedom risks provoking a desire for mass revolt. Finding its bearings in the familiar triangle of 'mommy–daddy–me', where it develops in separation from public life, desire under capitalism is left without a socially prescribed alibi for its incestuous longings, and its contingency finally becomes visible in plain view. The Oedipus complex fulfils the task of pacifying a desire without definite aim and of producing ascetic subjects who pose no threat to the capitalist social order once they have internalised the father's law of castration.

Clastres finds much in *Anti-Oedipus* to be worthy of admiration, claiming that in so far as it presents a general theory of society and societies, 'Deleuze and Guattari have written about Savages and Barbarians what ethnologists up to now have not' (Clastres in Deleuze 2004: 226). The accounts of savage coding and imperial overcoding, savage writing as a 'system of cruelty' and barbarian writing as a 'system of terror', the priority given to a genealogy of debt in relation to the structuralist theory of exchange, and, perhaps most importantly, the claim that 'the history of classless societies is the history of their struggle against the latent State', all borrow from and resonate strongly with Clastres's own work. But while Clastres is satisfied with Deleuze and Guattari's reliance upon the notion of the Urstaat to explain the movement from savagery to barbarism, he would still like an answer to the question of where the Urstaat had first come from. Deleuze and Guattari address this question more explicitly in *A Thousand Plateaus* – however, the answer already seems to be implicit in *Anti-Oedipus*, with their stated purpose of writing a universal history of contingency. In fact, the very question of the origin of the state would seem to adopt the point of view of the state, in the sense that it is the nature of the state to give a retrospective account of its own origins, upon which its efficacy as an organ of power is made contingent (Lundy 2012: 125). Before the emergence of the despotic state, the Urstaat would have existed only as an idea around which primitive societies were organised in an antagonistic manner. At some point, something precipitated this antagonism to become over-coded and, turning itself inward, desire was terrorised into a state of voluntary servitude. Yet the possibility of this happening would have always existed, which is perhaps why the state is always already a state of interiority. When Deleuze and Guattari go on to claim in *A Thousand Plateaus* that the state has always existed, they seem to literally mean that the Urstaat has always been immanent to existence, and then retrospectively fabricated its own origin myth through the medium of despotic actors in order to legitimate itself. According to them, Clastres was asking the wrong question, and his assumption that the state must have emerged by way of a clean political break demonstrates that he was looking at the problem the wrong way. How ironic that the trailblazing anarchist anthropologist had adopted the point of view of that which he most hated, in attempting to solve the mystery of its origin! But before moving on to Deleuze and Guattari's engagement with Clastres in *A Thousand Plateaus*, let us examine Clastres's own work more closely.

## The Amazonian War Machine

Some of Clastres's most penetrating insights into the nature of political power in primitive societies can be found in one of his earliest published works, an essay titled 'Exchange and Power', which he wrote before having ever visited South America. In it, he challenges the argument that chieftainship is based on a reciprocal exchange between a people and their chief. Without going so far as to outright challenge the structuralist assertion that primitive societies are founded upon exchange, as he would in his later writings, he argues here that what takes place between a people and their chief is in fact a negation of the very principle of exchange, whose purpose is to distinguish the political sphere from the social structure of the group. In order to be a chief in many indigenous cultures in South America, one must satisfy three criteria: one must play the role of a 'professional pacifier' capable of moderating conflicts; one must be limitlessly generous with the group; and one must be a gifted orator (Clastres 1987: 36). But to argue that in exchange for fulfilling these three criteria the chief is rewarded with the privilege of polygyny and allowed to take as many wives as he desires, would be to badly misinterpret the situation. In his critique of this argument, Clastres begins by distinguishing the first criterion by showing how the moderating role defines the *activity* of the chief, whereas the following two criteria, along with the privilege of polygyny, are the set of conditions that make the political sphere possible, or what amounts to the *nature* of the chief's role. To confuse the nature of chieftainship with its activity, he argues, is to confuse the transcendental and empirical aspects of the institution of political power (1987: 37). Strikingly, the three transcendental predicates of chieftainship mirror the three types of 'signs' whose exchange and circulation constitute society and distinguish it from the natural world: material goods correspond to the chief's obligation to be generous, words correspond to his oratorical talents, and women correspond to his right to polygyny. Could the political sphere possibly be isomorphic to the very structure of society? Clastres argues that to see any similarity between the exchange of goods, words and women that takes place between a people and their chief and the exchange of goods, words and women that constitute society itself would reflect a failure to understand the lengths to which the primitives go to protect their society from the corrupting influence of political power.

If anything, what takes place between a people and their chief is more like a parody of the very principle of exchange, since it is purposefully unequal and without reciprocity. The people can take without limit from their chief whatever goods they want, while the chief can expect no goods in return from them. And oration is as thankless a task as generosity: the words that the chief speaks when settling an internal dispute, or when negotiating with hostile groups on his people's behalf, are actively disrespected and mocked for their pretentiousness. Meanwhile, despite the chief producing daughters who will end up marrying the men of the group, he can accumulate without limit the daughters that they produce for him to take as wives. The circulation of women between the people and their chief is therefore asymmetrical, and can further be understood to occur in a unilateral fashion when we consider the impossibility of compensation by the chief, who could never produce enough daughters for each man to have as many wives as the chief is able to take for himself. For this reason, Clastres claims that the right to take many wives is a gift from the people to their chief, while the chief's generosity and speech are contrastingly seen as his ongoing fulfilment of an infinite debt to his people. The political sphere is distinguished from society on the basis of the negation of any reciprocity or exchange value when the two realms come into contact. Not only does this remove the political sphere from the structure of the group, but it also plays out a drama in which the political sphere becomes, like nature itself, the negation of the structure of the group, since to reject reciprocity is to reject society (1987: 41–2). With the respective transcendental conditions of power and society put at odds with one another, they can only coexist empirically once power has been rendered impotent and the chief has been reduced to playing the emasculated role of a 'professional pacifier' in the service of his people. Because power is apprehended as the very resurgence of nature, culture is forced to become the negation of both nature and power (44). Does this not seem to answer the question as to where the Urstaat comes from? To borrow a recent line from Marshall Sahlins and David Graeber that echoes Clastres's analysis: 'The state of nature has the nature of the state' (Graeber and Sahlins 2017: 3). This leaves one to wonder: what led Clastres to continue seeking the solution to a problem that he had apparently already solved before his real work as an ethnographer had even begun?

Clastres is critical of social evolutionism for the way it presents primitive societies as suffering from a sort of incompleteness: lacking the discipline and technological know-how to increase their productivity beyond the level of a mere subsistence economy and, also, lacking the political will to establish a state institution that would complete their society with a governing body. These are the ideas that guided Western civilisation in its destructive advance into the New World, and the misunderstandings that they exacerbated are still with us today. But what if, instead of deriving from a lack, subsistence economy in fact reflects the refusal of a useless excess, as Sahlins argues in his famous essay 'The Original Affluent Society' (Sahlins 1972: 1–39)? What if primitive peoples simply valued their leisure time too much to work beyond what was necessary to satisfy their basic needs? And what if, in addition to finding its purpose in the freeing up of time for the pursuit of leisure, the rejection of surplus labour is also motivated by a rejection of political power? The evolutionist argument presents the lack of economic development in primitive societies as the reason for the lack of political institutions. But what if the reverse is true? This is exactly what Clastres argues in his essay 'Society Against the State': that 'the political relation of power precedes and founds the economic relation of exploitation' (1987: 198). While the Amazonians would only surrender their leisure to work more than their needs required them to if they were violently coerced into doing so, this would have already been accomplished for the Indians of the Inca Empire, who rather than simply working for the satisfaction of their own needs, also worked for the needs of their rulers. The division of society into antagonistic social classes of rulers and ruled would have carried over into the unequal division of labour, and not vice versa. Neither is there any reason to assume that the transition from nomadism to sedentarisation, nor the transition from hunting and gathering to the domestication of animals and agriculture, would have necessarily catalysed the emergence of the state. Denying that the Neolithic revolution could have brought about an overturning of the social order in hunter-gatherer societies by itself, Clastres argues that there are various indigenous American societies that clearly illustrate the independence of the economy and society with respect to one another (200–2). Some groups of hunter-gatherers present the same sociopolitical characteristics as their sedentary agriculturalist neighbours, while these same sedentary agriculturalists may have completely opposed sociopolitical characteristics vis-à-vis the imperial societies whose mode of agriculture is only slightly more intensive than their own. For Clastres, this stands as proof that the decisive moment that brought about the overturning of one social order in favour of another must have been a political break rather than an economic transformation. Consequently, if one wants to preserve the Marxist infrastructure/superstructure distinction, one must acknowledge that the base is political and the superstructure is economic (202–3).

One explanation for the emergence of the state that Clastres does give some serious consideration to is the hypothesis of demographic determinism. Primitive societies purposely try to keep their numbers below a certain threshold, sometimes even resorting to infanticide in order to accomplish this, and break off into independent segmentary groups when their numbers do become too great. Somehow, there is an implicit understanding that society cannot continue to be egalitarian if its population rises above a certain limit. This seems to have been the very problem that the Tupi-Guarani faced in the sixteenth century around the time that they were first encountered by French and Portuguese colonisers who observed that the 'provincial kings' or 'kinglets' wielded a considerable degree of power over the inhabitants of their villages, whose populations then numbered in the several thousands (1987: 213–14). While these descriptions do not point to the existence of despotism among the Tupi-Guarani, Clastres does acknowledge the possibility of some primitive form of state power emerging during this period. But what interests him more than this are the descriptions of the prophets who would incite the Tupi-Guarani to forsake life in the villages and embark upon a quest for the Land Without Evil, an earthly paradise that would have delivered them from the 'evil' taking root at home (215). The prophets identified the One as the root of Evil, which Clastres understands to have amounted to an intuition of the universal 'essence' of the state (216–17). Apparently, these prophets were so persuasive with their rhetoric that the people followed them out of the villages in a mass exodus. How did this equation of the One with Evil have such a powerful effect? In a related text, Clastres explains how, among the Guarani, to claim that 'things in their totality are one' amounts to a strict application of the identity principle; for instance, that a man is only a man, and that a man cannot be a god. To assign limits, finitude and incompleteness to things thus reflects the authority to designate the world and define its beings, which itself acts as an apology for a secret potential to silently declare that, for instance, a man can be both man and god at the same time (173). The prophets exercised this very potential when, through the equivocations of prophetic speech, they seduced the masses into believing that heaven on earth was attainable, demonstrating an efficacy of power that the 'provincial kings' and 'kinglets' could only have dreamt of. Rejecting the hypothesis of demographic determinism as a viable explanation on its own, Clastres instead suggests that the prophets' power to tell the masses what they desired may have contained the seeds of a new discourse on political power (218). The Tupi-Guarani prophets, like the one-eyed magician-emperor god Varuna, may very well have been despots in the making with their ability to capture the attention of the masses. By equating the One with Evil while overcoding the world in their own image, they perhaps led the people back towards the very thing that they claimed to be saving them from.

For Clastres, the fundamental condition allowing primitive societies to avoid state capture is war: the threat of war from within, which is warded off by preventing the concentration of power in the chieftainship, and the threat of war from without, which unites the people against enemies and supports the formation of alliances with neighbouring communities. In one of his final essays, titled 'Archeology of Violence: War in Primitive Societies', Clastres is careful to consider three competing discourses that address the issue at hand before presenting his own theory. The naturalist discourse claims that war is the double of hunting and can be understood purely in terms of the biological tendency towards aggressiveness (Clastres 2010: 253–6). Clastres dismisses this discourse for completely overlooking the social dimension of primitive

war and treating its subjects as if they were mere animals. The econo-
mist discourse, which is best articulated by Marxist anthropologists,
contends that violence is linked to poverty and that primitive war is the
outcome of a competition for scarce goods (246–50). Clastres dismisses
this discourse on the basis of Sahlins's discovery that hunter-gatherer
societies are in fact societies of leisure and that the issue of scarcity rarely
enters the picture. Finally, the exchangist discourse put forward by Lévi-
Strauss holds that exchanges are the peaceful resolution of potential wars
and that wars are the outcome of unsuccessful exchanges (252). Clastres
gives his teacher's argument the most serious attention and spends the
rest of his essay refuting it. To reduce the social being of primitive
society exclusively to exchange, he argues, would not only disregard the
ideals of economic autarky and political independence, but also confuse
the levels on which war and exchange respectively function (253–6). The
refusal of social division, the exclusion of inequality and the prohibition
of alienation in primitive society would not allow a hypothetical savage
entrepreneur from ever realising a successful exchange with his surplus,
for instance, because it would sooner be expropriated from him and
consumed by his fellow tribesmen. Between neighbouring communities,
on the other hand, exchanges are only a means to establish alliances
for the purpose of waging war more efficiently against non-allied communities. Externally, a law of opposition and multiplicity ensures the
absolute difference between these undivided neighbouring communities, which Clastres likens to 'neo-monads' opening themselves up to
one another 'in the extreme intensity of the violence of war' (261–2).
Why would primitive communities be content with simply exchanging
women with one another, Clastres asks, when they could instead wage
war and win women without losing any? Complementing the external
policy of war is an internal policy that Clastres likens to an 'intransigent
conservatism', which seeks to preserve its traditional system of norms
and prevent any social innovation that would undermine the 'undivided
We' of the community. The 'war machine', with its centrifugal logic of
dispersion, is the motor of this conservative 'social machine', giving to
it its reason for being. But what distinguishes the conservative refusal
of social division from the centripetal logic of the One that the war
machine is focused on counteracting? The logic of the One seeks to
institute a unifying authority capable of separating itself from society
and dividing its people into Masters and Subjects (275), which would
seem to be a far cry from the 'undivided We' of the primitive monad.
One is left wondering, however, why Clastres stops short of questioning
whether the logic of the One may not already be at work in the war over

women. Does it not clearly show how the men are acting as a sort of unifying authority, separated from the women whom they dominate?

Clastres does not believe that there is any significant inequality between the sexes in the primitive societies he has studied. In 'Sorrows of the Savage Warrior', he goes so far as to claim that men are '*in a defensive position in regards to women,* because they recognize the superiority of women' (Clastres 2010: 314). As men, they must constantly be available for war and, in the extreme case of the warrior society (which Clastres distinguishes from primitive societies for turning the *permanent state of war* into *actual permanent war*) (303), they are dominated by an insatiable desire for glory and prestige that in most cases leads them to an early death. Like the levelling mechanisms that prevent the chief from asserting power over the group, a similar mechanism is in place to prevent warriors from doing the same. This mechanism has to do with how glory and prestige are viewed by a society as a whole. After each conquest, Clastres writes, the warrior 'must continuously start over, for each exploit accomplished is both a source of prestige and a questioning of this prestige' (301–2). More often than not, this leads the most zealous of warriors to a self-destructive end. But if they attain success enough times, a group of warriors could conceivably use their prestige to push the rest of society into following them down the path of ever-intensifying war. Here, Clastres admits to 'a remarkable paradox: on the one hand, war permits the primitive community to persevere in its undivided being; on the other hand, it reveals itself as the possible basis for division into Masters and Subjects' (304). But what of the treatment of women as goods of exchange and consumption – does this not put them into a subordinate role in relation to the men who kidnap them from their homes and kill off their fathers and brothers? Clastres is determined to analyse the workings of primitive society on its own terms and he rejects what he perceives to be Marxist and feminist attempts to discover class struggle where it does not exist – in this case, taking the form of a 'battle of the sexes' where the women are the 'losers' (314). To fully understand relations between men and women in primitive societies, Clastres argues, one must look at how the difference between the sexes is understood through their myths and rites. If man, as a warrior, is a being-for-death, then woman, as a mother, is a being-for-life. Women produce the future of the community and, if they are not happy with what is happening in their society, they have the power to decide its death by refusing to have children. The glorification of the masculine destiny in war through myths and rituals appears to Clastres as compensation 'for the too obvious truth that this destiny is feminine' (316).

Does Clastres make a valid point here, or is he simply apologising for male domination in primitive society – a type of society that he perhaps unduly presents as egalitarian? Critics have commonly described his account of primitive society as suffering from a sort of naïve romanticism, and some have even accused him of misogyny and homophobia (Graeber 2004: 23; Goldberg 1993: 12–15). When considering such responses to his work, we should remember that, as an anthropologist, Clastres would have sought to leave his own values behind and undergo full cultural immersion so he could study his subjects with an impartial eye. The ideals of individual autonomy and personal freedom that are practically axiomatic to anarchist thought and practice in the developed world would have found no place among the Amazonians. Clastres may be guilty of glossing over some important inconsistencies in his analysis and romanticising his subjects to a degree, but he never allows himself to make any claims about the superiority of the primitive way of life, as some of today's anarcho-primitivists have a tendency to do on the basis of far less nuanced idealisations.

## 'There Has Always Been a State'

While Clastres may have significantly informed Deleuze and Guattari's concept of the war machine in *A Thousand Plateaus* (even giving to it its name), this second time around they are decidedly more critical in their reception of his work. Quite simply, they fault him for the way in which he frames the problem of the origin of the state. By maintaining the self-sufficiency of primitive societies, he not only deprives himself of a way of explaining how the state first arose, they argue, but also returns to the very evolutionism that his entire approach to studying primitive societies had been focused on circumventing (Deleuze and Guattari 1987: 359). They liken Clastres's preferred scenario of the clean political break to a sudden and irreversible mutation and appear baffled as to why he remained so indifferent to the findings of archaeology, which confirm that the first empires dated as far back as Palaeolithic times. Taking this time span into account, it remains highly doubtful to Deleuze and Guattari that primitive societies would not at some point have come into contact with these prehistoric empires. On this assumption, they conclude that 'there has always been a State' (360). Yet somehow, their critique seems a bit disingenuous. While Clastres may not have much to say about the findings of archaeologists when he insists upon the self-sufficiency of primitive societies, does he actually mean this in an absolute sense for all of time? Would such a claim really preclude the possibility that primitive societies could have at some point encountered or even broken away from state societies in their very distant past? Clastres does, after all, appear to be more perplexed with the origins of the virtual Urstaat than he is with the emergence of actual state authority – so much is evident in his remarks on *Anti-Oedipus* (Deleuze 2004: 227). Neglecting to fully take this into account affects the cogency of Deleuze and Guattari's critique. For instance, there is nothing in Clastres to contradict the possibility that non-state societies could have transformed into state societies and then back again many times over, each time through a clean political break that could have been precipitated by a population explosion, the false promises of prophetic speech, the abuse of prestige for waging war and/or other unknown factors.[2] In any case, to simply conclude that 'there has always been a State' does not seem to answer the question in a way that would likely satisfy an empirically minded ethnographer. Do Deleuze and Guattari simply mean that there has always been a state in the non-literal sense, so that, as an institution of power, it has been around for hundreds of thousands of years, or do they mean it in the more literal sense of it being immanent to the workings of human thought (and by extension the social)?

If Clastres is still guilty of evolutionism for claiming that 'all civilized peoples were first primitives' (Clastres 1987: 205), then Deleuze and Guattari are no less guilty of the same charge in *Anti-Oedipus*, for the evolutionary character of their historical stages. It is perhaps for this reason that, in *A Thousand Plateaus*, they present the reality of both the war machine and the state apparatus in ahistoricist terms, maintaining their perpetual coexistence and denying that either could have had historical priority over the other. Whereas their universal history presented three successive epochs whose narratives were assembled retrospectively, the war machine operates outside any definite historical context as a pure form of exteriority, relative to the state apparatus, which functions as a pure form of interiority (and of which the despotic state is but one iteration). While the state overcodes flows and territories in order to install and legitimate stable powers, the war machine works in the opposite direction, decoding and deterritorialising flows into a fabric of immanent relations. And yet for Deleuze and Guattari, it is never a question of 'all or nothing' with regard to whether or not the state is present (Deleuze and Guattari 1987: 360). Contrary to Clastres's analyses, the conservative tendencies and strict social codes pervasive in primitive societies would already seem to be embryonic manifestations of state power.[3] Where would this leave the anti-statist aspirations of the anarchist ideology? If it is true that the state can never be completely suppressed, then it should be equally true that 'smashing the state' will not necessarily abolish the oppressive social relations that are reproduced through its institutions. In the words of Deleuze and Guattari, 'Never believe that a smooth space will suffice to save us' (1987: 500).

Ultimately, the Amazonian societies studied by Clastres are only one possible iteration of what Deleuze and Guattari call the war machine. When relating it to what lies outside of the state, they trace two simultaneous directions in which the war machine goes: on the one hand, worldwide organisations (commercial, industrial and religious) that enjoy a high degree of autonomy in relation to states, and on the other hand, local bands, margins and minorities that struggle for the rights of segmentary societies against the power of states (1987: 360). When the anticipation-prevention mechanisms break down and the state succeeds in appropriating the war machine, the result is the military institution. But the state also appropriates the anticipation-prevention mechanisms for its own purposes of warding off capitalism (437). The formation of the modern welfare state, for instance, is owed to the success of these mechanisms. When they break down, however, the war machine may succeed in appropriating the state, which results in fascism (230). Fascism, as defined by Giovanni Gentile, is the 'merger of state and corporate power'. While the primitive anarchists of the Amazon Basin had encoded a negation of nature and power into a local culture of freedom and equality that was nonetheless devoid of 'individuals' properly understood, today's anarcho-capitalists recast the war machine under the guise of the free market as if it were the global resurgence of nature and power, against a state that, if left unchecked, is purported to oppress its aspiring 'individuals' on the pretext of social justice. It is in this sense that the provisions of the welfare state are undermined in order to give free rein to forces that appropriate political power and manifest a sort of fascism from the side of the war machine. The question then remains: should the response of the local bands, margins and minorities simply be to continue to fight for the rights of segmentary societies against these appropriated states, or should they also be aiming to save the states themselves from the cancer that is taking root within them?

## Notes

1. For the sake of remaining faithful to the texts of Clastres, Deleuze and Guattari and not confusing the reader, I have chosen not to replace outdated terms such as 'primitive' or 'savage' with their more contemporary equivalents. However, I do recognise that these terms are deeply problematic, and in no way support the negative stereotyping of indigenous peoples with which they are associated.

2. While Deleuze and Guattari are critical of Clastres for insisting that the state emerged by way of a clean political break, Clastres's hypothesis regarding prophetic speech suggests a possibility for how the state could have emerged through a more ambiguous sort of process. For if, according to the Guarani prophets, man can be both man and god at the same time, then could primitive society similarly be both with and without state authority at the same time? Hélène Clastres (writing after her partner's death) presents the colonial-era Guarani in search of the Land without Evil as being faced with the ambivalence between a collective ethic of respect for the social order, and an ethic of salvation that is individualistic for negating the collective ethic that acts as its condition of possibility (Clastres 1995: 84). To believe that a mortal man can be realised as an immortal god entails the belief that 'the twofold limitation that assigns humans to death and destines them to be dependent on others can be abolished' (87). In perhaps the same sense that Deleuze and Guattari 'conceptualize the contemporaneousness or coexistence of the two inverse movements, of the two directions of time – of the primitive peoples "before" the State, and of the State "after" the primitive peoples' (Deleuze and Guattari 1987: 431), the past-oriented collective ethic and the future-oriented ethic of salvation can likewise be said to unfold simultaneously in a micropolitical field.
3. Indeed, what could the 'conservative social machine' in Clastres's analysis possibly have to do with the 'power of metamorphosis' that defines the war machine for Deleuze and Guattari (Deleuze and Guattari 1987: 437)?

# References

Clastres, H. (1995) [1975], *The Land-Without-Evil: Tupí-Guaraní Prophetism*, trans. J. G. Brovender, Urbana: University of Illinois Press.

Clastres, P. (1987) [1974], *Society Against the State: Essays in Political Anthropology*, trans. R. Hurley with A. Stein, New York: Zone Books.

Clastres, P. (1998) [1972], *Chronicle of the Guayaki Indians*, trans. P. Auster, New York: Zone Books.

Clastres, Pierre (2010) [1980], *Archeology of Violence*, trans. J. Herman, Los Angeles: Semiotext(e).

Clastres, P. (2012) [1974], *The Question of Power: An Interview with Pierre Clastres*, trans. H. Arnold, Los Angeles: Semiotext(e).

Deleuze, G. (2004) [2002], *Desert Islands and Other Texts, 1953–1974*, trans. M. Taormina, Los Angeles: Semiotext(e).

Deleuze, G. and F. Guattari (1983) [1972], *Anti-Oedipus: Capitalism and Schizophrenia*, trans. R. Hurley, M. Seem and H. R. Lane, Minneapolis: University of Minnesota Press.

Deleuze, G. and Guattari, F. (1987) [1980], *A Thousand Plateaus: Capitalism and Schizophrenia*, trans. B. Massumi, Minneapolis: University of Minnesota Press.

Goldberg, J. (1993), 'Sodomy in the New World', in M. Warner (ed.), *Fear of a Queer Planet: Queer Politics and Social Theory*, Minneapolis: University of Minnesota Press, pp. 3–18.

Graeber, D. (2004), *Fragments of an Anarchist Anthropology*, Chicago: Prickly Paradigm Press.

Graeber, D. and M. Sahlins (2017), *On Kings*, Chicago: Hau Books.

Holland, E. (1999), *Deleuze and Guattari's* Anti-Oedipus: *Introduction to Schizoanalysis*, New York: Routledge.

Lévi-Strauss, C. (1969) [1949], *The Elementary Structures of Kinship*, trans. J. H. Bell and J. R. von Sturmer, Boston: Beacon Press.

Lundy, C. (2012), *History and Becoming: Deleuze's Philosophy of Creativity*, Edinburgh: Edinburgh University Press.

Moyn, S. (2004), 'Of Savagery and Civil Society: Pierre Clastres and the Transformation of French Political Thought', *Modern Intellectual History*, 1(1): 55–80.

Nietzsche, F. (1967) [1887], *On the Genealogy of Morals and Ecce Homo*, trans. W. Kaufmann and R. J. Hollingdale, New York: Vintage Books.

Sahlins, M. (1972), *Stone Age Economics*, Hawthorne, NY: Aldine de Gruyter.

Viveiros de Castro, E. (2014) [2009], *Cannibal Metaphysics: For a Post-Structural Anthropology*, trans. P. Skafish, Minneapolis: Univocal.

Chapter 13

# From the Autochthonousphere to the Allochthonousphere: Escaping the Logics of Plantations and the Moving Target

*Chantelle Gray van Heerden*

## The Autochthonousphere, or, The Logics of the Plantation

> Movement always happens behind the thinker's back, or in the moment when he [*sic*] blinks. Getting out is already achieved, or else it never will be. (Deleuze and Parnet 2007: 1)

This movement, Deleuze and Guattari remind us, is all about the three great strata – the organism, *signifiance* and subjectification – about how we might succeed in 'freeing lines of flight' and generate 'continuous intensities for a BwO' through a 'meticulous relation with the strata' (Deleuze and Guattari 1987: 161). These strata give form to the world as we know it; they capture and code intensities and affects; they inform subjective possibilities; they binarise thought through a double articulation that shifts even as it stratifies. The folding and unfolding of the earth. The first articulation of the autochthonousphere – the logics of the plantation – creates a particular appreciative of the spatial coordinates of histories. As Katherine McKittric reminds us,

> Spatially, then, the plantation folds over into the prison which expresses its carceral underpinnings within the urban and which are mapped onto the tourist island and back again to the plantation and forward to asymmetrical and racist residential patterns that keep the poorest poor on our planet in slums . . . Put differently, the system itself does not change: plantation logic steadies different kinds and types of racial violence; and, our analyses honour the violence by naming it (as wrong and unjust) and asking the condemned to escape violence and join to the very system that thrives on anti-blackness! (Quoted in Hudson 2013: 240)

This kind of facialisation of power is always reliant on binarisation and biunivocalisation. In order, therefore, to bring about any real change in the world, anarchism has to shed this weight, becoming-imperceptible

– which is not the same as making whiteness invisible – being a necessary step towards the deterritorialisation of stratified micro-powers,
of the dogmatic image of thought, of the sedentary 'arrangements of
enunciation' and 'of subjectivization' (Guattari 1996: 179). There is a
violence here, both in terms of the strata that maintain the logics of the
plantation and in breaking free from it. The 'ascendancy of whiteness'
implies that while white bodies are subject to plantation logics under
capitalism, whiteness continues to act biopolitically as an apparatus of
violence (Chow 2002: 3). Their monstrous Frankenstein, now turned on
them, has resulted in the schizophrenic temperament of capitalist formations. Them – us – being creators, we must insist on a hauntological
praxis: ontological and epistemological 'correctives' are not sufficient in
themselves. Models of inclusion and diversity do not allow for political
capacitation so much as they do political pacification. Hauntology, on
the other hand, invites the temporality of the ghost – neither here nor in
the past, yet present and waiting in the future.

A problem of whiteness continues to pervade anarchism – certainly
in the stratified histories of the Global North. As a result, anarchism is
often seen as belonging to Western – white – thought and praxis (see, for
example, Ervin n.d.). This is not surprising given the canon consisting
of figures such as Mikhail Bakunin, Peter Kropotkin, Max Stirner, Peter
Gelderloos, Colin Ward, Daniel Guérin, Alexander Berkman, Pierre-
Joseph Proudhon, Eric Malatesta and so on. Like most Western canons,
this one too slants towards male representation. When the history of
anarcha-feminism is presented, it characteristically includes Emma
Goldman, Voltairine De Cleyre and *Mujeres Libres*. Lucy Parsons may
be included as the 'black representative'. Important contributions that
disrupt the canon include the Black Rose Anarchist Federation's *Black
Anarchism: A Reader*, and the recently published *Anarchism in Latin
America* (AK Press). Yet, although contributions such as these disrupt
the idea that anarchism is white, they simultaneously bring the issue
into sharp focus. Why is it necessary to talk about black anarchism or
anarchism in Latin America in the first place? Why have these histories
been occluded from mainstream anarchist publications for so long? In
order to break through these autochthonous strata, Romina Akemi and
Bree Busk suggest that, instead of focusing on individuals or particular
groups, we should learn from the entire history of anarchism. This, they
argue, is essential if we are to start prefiguring a praxis that has a clear
politics, is distinct from what Foucault referred to as the liberal 'entre-
preneurship of the self', and can collectively and effectively challenge the
very existence and imbrication of the State and capitalism (Akemi and

Busk 2016). If we *are* to learn from our entire history, the implication is that we include indigenous and other relegated forms of anarchism.

There is a rich history of indigenous anarchisms in many countries in the world, from both the so-called Global North, for example Canada and the United States, and the Global South, for example Bolivia, Brazil and Zimbabwe. Furthermore, as Sam Mbah and I. E. Igariwey, the authors of *African Anarchism*, argue, although anarchism 'as a social philosophy' and 'theory of social organisation' is underdeveloped in African theorisation, with the exception of South Africa, 'anarchism as a way of life is not at all new to Africa' (Mbah and Igariwey 1997: 2). The case of Canada is particularly useful for further thought about knowledge production in anarchist circles. Laura Hall writes, for example, that indigenous women 'like Winona LaDuke and Katsi Cook' have breathed life into their own worldviews to 'talk about food security, our connections to environment, to Creation, and our responsibilities' (Hall 2017). Creation stories have been revived from their ossification as 'truth and reality unfolding'. As such, these stories are 'not myth or metaphor or constructed reality'. As Cook says,

> women are the 'first environment' and Indigenous women are harmed by the toxification of the water, in health and physical embodiment of that direct and intentional harm, and also as leaders and keepers of the water, in the sense that a whole governance system, familial organization, and community wellbeing are equally undone. (Quoted in Hall 2017)

One of the many ways in which indigenous women challenge biopolitical control over their lives is by becoming allochthonous. Moved from their original habitat, they refuse to follow models of inclusion and diversity, nor do they attempt to return to a utopianised past where the ghost of the noble savage lies in wait.[1] Rather, they follow a logic entirely different to that of the plantation. The facialised, raced geologies that displaced them and stratified their culture are prised open as they produce intensities and affects that create speculative cracks into the Cosmos. These practices do not affirm the spatial logics of the State and capitalism, but follow flows of contamination and collaboration. As Anna Lowenhaupt Tsing puts it:

> We are contaminated by our encounters; they change who we are as we make way for others. As contamination changes world-making projects, mutual worlds – and new directions – may emerge. Everyone carries a history of contamination; purity is not an option. (Tsing 2015: 27)

Notions of purity, in any event, are profoundly colonial and, as Deleuze reminds us, the 'revolutionary problem today is to find some unity in our various struggles without falling back on the despotic and bureaucratic organisation of the party or State apparatus' (Deleuze 1994: 260). This demands a contaminated, collaborative, prefigurative praxis. At any rate, each stratum is made up of several layers which go 'from a center to a periphery, at the same time as the periphery reacts back upon the center to form a new center in relation to a new periphery' (Deleuze and Guattari 1987: 50). The intermediate processes that allow for decoding or drift between milieus (or blocks of space-time) are the epistrata. Milieus, together with the organism, form the two pincers of subjectivity because milieus (which are not territories) 'always act, through selection, on entire organisms' (1987: 52). These selections depend on local movements, codes, drift and deteritorrialisation. Hakim Bey's notion of 'temporary autonomous zones' comes to mind in thinking about these emergent modes of organisation, knowledge production and the interwoven processes of different/ciation that are exerted on the stratified grids we move through.[2] Hauntology can create such temporary autonomous zones, driven by the kinds of experimentation that produce the making of *a* life which 'is everywhere, in every moment which a living object traverses and which is measured by the objects that have been experienced'; *a* life which 'coexists with the accidents of *the* life that corresponds to it' even though they are arranged and distributed differently, as relations between milieus and associated milieus (Deleuze 2001: 29).

In *Cannibal Metaphysics*, Eduardo Vivieros de Castro argues that 'European praxis consists in "making souls" (and differentiating cultures) on the basis of a given corporeal ground – nature – while indigenous praxis consists in "making bodies" (and differentiating species) on the basis of a socio-spiritual continuum' (Vivieros de Castro 2014: 53). The consequence of these two different operations is that, in Western epistemology, the Other is an object – a thing – whereas indigenous praxis aims to personify so that the Other is always worth knowing (2014: 60). Contamination between white, indigenous and 'Other' anarchisms from this latter point of view thus catalyses intermediate processes in the epistrata that disrupt linear striations of temporality, captivity, control, faciality and the strata that ensconce them. The spectrality of *being* (which is not equivalent to *presence* as Derrida 2006 argues) is, then, the hauntology that 'confront[s] "white" culture with the kind of temporal disjunction that has been constitutive of the Afrodiasporic experience since Africans [and other indigenous peoples] were first abducted by slavers and projected from their own lifeworld into the abstract space-time of Capital' (Fisher 2013: 46). To know is to personify, to invite the ghosts that bear witness.

The problem, I would argue, lies at the surface, when surface equals ground as a condition, because one is then 'perpetually referred from the conditioned to the condition, and also from the condition to the conditioned' (Deleuze 1990: 19). From within this circular logic, the surface-ground is the *cause* that attributes to 'above' the ascendency of whiteness. No other condition is possible while the surface 'grounds itself on the finite synthetic unity' of transcendental apperception (1990: 138), because this unity is tied to the four aspects that subordinate difference to diversity, namely identity, analogy, resemblance and opposition.[3] Plantation logics, with its insistence on differentiating cultures – in other words, diversifying ontologies rather than starting from Difference – traps subjectivities in the division of simple height and depth where the one is the binary opposite of the other along a single vertical axis. Thus, because whiteness ascends, it is analogous to height, rendering blackness in opposition to white and trapping it in the negative connotations of depth – all the way to hell. Deleuze, in *The Logic of Sense*, invites us to reconsider the surface and the ground: 'what is most deep is the skin' (1990: 10). As in *Difference and Repetition*, we are called to consider the metaphysics of the groundless ground. This calls to mind Deleuze's articulation of the *event* as 'the identity of form and void. It is not the object as denoted, but the object as expressed or expressible, never present, but always already in the past and yet to come' (1990: 136). The event is thus not an aspect of height or depth but, rather, an effect of the surface – a quasi-causal, incorporeal entity that is 'independent of the spatio-temporal actualization in a state of affairs' (136). The event takes place within the temporality of the ghost; that is, it is a hauntological surface effect that reorders the coordinates between height, depth and surface. Instead of plantation logics, we now enter the logic of sense where the surface is a real effect between depth and height. As in *A Thousand Plateaus*, where 'every assemblage has two sides – the machining of bodies or objects, and group enunciation' (Deleuze and Guattari 1987: 429) – the surface, in *The Logic of Sense*, also faces two sides, namely height or Ideal (virtual) events, and depth or actual(ised) causes. To put it differently, the surface is the 'impersonal and pre-individual transcendental field, which does not resemble the corresponding empirical fields [or *bodies*], and which nevertheless is not confused with an undifferentiated depth [or *propositions*]' (Deleuze 1990: 102). Importantly, the surface, like Difference, cannot be reduced to a space '"between" in the ordinary sense of the word' (Deleuze 1994: 65). 'Nothing', writes Deleuze, 'ascends to the surface without changing its nature' (1990: 165). Thus, depth is a field or plane unto its own, different in nature from the surface which, in turn, differs in nature from height which, as implied, differs in nature from depth so that height and depth cannot be reduced to dual counterparts along a single vertical line:

> Here even the barometer neither rises nor falls, but goes lengthwise, sideways, and gives a horizontal weather. A stretching machine even lengthens songs. And Fortunatus' purse, presented as a Möbius strip, is made of handkerchiefs sewn in the wrong way, in such a manner that its outer surface is continuous with its inner surface: it envelops the entire world, and makes that which is inside be on the outside and vice versa ... surface effects in one and the same Event, which would hold for all events, bring to language becoming and its paradoxes. (1990: 11)

Taking into account that these three coordinates differ in nature, and thinking about surface effects as events, has certain consequences when brought into relation with plantation logics – at least in thinking about how to disrupt the spatial coordinates of the plantation and the racial violence it portends. This is one of the main concerns of anarchism, though, as I have argued, knowledge production continues to be an aspect we need to think about and change. If we take Vivieros de Castro's distinction between making souls and differentiating cultures as the corporeal height (Western praxis), and making bodies or differentiating species as the metaphysical depth (indigenous praxis), we have the hauntological plane as surface effect (the event). What takes place here is neither individual, nor personal but,

> on the contrary, emissions of singularities in so far as they occur on an unconscious surface and possess a mobile, immanent principle of auto-unification through a *nomadic distribution*, radically distinct from fixed and sedentary distributions as conditions of the syntheses of consciousness. (1990: 102)

This is possible on Deleuze's surface because, as a kind of Möbius strip, it has the property of being unorientable. Thus, whereas surfaces usually have a *normal* (or *surface normal*) – in other words, a line or (Euclidean) vector perpendicular to a given object – a Möbius strip does not. The effect of this is that while objects can usually be oriented according to lines and points so that, for example, each set of points on a Euclidean plane can be determined by – or, more correctly, expressed as – distance and angle, a Möbius surface cannot. It remains unorientable because the corresponding line or directrix of every point is reversed around a closed path or loop. As such, it has the 'immanent principle of auto-unification through a nomadic distribution' (1990: 102). While not the same as the undiffentiated depth of the Ideal, we do move from the ground to groundlessness; from the individual to impersonal individuations; from the personal to pre-individual singularities; from diversity to ontological repetition 'ordered in the pure form of time', this 'pure form or straight line' where 'all that returns, the eternal return, is the unconditioned' (Deleuze 1994: 240, 294, 297). What we see here, then, is the potential of a hauntological praxis to redistribute singularities-events or the 'potentials [that] haunt the surface' as 'all dice throws, in a single cast' (Deleuze 1990: 103).

I return to the notions of time, surface and event, but first I think about the kinds of subjectivity the plantation produces.

## The Migrant, or, The Logics of the Moving Target

It would be false to think that plantation logics works simply because it has a strong signifier with direct feedbacks to or resonances with mass identity. The spatio-temporal logics of the State and capitalism are not reducible to signifier or signified, even though identity politics are incorporated into the rhetoric. What is important, then, is not so much the individual and collective meaning these logics produce (although signification does play a part); rather, it is *the way* in which they stratify the subjectivity of the milieu, *the conditions* under which they stratify the entire organism, and the micropolitical semiotics they employ (which implies more than mere signification). 'Resonance, or the communication occurring between the two independent orders [content and expression], is what institutes the stratified system' (Deleuze and Guattari 1987: 57). What makes it powerful, though, is that it 'works directly at the style of life, at the semiotisation of a world' (Guattari 2016: 209). In other words, while language and signifiance are used to create resonance between content and expression, there is no direct, linear referential as in Saussure's linguistic model or many, especially older, communication models. While meaning is produced individually, it is always already social and thus informed by larger apparatuses. This is why stratification is the more important aspect: it draws on different kinds of semiotisation to create resonance by overcoding (the State) and decoding (capitalism) flows. As a result, the semiotisation of a world is absorbed by the stratifying logics of the plantation because the carceral is directly related to representation and recognition. Moreover, to identitarian rhetoric an affective dimension is added – an *I feel*. In Schreber's words:

> And if, in this process, a little sensual pleasure falls to my share, I feel justified in accepting it as some slight compensation for the inordinate measure

of suffering and privation that has been mine for so many past years. (Deleuze and Guattari 1983: 16)

What we have here is thus the segregative and biunivocal use of the conjunctive syntheses. And it is precisely these libidinal restrictions that enable the plantation war machine to resonate with the machinic assemblages to which it is coupled (*plugged into*). In short, it is the creation of a people; in this case, a filial affair of fathers and patriots, States and families, the production of mass-man.[4]

Although 'all filiation is imaginary' (Deleuze and Guattari 1987: 238), it is *believable* because it is supported by the fascist war machine (*we all have one lurking somewhere*), which connects to the abstract machine of facialisation which, in turn, produces a geology of incorporeal transformations. The 'passage from the state of nature to the social state is like a leap in place,' Deleuze and Guattari write, 'an incorporeal transformation occurring at zero hour' (1987: 81). Relays of every kind. Whole systems of facialisations and incorporeal transformations, too many regimes of power to account for, too many desiring-machines. The problematic lies in the tension between that which is and can be stratified – and therefore regulated – and that which presumably cannot. I say 'presumably' because the intensification of algorithmic regulation and recognition under disciplinary control societies means that moving bodies have increasingly come under political governance, which at once owns and disowns them as the figure of the migrant, the moving target par excellence of our time, in part due to this double bind.

The moment bodies are marked as 'migrant', the incorporeal transformation renders them not refugees, but drifters, interlopers, runaways. Geopolitical apparatuses and stratifications lock these bodies concurrently into the logics of the plantation and the logics of the moving target. 'The prime function incumbent upon the socius has always been to codify the flows of desire, to inscribe them, to record them, to see to it that no flow exists that is not properly dammed up, channeled, regulated' (Deleuze and Guattari 1983: 33). These biopolitical control measures are further intensified through spectacle politics or *I feel* identitarian frames that give the State power to increase their securitisation policies and practises. Migrants are as much Syrian refugees as black bodies (particularly in the USA). Fast death or 'slow death', it does not matter, necropolitics demands the elimination of moving targets either way (see Berlant 2007: 760). Thus, argues Thomas Nail, the 'twenty-first century will be the century of the migrant' (Nail 2015: 1):

However, not all migrants are alike in their movement. For some, movement offers opportunity, recreation, and profit with only a temporary expulsion. For others, movement is dangerous and constrained, and their social expulsions are much more severe and permanent. Today, most people fall somewhere on this migratory spectrum between the two poles of 'inconvenience' and 'incapacitation'. But what all migrants on this spectrum share, at some point, is the experience that their movement results in a certain degree of expulsion from their territorial, political, juridical, or economic status. (Nail 2015: 2)

The logics of the moving target necessarily take place within a facialised geology and the value extraction of capitalism. Bodies that do not produce are relegated to migrant frames of inconvenience and incapacitation. According to this logic – propelled once more by the ascendancy of whiteness – certain groups of people are stratified across registers of the migrant and shifted to geographical locations marked for the 'subhuman or not quite human' (Puar 2017: 25). Owned and disowned. This is how it gets into the strata – these special little signs, these regimes of signs and assemblages of power – it is all a matter of arrangements, and of assemblages of individuals, 'but also ways of seeing the world, emotional systems, conceptual machines, memory devices, economic, social components, elements of all kinds' (Guattari 1996: 179–80). In this way, then, the 'trajectory merges, not only with the subjectivity of those who travel through a milieu, but also with the subjectivity of the milieu itself, insofar as it is reflected in those who travel through it' (Deleuze 1997: 61) – the semiotisation of a world complete.

Migrant frames, as memory devices, signal a problematic related to the temporal dimensions that memory inhabits and catalyses. It is particularly the commemorative function of psychoanalysis, Deleuze and Guattari argue, which inhibits experimentation. Moreover, it is *this* memory that the socius inscribes on our bodies:

For it is a founding act – that the organs be hewn into the socius, and that the flows run over its surface – through which man [*sic*] ceases to be a biological organism and becomes a full body, an earth, to which his organs become attached, where they are attracted, repelled, miraculated, following the requirements of a socius. Nietzsche says: it is a matter of creating a memory for man; and man, who was constituted by means of an active faculty of forgetting (*oubli*), by means of a repression of biological memory, must create an *other* memory, one that is collective; a memory of words (*paroles*) and no longer a memory of things, a memory of signs and no longer of effects. (Deleuze and Guattari 1983: 144)

No longer of effects, we see a movement away from the surface. No hauntological praxis to invite the ghosts that bear witness, memory folds into the fascist war machine to unfold as commemoration through collective enunciations. Individual and personal rather than impersonal individuations and pre-individual singularities. Reverse racism is a good example of this kind of memory. However, as Lorenzo Kom'boa Ervin remarks, 'whites are not being herded into ghetto housing; removed from or prohibited from entering professions; deprived of decent education; forced into malnutrition and early death; subjected to racial violence and police repression' (Ervin 2016: 14). Thus, the memory inscribed by the socius catalyses migrant frames (the logics of the moving target) which, in turn, connect with the fascist war machine reliant on the spatio-temporal dimensions of plantation logics. Memory of this kind is indeed a powerful weapon in the creation of exceptionalism because it constructs a ruling elite 'selected by the reinforcement of systems of self-repression and by the promotion of segregatory models that result in a contempt for those' who fail to learn the game (Guattari 2016: 78). Canons and histories are replete with the semiotics of the order-word and the incorporeal transformations it instantiates, as well as the strati-fication functions it capacitates in the memory of milieus which, in turn, act on an entire organism. The logics of the plantation and the moving target are employed to their fullest extent through historiographies sup-ported by migrant frames that objectify and differentiate humans and non-humans alike on the basis of faciality and the strata it maintains for the State and capitalism. Experimentation is foreclosed at the outset, the strata of signifiance and subjectification rigidified in their organisation. How, then, do we get from the traversing migrant subject to the destrati-fying transversal one? How do we get from hostile departure to passage?

## Dismantling Love in Order to Become Capable of Loving: Escaping the Double Logics of the Autochthonousphere

To reiterate, the problem is that exceptionalism is too tied to memory, to memorialisation, the black hole of involuntary memory (redundancy), now 'fall[ing] back onto the strata, into the strata's relations and milieus' (Deleuze and Guattari 1987: 56). We must understand, '[d]esire does not "want" revolution, it *is* revolutionary in its own right' (1987: 127). 'It's revolutionary by nature because it builds machines capable – when inserted into the social structure – of exploding things, of disrupting the social fabric' (Guattari 2009: 54). Which is indeed why it can be said that fascism and anarchism have the same abstract machine, although this does not render anarchism the flipside of fascism. Which is indeed why we need to analyse the local conditions, the thresholds of identity, the associated milieus, the codes, the processes of decoding or drift, the movements of deterritorialisation and reterritorialisation. (What kinds of assemblages brought about the Mexican Revolution, the Paris Commune, the Spanish Revolution, Nazism, the election of Donald Trump?) Taking these many facets into consideration changes our conception of subjectivity which, in psychoanalysis, but also in fascism, 'establishes a profound link between the unconscious and memory', so that it is 'a memorial, commemorative or monumental conception that pertains to persons or objects', rendering milieus 'nothing more than terrains capable of conserving, identifying or authenticating' these memories (Deleuze 1997: 66). The social memory is *all* memory, inscribed on the social body through histories and canons. The order-word. Mythmaking. It works like this: 'A depressed patient speaks of his memories of the Resistance and of a chief of the network called René. The psychoanalyst says, "Let us keep René". René [reborn] is no longer Resistance, it's Renaissance.' Nothing more than a shift of vowels and consonants to effectuate displacement – migrancy – 'which gives a falsified apparent image that is meant to trap desire' (Deleuze and Guattari 1983: 115). To put it differently, memorialisation is a structural problem, closely tied to that of facialisation and exceptionalism in that it modulates desire according to plantation logics, producing migrant subjectivities. This is a politics of black holes, the void and white walls. Nevertheless, while it creates a void, it simultaneously expresses 'the semiotic seizure of power' – and *this* relies on memory: both involuntary and voluntary (Guattari 2016: 180).

Involuntary memory, which constitutes sensuous signs, or reminiscences and discoveries, are basically sensations that interfere and superimpose themselves so that 'we feel an imperative that forces us to seek [their] meaning' (Deleuze 2008: 35). It is the kind of memory that induces sentimentality (2008: 14) through simplistic signification systems capacitated by affective structures. Example: *Let's make America great again!* Relatively simplistic frames are drawn from here in order to reminisce about a 'better past', simultaneously invoking certain sentiments to resonate with the frames. Importantly, there are no causal propositions at play in this example, as that would reduce the analysis to simple source–receiver or signifier–signified models. In Deleuze's words, the 'problem bears resemblance neither to the propositions which it subsumes under it, nor to the relations which it engenders in the proposition: it is not propositional, although it does not exist outside of the propositions which express it' (Deleuze 1990: 122). What we are dealing with, then, are the two orders or articulations, content and expression – 'two variables of a function of stratification' (Deleuze and Guattari 1987: 44). And this lands us neatly in plantation logics, although this is not to say that involuntary memory – even a kind of romanticism – cannot be used affirmatively. Rather, what I am trying to get at is that memory used to undergird notions of nationalism or the nation-state is more often than not, if not always, reliant on the illegitimate (segregative and biunivocal) use of the conjunctive syntheses (Deleuze and Guattari 1983: 110): the familial application of Oedipus.

On the other hand, we have voluntary memory, which recalls in snapshot fashion and can only proceed from 'an actual present to a present that "has been", to something that was present and is so no longer'. In other words, it cannot 'apprehend the past directly' – that is, the past as being past – but apprehends or composes it as another present (Deleuze 2008: 35). What Deleuze finds problematic with this is that such a view subordinates time to memory, which 'fulfils the conditions of normality' and remains locked within the extrinsic conditionings of identity and representation (Deleuze 1989: 36; see also Deleuze 1994). Thus, both involuntary and voluntary memory are used by the social machine, especially State-capitalist arrangements, to effectuate exceptionalism through the use of identitarian frames invoked by reminiscence and recall. Although each of these kinds of memory employ different modes, they are activated by State-capitalist assemblages to bind, localise and integrate the decoded material of social and semiotic flows. In this way, memory grounds itself on the finite synthetic unity of apperception so that it remains within the circular logic of condition/conditioned, which itself is arrested by the 'power formations' and 'hegemonic mission' of faciality (Guattari 2016: 180).

As with plantation logics, migrant frames subordinate Difference to identity, informed by the condition of the ascendancy of whiteness, actualised as exceptionalism – the hyper-stratification of the visual components of facialisation. The effect of this is that desire is semiotised according to a politics of black holes. Thus, by 'emptying the world of the polyvocity of its contents, it installs behind each gaze an empty point, a black hole' (Guattari 2016: 183). Once created, these exceptional states make it very difficult to escape the processes of subjectivation produced and maintained by these kinds of assemblages of enunciation. This is quite evident when thinking about migrants who are, as I have said, both owned and disowned – neither exceptional nor unexceptional, yet both simultaneously. As such, they are always moving targets propelled by hostile departure rather than passage. In thinking about ways in which anarchism can respond to the logics of the plantation and the moving target, we might begin by heeding Deleuze. 'Revolution', he writes, 'has nothing to do with an attempt to inscribe oneself in a movement of development and in the capitalization of memory, but in the preservation of the force of forgetting' (Deleuze 2004: 278). Forgetting is, therefore, the condition of experimentation, the condition for creating a people with an unexceptional status. In fact, Deleuze argues, a revolutionary 'breaks free by forgetting and remains unmoved by the reproach their critics constantly make: "It has existed, therefore it will always exist"' (Deleuze 2004: 277). *The State has always existed, capitalism will always exist.* Instead, the revolutionary relies on '[a]cts of thought without image against the image of thought' as 'the force of forgetting against memory' (Deleuze and Parnet 2007: 34). In short, in order to respond meaningfully to the logics of the plantation and the moving target, anarchism has to desire a politics of time – and I argue that it does – rather than one of memory because, by forgetting, we return to the groundless ground of the surface, leaving behind the conditions that memory ties us to.

These conditions, Guattari reminds us, inform subjectivity, but they are never individual; they are always 'in circulation in social complexes of various sizes'; they are 'essentially social, and [are] assumed and experienced by individuals in their particular existences' (Guattari and Rolnik 2008: 46). Generally, these experiences of subjectivity flow between two poles of relationality – that of 'alienation and oppression' and that of 'expression and creation' (2008: 46), but it is the second iteration that leads to processes of singularisation, produces them, in fact, and propulses the traversing migrant subject into transversality:

> To become imperceptible oneself, to have dismantled love in order to become capable of loving. To have dismantled one's self in order finally to be alone and meet the true double at the other end of the line. A clandestine passenger on a motionless voyage. To become like everybody else; but this, precisely, is a becoming only for one who knows how to be nobody, to no longer be anybody. To paint oneself gray on gray. (Deleuze and Guattari 1987: 197)[5]

What Deleuze and Guattari describe here is the imperceptible rupture of the passage of the nomad – a distinctly different movement to that of the signifying break of the migrant. Two things are important here. First, the migrant is State-owned/disowned and, as such, *of* the State war machine, whereas the nomad 'invented a war machine *in opposition to* the State apparatus' (Deleuze and Guattari 1987: 24, emphasis added). Second, the signifying break of migrant frames is tied to memory, whereas the imperceptible rupture of the passage of the nomad is one of time. *To become imperceptible oneself* – a passage of becoming rather than the hostile departure of filial affairs; *to have dismantled love in order to become capable of loving* – a destratifying transversal protocol rather than that of the traversing migrant subject, caught in the striating logics of the plantation and the moving subject. But how do we get from memory to time?

In *Difference and Repetition*, Deleuze argues that the first passive synthesis of time or habit (Habitus) poses a paradox, namely that it constitutes time 'while passing in the time constituted' (Deleuze 1994: 79). He argues that we can conclude from this that 'there must be another time in which the first synthesis of time can occur' (1994: 79) which he calls the second passive synthesis of Memory. Accordingly, whereas the first synthesis contracts time as living and passing presents, the second synthesis contracts the pure past, while also allowing the present to pass. In Deleuze's words: 'The present exists, but the past alone insists and provides the element in which the present passes and successive presents are telescoped' (85). A question arises from this relation between the first two syntheses, namely: How might we move from memory to 'forgetting as a force' – 'an integral part of the lived experience of eternal return' (8)?

It may appear at first that this is merely a problem of identity and representation, for it seems obvious to assume that memory is always tied to 'infinite representation' (Deleuze 1994: 54), but this would render time subordinate to the movement of memory. One way in which Deleuze overcomes this problem is to argue that the pure past is virtual and determines the actual (living and passing presents), while simultaneously being determined by it. This is why it can be argued that memory is tied to desire. *Memory as desire.* In order to get from memory to forgetting – from the signifying break of migrancy to the imperceptible rupture of nomadism – Deleuze proposes a third synthesis of time, and it is really this synthesis that opens our understanding to permanent revolution through the concept of the eternal return, because it is the third synthesis that eliminates the hypotheses of time as 'intracyclic and extracyclic', putting time into a straight line, a pure form. This third repetition or eternal return thus 'takes time out of "joint"' and 'renders the repetition of the other two impossible' (1994: 296). What this means, in effect, is that this repetition, which we name the eternal return, is that which allows the 'past to be lived within Forgetting' (85). In other words, this is the in-itself of revolution, the in-itself of desire. What we see here, then, is that while fascism is reliant on memory and memorialisation, anarchism is a problem of time in that it is concerned with the conditions of the *real* rather than the *possible*:

> It is the Aion. We have seen that past, present, and future were not at all three parts of a single temporality, but that they rather formed two readings of time, each one of which is complete and excludes the other: on one hand, the always limited present, which measures the action of bodies as causes and the state of their mixtures in depth (Chronos); on the other, the essentially unlimited past and future, which gather incorporeal events, at the surface, as effects (Aion). (Deleuze 1990: 61)

We should not, however, be tempted to think that anarchism is free of facialisations, memorialisation, arborescence or even microfascisms – the canon betrays ongoing epistemological and ontological aspects that need urgent attention. What can be said of anarchist subjectivities (for there are many, each already a multiplicity) is that the internal and external structuring – structuration – lend themselves to immanent critique and the exploration of new desiring coordinates which may be thought of in terms of a politics radically different to that of the black hole of memory (see, for example, the special issue of *Anarchist Development in Cultural Studies* entitled 'Blasting the Canon'). Thus, it is a politics aimed at creating life and finding a weapon 'capable of overturning all orders and representations in order to affirm Difference in the state of permanent revolution which characterizes eternal return' (Deleuze 1994: 53). Permanent Revolution: not so much a double articulation as a 'folding, unfolding, refolding', the overtaking of migrancy with nomadology (Deleuze 2006: 158). The war machine: not so much an objective pertaining to an *I feel* as to annihilation: the annihilation of 'the forces of the State', the destruction of 'the State-form' (Deleuze and Guattari 1987: 417). To live in the folds, as Michaux writes (Deleuze 2006: 38), is to live the fold as the caesura – a *Zweifalt* – the line of the fracture, the cut or imperceptible rupture that orders the before and after in the encounter of the new.

No longer in the realm of the possible that attends to the content of concepts, we enter the realm of the virtual content of Ideas. This is how anarchy as a politics of time accounts for the genesis of new experience that forms the groundless conditions of Difference-in-itself, rather than it being subject to diversity as external conditioning. This is also how we disrupt the double logics of the autochthonous strata that capture traversing subjects even as they are relinquished. As a transversal politics, it does not look the other way, yet refuses to commemorate and in that memory reify the logics of the plantation and the moving target. It is a hauntological praxis: ghosts are invited to the surface. They apparate as potentials that haunt the surface without ever assuming a face. These apparitions are all dice throws in a single cast, the redistribution of singularities-events. If 'human beings have a destiny,' write Deleuze and Guattari, 'it is to dismantle the face and facializations, to become imperceptible', to escape the memorialisation of the face (Deleuze and Guattari 1987: 171). This is what it means to live the past within Forgetting:

> Only bodies penetrate each other, only Chronos is filled up with states of affairs and the movements of the objects that it measures. But being an empty and unfolded form of time, the Aion subdivides ad infinitum that which haunts it without ever inhabiting it – the Event for all events. This is why the unity of events or effects among themselves is very different from the unity of corporeal causes among themselves. (Deleuze 1990: 64)

We who remember technoscapes only, let us open ourselves again to this living within forgetting, for such an anarchic hauntology allows for the exploration of non-Western perceptions of time and reality unfolding, where a multiplicity of voices rupture the plane of organisation. The disappearance of representation proper is the hauntological becoming-imperceptible. A passing, merely a passing.

## Notes from Utopia

Disarticulated and deterritorialised, Challenger mutters that she is taking the Earth with her, that she is leaving for the mysterious world, her poison garden. She whispers something else: it is by headlong flight that things progress and signs proliferate – to have dismantled one's self in order finally to be alone and meet the true double at the other end of the line. A clandestine passenger on a motionless voyage.

The figure slumps oddly into a posture scarcely human, and begins a curious, fascinated sort of shuffle towards a coffin-shaped clock, enters and pulls the door shut after it. The abnormal clicking goes on, beating out the dark, cosmic rhythm that underlies all mystical gateopenings – the Mechanosphere, or rhizosphere, the Allochthonousphere.[6]

## Notes

1. 'Autochthonous' refers to both indigenous habitants and geological deposits that formed in their current position. Here I am referencing both aspects. 'Allochthonous' geological formations, on the other hand, refers to deposits that have moved from their sites of origin.
2. Emergent forms of knowledge production – if we take it seriously – is an attempt to find ways of thinking that run counter to the great modernist narratives of colonial 'progress'. As race, gender and sexuality form the bedrock condition of the colonial – and now capitalist – enterprise, any attempt to reconfigure positionality requires that we interrogate and change the ways in which these hierarchies have become stratified and continue to be reproduced (see Stoler 1985). However, as Frantz Fanon argues, the colonial system did not so much bring about the death of cultures as keep them in 'a continued agony'. Thus, a 'culture, once living and open to the future, becomes closed, fixed in the colonial status, caught in the yoke of oppression. Both present and mummified, it testifies against its members' (Fanon 1967: 33–4). In thinking about knowledge production, we thus have to reach towards the possibility of non-Eurocentric modes of being and seeing without negating the complex co-imbrication of and contamination between indigeneity, coloniality and modernity.
3. Deleuze reminds us that difference 'is not between species, between two determinations of a genus, but entirely on one side, within the chosen line of descent' (Deleuze 1994: 60). It is not '"between" in the ordinary sense of the word' and neither is it 'an object of representation' (65). 'Difference is not diversity' (222).
4. A term borrowed from the Spanish philosopher José Ortega y Gasset.
5. I want to clarify two points of my argument that relates to *becoming-imperceptible* and *forgetting*. Most importantly, these terms do not pertain to epistemology – if that were so I would not in fact be suggesting anything of worth here. At no point am I implying that histories – especially those that have been invisible, erased, overlooked or distorted – be made imperceptible or be forgotten. Thus, *becoming-imperceptible* is not *being made invisible* and *forgetting* is not *disremembering* (this would be an epistemological argument which mine is not). In fact, and I do think this is clear, I am contending quite the opposite. The becoming-imperceptible and forgetting that I am arguing for is ontogenetic which makes a radical break from the predetermined conditions of possible experience to the genetic conditions of real experience. Thinking about subjectivity (in fact *producing* subjectivities) is thus more about foldings and openings than processes of subjectification according to hierarchical and dominant modes of being.
6. Adapted from *A Thousand Plateaus*, pp. 72, 73–4.

## References

Akemi, R. and B. Busk (2016), 'Breaking the Waves: Challenging the Liberal Tendency within Anarchist Feminism', *Institute for Anarchist Studies*, 29 June, https://anarchiststudies.org/2016/06/29/breaking-the-waves-challenging-the-liberal-tendency-within-anarchist-feminism-by-romina-akemi-and-bree-busk/ (last accessed 20 August 2018).

Berlant, L. (2007), 'Slow Death (Sovereignty, Obesity, Lateral Agency)', *Critical Inquiry*, 33: 754–80.

Chow, R. (2002), *The Protestant Ethnic and the Spirit of Capitalism*, New York: Columbia University Press.

Deleuze, G. (1989), *Cinema 2: The Time-Image*, trans. H. Tomlinson and R. Galeta, Minneapolis: University of Minnesota Press.

Deleuze, G. (1990), *The Logic of Sense*, trans. M. Lester with C. Stivale, New York: Columbia University Press.

Deleuze, G. (1994), *Difference and Repetition*, trans. P. Patton, New York: Columbia University Press.

Deleuze, G. (1997), 'What Children Say', in *Essays Critical and Clinical*, trans. D. W. Smith and M. A. Greco, Minneapolis: University of Minnesota Press, pp. 61–7.

Deleuze, G. (2001), *Pure Immanence: Essays on a Life*, trans. A. Boyman, New York: Zone Books.

Deleuze, G. (2004), 'Five Propositions on Psychoanalysis', in G. Deleuze, *Desert Islands and Other Texts 1953–1974*, trans. M. Toarmina, Los Angeles and New York: Semiotext(e), pp. 274–80.

Deleuze, G. (2006), *The Fold: Leibniz and the Baroque*, trans. T. Conley, London and New York: University of Minnesota Press.

Deleuze, G. (2008) *Proust and Signs*, trans. R. Howard, London and New York: Continuum.

Deleuze, G. and F. Guattari (1983), *Anti-Oedipus. Capitalism and Schizophrenia*, trans. R. Hurley, M. Seem and H. R. Lane, Minneapolis: University of Minnesota Press.

Deleuze, G. and F. Guattari (1987), *A Thousand Plateaus: Capitalism and Schizophrenia*, trans. B. Massumi, Minneapolis: University of Minnesota Press.

Deleuze, G. and C. Parnet (2007), *Dialogues II*, trans. H. Tomlinson and B. Habberjam, New York: Columbia University Press.

Derrida, J. (2006), *Specters of Marx*, New York and Abingdon: Routledge.

Ervin, L. K. (n.d.), 'The Progressive Plantation: Racism Inside White Radical Social Change Groups', *The Anarchist Library*, https://theanarchistlibrary.org/library/lorenzo-kom-boa-ervin-the-progressive-plantation-racism-inside-white-radical-groups (last accessed 20 August 2018).

Ervin, L. K. (2016), 'Anarchism and the Black Revolution', *The Anarchist Library*, https://theanarchistlibrary.org/library/black-rose-anarchist-federation-black-anarchism-a-reader.pdf (last accessed 20 August 2018).

Fanon, F. (1967), *Toward the African Revolution*, trans. H. Chevalier, New York: Grove Press.

Fisher, M. (2013), 'The Metaphysics of Crackle: Afrofuturism and Hauntology', *Dancecult: Journal of Electronic Dance Music Culture*, (5)2: 42–55.

Guattari, F. (1996), *Soft Subversions*, ed. S. Lotringer, trans. D. L. Sweet and C. Wiener, New York: Semiotext(e).

Guattari, F. (2009), *Chaosophy: Texts and Interviews 1972–1977*, trans. D. L. Sweet, J. Becker and T. Adkins, New York: Semiotext(e).

Guattari, F. (2016), *Lines of Flight*, trans. A. Goffey, London and New York: Bloomsbury.

Guattari, F. and S. Rolnik (2008), *Molecular Revolution in Brazil*, trans. K. Clapshow and B. Holmes, Los Angeles: Semiotext(e).

Hall, L. (2017), 'Indigenist Intersectionality: Decolonizing an Indigenous Eco-Queer Feminism and Anarchism', *Institute for Anarchist Studies*, 15 February, https://anarchiststudies.org/2017/02/15/indigenist-intersectionality-decolonizing-an-indigenous-eco-queer-feminism-and-anarchism-by-laura-hall/ (last accessed 20 August 2018).

Hudson, P. J. (2013), 'The Geographies of Blackness and Anti-Blackness: An Interview with Katherine McKittric', *The CLR James Journal*, 20(1–2): 233–40.

Mbah, S. and I. E. Igariwey (1997), *African Anarchism: The History of a Movement*, Tucson: See Sharp Press.

Nail, T. (2015), *The Figure of the Migrant*, Stanford: Stanford University Press.

Puar, J. (2017), *The Right to Maim: Debility, Capacity, Disability*, London and Durham, NC: Duke University Press.

Stoler, L. A. (1985), *Capitalism and Confrontation in Sumatra's Plantation Belt 1870–1979*, Ann Arbor: University of Michigan Press.

Tsing, A. L. (2015), *The Mushroom at the End of the World*, Princeton: Princeton University Press.

Vivieros de Castro, E. (2014), *Cannibal Metaphysics*, trans. Peter Skafish, Minneapolis: Univocal.

# Notes on Contributors

Jesse Cohn lives and works in northwest Indiana and is a part of the vast academic desiring-machine that is already caught up in revolutionary agitation against itself. In particular, he enjoys masochistically overidentifying with the academy's demand to turn the universe into readable text by continually translating works from other languages to English. His translation of Daniel Colson's *Petit lexique philosophique de l'anarchisme: De Proudhon à Deleuze* will soon be published by Minor Compositions.

Aragorn Eloff is an independent researcher with a long-standing interest in the work of Gilles Deleuze and Félix Guattari. He is the co-convener of the biennial South African Deleuze and Guattari Studies Conference and a director of the Institute for Critical Animal Studies in Africa. His work focuses on the application of Deleuze and Guattari's thought to questions around anarchism, algorithmic governance and earth/animal liberation. He also works in the field of experimental music and performance.

Elmo Feiten writes on the relations between Max Stirner, poststructuralist anarchism and the life sciences. He studied English, cultural studies and cognitive science at the University of Freiburg and has published and presented on the reception of Stirner's thought within the anarchist tradition, as well as on the similarities and differences between Stirner and Foucault. His recent research focuses on the link between brain and subjectivity as a challenge for materialism, on the implications of neuroplasticity for self-empowerment, and on the connections between Stirner, phenomenology and radical constructivism.

Chantelle Gray van Heerden (PhD) is employed as a senior researcher at the Institute for Gender Studies at the University of South Africa (UNISA).

Her research centres on the philosophical collaboration between Gilles Deleuze and Félix Guattari and she is one of the organisers of the biennial South African Deleuze and Guattari Studies Conference. She is a member of the editorial collective of *Gender Questions* and served as editor-in-chief during 2017. Chantelle also makes experimental music and is one of the organisers of the annual Edge of Wrong festival.

**Christoph Hubatschke** is a philosopher and political scientist based in Vienna. He is a DOC-Fellow of the Austrian Academy of Science working as PhD researcher at the University of Vienna, Department of Philosophy, on Deleuze, Guattari and social movements. From 2017 to 2018 he was a visiting research fellow at the Department for Visual Cultures, Goldsmiths University, London. Publications and presentations cover different fields of research: poststructuralist political theory, Deleuze/Guattari studies, anarchist theory, philosophy of technology, social movement studies, the politics of humanoid robots and AI, and monster studies.

**Nathan Jun** is Associate Professor and Coordinator of the Philosophy Program at Midwestern State University. He is the author of *Anarchism and Political Modernity* (2011) and has published several edited volumes and journal articles on political theory, the history of political thought, and contemporary European philosophy.

**Gregory Kalyniuk** is an independent researcher with a long-standing interest in anarchy and anarchism, as well as the work of Deleuze and Guattari.

**Thomas Nail** is an associate professor of philosophy at the University of Denver. He is the author of *Returning to Revolution: Deleuze, Guattari and Zapatismo* (Edinburgh University Press, 2012), *The Figure of the Migrant* (Stanford University Press, 2015), *Theory of the Border* (Oxford University Press, 2016), *Lucretius I: An Ontology of Motion* (Edinburgh University Press, 2018), *Being and Motion* (Oxford University Press, forthcoming 2018), *Theory of the Image* (Oxford University Press, forthcoming 2018) and co-editor of *Between Deleuze and Foucault* (Edinburgh University Press, 2016). His publications can be downloaded at http://du.academia.edu/thomasnail

**Paul Raekstad** has a PhD in philosophy from the University of Cambridge and is currently a postdoctoral research fellow at the University of

Amsterdam. He works on methodological questions in political philosophy, democracy, alternative economic institutions and social practices seeking to introduce them – with particular interests in anarchism and Marxism. He is currently working on three books: on a realist reconstruction of Karl Marx's critique of capitalism; on prefigurative politics (with Sofa Gradin); and on radical approaches to realism, genealogy and ideology critique (with Enzo Rossi).

**Andrew Stones** is an early career fellow at the Institute of Advanced Study, University of Warwick, researching climate fiction, extinction and postcolonial critiques of the Anthropocene. He completed his PhD research in world literature and the philosophy of Gilles Deleuze at the Department of English and Comparative Literary Studies, University of Warwick, in 2018. He is currently working on a book-length project focusing on the politics and aesthetics of climate change, dystopia and indigeneity.

**Alejandro de la Torre Hernández** is a researcher at the Department of Historical Studies at the National Institute of Anthropology and History (Mexico) where he coordinates the Workers' Culture Workshop as well as the Tradition and Radical Culture project. His research focuses on the history of the press and cultural practices of international anarchism. He has contributed to the critical edition of the Complete Works of Ricardo Flores Magón.

**Gerónimo Barrera de la Torre** is a PhD student at the Institute of Latin American Studies at the University of Texas, Austin. For his research project, he works with indigenous people in Mexico on forest conservation programmes and alternatives through community organisation. His interests include political ecology, indigenous onto-epistemologies, decoloniality and critical landscape studies. He has published work on the critical geographies of tourism and political geography.

**Natascia Tosel** received her PhD in philosophy with honours at the University of Padua (Italy) with a foreign co-advisor in Paris (Éric Alliez, University Paris8). Her research is in the field of political philosophy and her interests concern especially contemporary French philosophy. She did her doctoral thesis on the role of the law in Gilles Deleuze and she is now developing her research on the Deleuzian readings of Gabriel Tarde and Maurice Hauriou. She has participated in international conferences and worked as a lecturer, and has published articles in many scientific journals. She is a member of the editorial board of *Materiali Foucaultiani.*

**Elizabet Vasileva** is a PhD candidate at Loughborough University in the Department of Politics, History and International Relations. She is a contributor to the Anarchist Studies Network and is a tutor for the Free University of Brighton education project. She lives a nomadic life on a narrowboat, enjoying the company of friends and Min the dog. Elizabeth's interests include neo-materialism, radical politics, ethics and the intersection of philosophy and neuroscientific practice.

# Index

EU representative:
Easy Access System Europe
Mustamäe tee 50, 10621 Tallinn, Estonia
Gpsr.requests@easproject.com

www.ingramcontent.com/pod-product-compliance
Lightning Source LLC
Chambersburg PA
CBHW070843300326
41935CB00039B/1384